TEACHINGS OF PRESIDENTS OF THE CHURCH
HOWARD W. HUNTER

Published by
The Church of Jesus Christ of Latter-day Saints
Salt Lake City, Utah

Books in the *Teachings of Presidents of the Church* Series

To obtain copies of these books, go to your local distribution center or visit store.lds.org. The books are also available in digital formats at LDS.org and on the Gospel Library mobile application.

Your comments and suggestions about this book would be appreciated. Please submit them to:

Curriculum Development
50 East North Temple Street
Salt Lake City, UT 84150-0024 USA
Email: pth-development@ldschurch.org

Please give your name, address, ward, and stake. Be sure to include the title of the book. Then offer your comments and suggestions about the book's strengths and areas of potential improvement.

Contents

Howard W. Hunter

Introduction

The First Presidency and the Quorum of the Twelve Apostles have established the *Teachings of Presidents of the Church* series to help you draw closer to your Heavenly Father and deepen your understanding of the restored gospel of Jesus Christ. As the Church adds volumes to this series, you will build a collection of gospel reference books for your home. These books are designed to be used for personal study and for Sunday instruction. They can also help you prepare family home evening lessons, prepare other lessons or talks, and answer questions about Church doctrine.

This book features the teachings of President Howard W. Hunter, who served as President of The Church of Jesus Christ of Latter-day Saints from June 5, 1994, to March 3, 1995.

Personal Study

As you study the teachings of President Howard W. Hunter, prayerfully seek the inspiration of the Holy Ghost. The questions at the end of each chapter will help you ponder, understand, and apply President Hunter's teachings. The following ideas may also be helpful:

- Write thoughts and feelings that come to you from the Holy Ghost as you study.

- Underline passages you want to remember. Consider memorizing these passages or noting them in your scriptures next to related verses.

- Read a chapter or passage more than once so you can understand it more deeply.

- Ask yourself questions such as, How do President Hunter's teachings increase my understanding of gospel principles? What does the Lord want me to learn from these teachings?

- Ask yourself how the teachings in this book can help you with personal challenges and concerns.

- Share what you learn with family members and friends.

Teaching from This Book

The following guidelines will help you teach from this book, whether at home or at church.

Prepare to Teach

Seek the guidance of the Holy Ghost as you prepare to teach. Prayerfully study the chapter to become confident in your understanding of President Hunter's teachings. You will teach with greater power when his words have influenced you personally (see D&C 11:21).

Most chapters contain more material than you will be able to discuss in one meeting. Prayerfully select the teachings that you feel will be most helpful.

Encourage those you teach to study the chapter in advance so they will be better prepared to participate in discussions and edify one another.

In preparing to engage those you teach, give special attention to the "Suggestions for Study and Teaching" section at the end of each chapter. In that section you will find questions, scriptures, and a study help or teaching help. The questions and scriptures correlate with the material in the chapter. The study and teaching helps apply more broadly in learning and teaching the gospel.

Introduce the Chapter

As you introduce the chapter, seek to establish an atmosphere in which the Spirit can touch the hearts and minds of participants. You may want to use one or more of the following ideas:

- Read or review the section titled "From the Life of Howard W. Hunter" at the beginning of the chapter, and then discuss it.

- Discuss a quotation, picture, or scripture from the chapter.

- Sing a hymn together.

- Briefly share a personal experience about the topic.

Encourage Discussion about President Hunter's Teachings

As you teach from this book, invite others to share their thoughts, ask questions, testify, and teach one another. When they actively participate, they will be more prepared to learn and to receive personal revelation.

Allow good discussions to continue rather than trying to cover all the teachings. Guide the discussions so they focus on President Hunter's teachings.

The questions at the end of each chapter are a valuable resource for encouraging discussion. You may also develop your own questions that are specifically for those you are teaching. Some other ideas for encouraging discussion are provided below:

- Ask participants to share what they have learned from their personal study of the chapter. It may be helpful to contact a few of them in advance and ask them to come prepared to share what they have learned.

- Assign selected questions at the end of the chapter to individuals or small groups. Ask participants to look for teachings in the chapter that relate to the questions. Then invite them to share their thoughts and insights.

- Read together some of President Hunter's teachings in the chapter. Ask participants to share examples from the scriptures and from their own experiences that relate to those teachings.

- Ask participants to choose one section and read it silently. Invite them to gather in groups of two or three people who chose the same section and discuss what they learned.

Encourage Application and Sharing

President Hunter's teachings will be most meaningful when individuals apply them in their lives and share them with others. You may want to use one or more of the following ideas:

- Ask participants how they can apply President Hunter's teachings in their responsibilities at home, in the Church, and in other settings. For example, you could invite them to ponder and discuss how they can apply his teachings as husbands, wives, parents, sons, daughters, home teachers, or visiting teachers.

- Invite participants to share their experiences with applying what they have learned.

- Encourage participants to share some of President Hunter's teachings with family members and friends.

Conclude the Discussion

Briefly summarize the lesson or ask one or two others to do so. Testify of the teachings you have discussed. You may also want to invite others to share their testimonies.

Information about Source Materials

The teachings in this book are direct quotations from President Howard W. Hunter's sermons and articles. Quotations from published sources have retained the punctuation, spelling, capitalization, and paragraphing of the original sources unless editorial or typographic changes have been necessary to improve readability. Because the quotations maintain fidelity to published sources, you may notice minor stylistic inconsistencies in the text. For example, pronouns referring to Deity are lowercased in some quotations and capitalized in others.

President Hunter often used the terms *men, man,* and *mankind* to refer to all people, both male and female. He also frequently used the pronouns *he, his,* and *him* to refer to both genders. These language conventions were common in his era, and he was typically referring to both women and men when he used them.

Historical Summary

The following chronology provides a brief historical framework for the teachings of President Howard W. Hunter in this book.

November 14, 1907	Born to John William (Will) Hunter and Nellie Marie Rasmussen Hunter in Boise, Idaho.
April 4, 1920	Baptized and confirmed in Boise.
May 1923	Receives the Eagle Scout Award—the second Eagle Scout in Boise.
January and February 1927	With his band, Hunter's Croonaders, provides music during a two-month cruise to Asia.
March 1928	Moves to Southern California.
April 1928	Begins working at a bank in California.
June 10, 1931	Marries Clara May (Claire) Jeffs in the Salt Lake Temple.
January 1932	Loses his banking job due to bank closures brought on by the Depression; begins working a series of odd jobs.
January 1934	Begins working in the title department of the Los Angeles County Flood Control District.
March 20, 1934	Son Howard William (Billy) Hunter Jr. is born.
October 11, 1934	Son Howard William (Billy) Hunter Jr. dies.

September 1935	Enters the Southwestern University School of Law in Los Angeles (now Southwestern Law School).
May 4, 1936	Son John Jacob Hunter is born.
June 29, 1938	Son Richard Allen Hunter is born.
June 8, 1939	Graduates from law school, third in his class.
April 1940	Begins private law practice, working part-time and then full-time by 1945; continues practicing law until his call as an Apostle in 1959.
September 1940 to November 1946	Serves as bishop of the El Sereno Ward in California.
February 1950 to November 1959	Serves as president of the Pasadena Stake in California.
November 14, 1953	Sealed to his parents on his 46th birthday in the Mesa Arizona Temple.
October 9, 1959	Called by President David O. McKay to be a member of the Quorum of the Twelve Apostles.
October 15, 1959	Ordained an Apostle and set apart as a member of the Quorum of the Twelve by President David O. McKay.
1964 to 1972	Serves as president of the Church's Genealogical Society.
1965 to 1976	Serves as president of the Polynesian Cultural Center in Laie, Hawaii.
1970 to 1972	Serves as Church Historian.
1974 to 1979	Helps oversee the planning, funding, and building of the Orson Hyde Memorial Garden in Jerusalem.

November 1975	Directs the organization of 15 stakes in one weekend from what were 5 stakes in Mexico City.
1979 to 1989	Oversees the planning and construction of the Brigham Young University (BYU) Jerusalem Center for Near Eastern Studies.
October 24, 1979	Conducts dedicatory services for the Orson Hyde Memorial Garden in Jerusalem.
October 9, 1983	Claire Hunter dies after an illness of more than 10 years.
November 10, 1985	Set apart as Acting President of the Quorum of the Twelve Apostles due to the poor health of the quorum president, Marion G. Romney.
June 2, 1988	Set apart as President of the Quorum of the Twelve Apostles after the death of President Marion G. Romney.
May 16, 1989	Dedicates the BYU Jerusalem Center for Near Eastern Studies.
April 12, 1990	Marries Inis Bernice Egan Stanton in the Salt Lake Temple.
June 5, 1994	Set apart as the 14th President of The Church of Jesus Christ of Latter-day Saints.
October 1, 1994	Sustained as President of the Church in general conference.
October 9, 1994	Dedicates the Orlando Florida Temple.
December 11, 1994	Presides over the creation of the Church's 2,000th stake (Mexico City Mexico Contreras Stake).
January 8, 1995	Dedicates the Bountiful Utah Temple.
March 3, 1995	Dies at his home in Salt Lake City, Utah, at age 87.

The Life and Ministry of Howard W. Hunter

On June 6, 1994, the day after Howard W. Hunter was set apart as President of The Church of Jesus Christ of Latter-day Saints, he extended two invitations. Speaking with a tone of gentle encouragement, he said:

"First of all, I would invite all members of the Church to live with ever more attention to the life and example of the Lord Jesus Christ, especially the love and hope and compassion He displayed. I pray that we might treat each other with more kindness, more courtesy, more humility and patience and forgiveness." [1]

Encouraging people to follow the Savior's example had been a focus of President Hunter's teachings for decades. "Please remember this one thing," he had said a few years earlier. "If our lives and our faith are centered upon Jesus Christ and his restored gospel, nothing can ever go permanently wrong. On the other hand, if our lives are not centered on the Savior and his teachings, no other success can ever be permanently right." [2]

President Hunter's second invitation was for Church members to partake more fully of the blessings of the temple:

"I also invite the members of the Church to establish the temple of the Lord as the great symbol of their membership and the supernal setting for their most sacred covenants. It would be the deepest desire of my heart to have every member of the Church be temple worthy. I would hope that every adult member would be worthy of—and carry—a current temple recommend, even if proximity to a temple does not allow immediate or frequent use of it.

"Let us be a temple-attending and a temple-loving people. Let us hasten to the temple as frequently as time and means and personal circumstances allow. Let us go not only for our kindred dead, but

Howard W. Hunter as a child

let us also go for the personal blessing of temple worship, for the sanctity and safety which is provided within those hallowed and consecrated walls. The temple is a place of beauty, it is a place of revelation, it is a place of peace. It is the house of the Lord. It is holy unto the Lord. It should be holy unto us."[3]

President Hunter continued to emphasize these two invitations throughout his service as President of the Church. Although his time as President lasted only nine months, these invitations inspired Church members worldwide to be more Christlike and to seek the blessings of the temple with greater devotion.

Beginnings

In the mid-1800s, Howard W. Hunter's ancestors in four different countries joined The Church of Jesus Christ of Latter-day Saints. On his mother's side, these ancestors were from Denmark and Norway. After emigrating from their homelands, they were some of the earliest settlers of Mount Pleasant, Utah. A descendant of these stalwart pioneers, Nellie Rasmussen, would become the mother of a prophet.

On his father's side, Howard had ancestors with deep roots in Scotland and New England. Those who joined the Church sacrificed greatly, but most of them discontinued their affiliation after a few years. The birth of John William (Will) Hunter in 1879 marked the beginning of the third generation in the Hunter line that was no longer connected with the Church. And yet Will Hunter would become the father of a prophet.

When Will Hunter was 8 years old, his family moved to Boise, Idaho. About 16 years later, Will met Nellie Rasmussen when she came to Boise to stay with an aunt and uncle. Will soon began courting Nellie, and after two years he proposed marriage. Nellie hesitated for some time, but Will persisted, and she eventually accepted his proposal. The couple was married in Mount Pleasant, Utah, and returned to Boise to make their home. Their first child, Howard William Hunter, was born in Boise on November 14, 1907. Their only other child, a daughter they named Dorothy, was born in 1909.

Building a Foundation for Life

At the time of Howard's birth, the Church had only one small branch in Boise. Howard's mother was an active member of the branch who raised her children in the gospel. Of her, Howard said, "She was always faithful. . . . She served as president of the Primary and [Young Women]. I can remember going to church with mother, sometimes before the scheduled hour for the meetings, and then staying after so she could complete her work."[4] Although Howard's father was not a member of the Church, he did not object to the family's participation and occasionally attended sacrament meeting with them.

In addition to leading her children in Church activity, Nellie Hunter helped them build a strong religious foundation at home. "It was mother who took the lead in teaching us the gospel," Howard recalled. "It was at her knee that we learned to pray. . . . I received a testimony as a boy at my mother's knee."[5]

The Boise Branch was made into a ward in 1913, a few days before Howard's sixth birthday. Two years later, when Howard was eight, he was looking forward to being baptized. "I became very excited about the possibility," he said. However, his father would not give permission. Howard recalled, "Father . . . felt I should wait until I knew what course I wanted in life. I wanted to be baptized, though the time came and passed without that blessing."[6]

Because Howard had not been baptized, he could not be ordained a deacon when he turned 12. "By that time, all my friends had been ordained deacons," he said. "Because I wasn't an official member of the Church, I wasn't able to do many of the things that they did."[7] Howard was especially disheartened that he could not pass the sacrament: "I sat in sacrament meetings with the other boys. When it was time for them to pass the sacrament, I would slump down in my seat. I felt so left out."[8]

Howard again approached his father, this time with his 10-year-old sister, Dorothy: "[We] began coaxing our father to allow us to be baptized. We also prayed that he might say yes. We were overjoyed when he finally gave his consent."[9] Nearly five months after Howard turned 12, he and Dorothy were baptized in a public swimming pool. Soon afterward, Howard was ordained a deacon and passed the sacrament for the first time. "I was frightened, but thrilled to have the privilege," he recalled.[10] Among his other duties, Howard pumped the bellows for the organ and started the fire to warm up the chapel on cold Sunday mornings. "A whole new world opened up to me as I learned the responsibilities of being a member of the Church and holding the priesthood," he said.[11]

As a young man, Howard joined his ward's Boy Scout troop and worked hard toward earning the highest award—Eagle Scout. When he neared his goal, he became involved in a friendly competition. "There were two of us vying to be the first Eagle Scout in Boise," he remembered.[12] The other young man finished the requirements first, but Howard seemed satisfied to be the second person to earn the award.[13]

Howard learned to be industrious early in life. He helped widows and other neighbors, sold newspapers, and worked on his uncle's ranch. As he grew older, his jobs included caddying at a golf course, delivering telegrams, and working at a drugstore, a newspaper, a hotel, a department store, and an art store.

Dorothy Hunter said her brother had a "driving ambition" and a "brilliant mind."[14] Complementing these attributes were qualities of compassion and generosity. Recalling his caring ways, Dorothy said, "Howard always wanted to do good and to be good. A wonderful brother, he looked out for me. He was kind to our mother and father."[15]

Howard's compassion also extended to animals. "Every stray cat could find a haven at our house, even against family objections," he said.[16] One time some neighbor boys were tormenting a kitten by throwing it in an irrigation ditch near the Hunters' home. Every time it crawled out, the boys threw it back in. Soon Howard came along and rescued the kitten. "It was lying there almost dead," Dorothy recalled, "and he brought it home."[17]

"It won't live," his mother said.

"Mother, we have to try," Howard insisted.[18]

Dorothy said they "wrapped it in a blanket and put it near the warm oven and nursed it," and with this care the kitten revived and lived with the family for many years.

Howard was ordained a teacher in 1923, just before the creation of the Boise Second Ward. Needing another place to meet, and anticipating future growth, local Church leaders proposed building a stake tabernacle. The Saints in Boise were asked to contribute $20,000 toward the construction of the building.[19] In a meeting where leaders made an appeal for donations, young Howard W. Hunter was the first person to raise his hand and make a pledge. The amount he pledged—$25—was a large sum in 1923, especially for a 15-year-old. "I worked and saved until I was able to pay my commitment in full," he later said.[20] The tabernacle was completed in 1925, and President Heber J. Grant came to dedicate it that December.[21]

From a young age, Howard showed an aptitude for music, and as a teenager he learned to play several instruments. At age 16 he formed his own music group, which he called Hunter's Croonaders. This group performed frequently at dances, receptions, and other events in the Boise area.

When Howard was 19, he was given a contract to provide music on a cruise ship that was going to Asia. For the first two months of 1927, Howard's five-piece band played for dinners and dances as the ship crossed the Pacific and stopped at various cities in Japan, China, and the Philippines. The cruise was an enlightening experience for Howard, allowing him to learn about other people and their cultures. Although he spent most of his earnings on sightseeing and souvenirs, he reasoned, "The education has been worth what we spent."[22]

A Time of Big Decisions

Howard came home from the cruise to the joyful news that his father had been baptized while he was gone. The next Sunday, Howard and his father attended priesthood meeting together for the first time. A caring bishop had been encouraging Will Hunter to

Howard W. Hunter, center, with Hunter's Croonaders, 1927

be baptized, and Howard said that "it was through a [home] teacher that a greater interest was created on his part for the church."[23]

After the cruise, Howard was uncertain about his future. He kept busy with musical activities and other jobs, including his own business, but none of these held the prospect of a good career. When his business venture stalled in March 1928, he decided to visit a friend in Southern California. He originally planned to stay for only a week or two, but he soon decided to remain and seek what he described as "employment with opportunity."[24] In California he would find not only a career but also his wife, extensive opportunities to serve in the Church, and a home for more than three decades.

Howard's first jobs in California were selling shoes and working at a citrus packing plant, where some days he loaded between 45 and 50 tons of oranges into railroad cars. "I didn't know there were this many oranges in the world," he mused. One day he had "a terrible time" because he had to sort lemons according to color, and he could not differentiate the yellow and green shades due to color blindness. "Before the day was over I thought I would have a nervous breakdown," he recalled.[25]

After two weeks at the citrus plant, Howard applied for a job at a bank in Los Angeles, which hired him immediately and began promoting him quickly. He also continued his musical activities, playing with various bands in the evenings. In September 1928, about six months after Howard moved to California, his family was reunited when his parents and sister moved there.

During his youth, Howard had attended church but had not studied the gospel in great depth. In California he became much more attentive to gospel study. "My first real awakening to the gospel came in a Sunday School class in [the] Adams Ward taught by Brother Peter A. Clayton," he recalled. "He had a wealth of knowledge and the ability to inspire young people. I studied the lessons, read the outside assignments he gave us, and participated in speaking on assigned subjects. . . . I think of this period of my life as the time the truths of the gospel commenced to unfold. I always had a testimony of the gospel, but suddenly I commenced to understand."[26] For Howard, the experiences in that Sunday School class began a lifelong love for studying the gospel.

Howard enjoyed associating with other young adults in the Los Angeles area. They attended church together, sometimes going to two or three wards on a Sunday, and participated in a wide variety of activities. One of those activities had lasting significance for Howard. A few months after he arrived in California, he and some friends attended a Church dance and then went to the beach to wade in the surf. That evening, Howard met Clara May (Claire) Jeffs, who was on a date with one of his friends. Howard and Claire soon developed a mutual attraction that flowered into love.

They dated a few times in 1928 and became more serious the next year. "She had light brown hair and was a very beautiful girl," Howard later said. "I think the thing that impressed me most was the depth of her testimony."[27] On a spring evening in 1931, nearly three years after they met, Howard took Claire to an overlook above the Pacific Ocean. There he proposed marriage, and she accepted. Howard recalled:

"We drove to Palos Verdes and parked on the cliffs where we could watch the waves roll in from the Pacific and break over the rocks in the light of a full moon. We talked about our plans and I put a diamond ring on her finger. We made many decisions that night and some strong resolutions regarding our lives."[28]

Those resolutions influenced Howard to make a life-changing decision four days before the wedding. After his band performed that night, he packed up his instruments and never played again professionally. Providing music for dances and parties "was glamorous in some respects," he said, "and I made good money," but he felt that parts of the lifestyle were incompatible with the life he envisioned for his family. "This left a void of something I had enjoyed, [but] the decision has never been regretted," he said years later.[29] His son Richard observed, "I have often thought of the remarkable discipline (I call it grit) it must have taken to give up something he deeply loved because he valued something more."[30]

Challenges and Blessings during the Early Years of Marriage

Howard and Claire were married in the Salt Lake Temple on June 10, 1931, and returned to Southern California to begin their life together. Business conditions in the United States were deteriorating because of the Great Depression, and in January 1932, the bank where Howard worked was forced to close. For the next two years he worked at a variety of jobs, trying to make ends meet. He and Claire were determined to be independent as long as possible, but after a year they accepted an invitation to live with Claire's parents for a time.

On March 20, 1934, Howard and Claire's first child was born, a son they named Howard William Hunter Jr. and called Billy. That summer they noticed that Billy seemed lethargic. Doctors diagnosed him with anemia, and Howard twice gave blood for transfusions, but Billy's condition did not improve. Further tests revealed a severe intestinal problem for which doctors recommended surgery. Howard recalled: "I was taken into the room on a table beside him and gave blood during the operation. At the conclusion, the doctors were not encouraging."[31] Three days later, seven-month-old Billy passed away as his parents sat beside his bed. "We were grief-stricken and numb as we left the hospital into the night," Howard wrote.[32] "This was a severe blow to us."[33]

Two months before Billy was born, Howard had obtained employment with the Los Angeles County Flood Control District. His work there introduced him to legal documents and court proceedings, and he decided to pursue a career as an attorney. Fulfilling that goal required years of resolve and hard work. Not having an undergraduate degree, Howard had to complete many classes before he could be admitted to law school. He took the classes at night because he needed to keep working. Even during his years in law school, he continued to work full time. "To work all day and go to school at night, and, in addition, to find the time to study was not an easy task," he wrote.[34] "It was not unusual for me to study far into the night."[35] Howard maintained that rigorous schedule for five years, finally graduating in 1939 as third in his class.

While Howard was in law school, two other sons were born to Claire and him—John in 1936 and Richard in 1938. Because of Howard's job with the Flood Control District, the family was able to buy a small home.

Bishop of the El Sereno Ward

In 1940, about a year after Howard graduated from law school, he was called to serve as bishop of the newly created El Sereno Ward in California. Surprised by this calling, he said, "I had always thought of a bishop as being an older man, and I asked how I could be the father of the ward at the young age of thirty-two." The stake presidency responded by assuring him that he could be "equal to the assignment." Although Howard felt overwhelmed, he promised, "I will do my best."[36] He fulfilled that promise with great commitment, inspiration, and compassion during his more than six years of service as bishop.

Once again, Howard faced heavy demands on his schedule and energy, but he felt that his service returned many blessings. "I found myself inundated with consuming responsibilities," he said. "It was a glorious work and a great blessing."[37]

An immediate need for the new ward was finding a place to meet. The bishopric leased some rooms in a local building, and ward members began to raise funds for their own meetinghouse. The construction of Church buildings was soon put on hold because of World War II, but ward members looked to the future and continued to raise money. For one of the fundraisers, known as the "onion project," they went to a pickle plant to trim onions. The odor of the onions would linger, which prompted Bishop Hunter to quip, "It was easy to tell in sacrament meeting if a person had been snipping onions."[38]

Other fundraisers included shredding cabbage in a sauerkraut plant and packaging and selling surplus breakfast cereal. "These were happy days when we worked together, people of all classes and ability supporting the bishopric in raising funds to build a chapel," Bishop Hunter recalled. "Our ward was like a big, happy family."[39] After much patience and sacrifice, the goal of the ward's own meetinghouse was finally realized in 1950, nearly four years after Howard was released as bishop.

Being a bishop during World War II presented unique challenges. Many male members of the ward were serving in the military, leaving families without husbands and fathers at home. The shortage of men also presented challenges in filling Church callings. Consequently, during part of his tenure as bishop, Howard also served as Scoutmaster. "We had a group of fine young men who could not be neglected," he said. "I worked with the boys for nearly two years and they made excellent progress."[40]

Howard was released as bishop on November 10, 1946. "I will always be thankful for this privilege and the education of those years," he said. Although the experience was "difficult in many ways," he and Claire "were grateful for the values it brought to our family."[41] Expressing gratitude for Bishop Hunter's service, one ward member wrote: "He brought our small ward membership together in a united effort and taught us to accomplish goals that seemed beyond our reach. We worked together as a ward, we prayed together, played together, and worshipped together."[42]

Although Howard was released in 1946, his special bond with members of the El Sereno Ward continued. His son Richard said that "to the end of his life, he stayed in contact with them and knew where they were and what their circumstances were. Whenever he traveled to a place where one of the old ward members [lived], he would make contact with them. The love he had for the ward members lasted his whole life."[43]

Raising a Family and Building a Career

Howard and Claire Hunter were loving parents who taught their sons values, responsibility, and the importance of the gospel. Long before the Church designated Monday night for family home evening, the Hunter family set aside that night as a time for teaching, telling stories, playing games, and going places together. When the family traveled, they sometimes went to temples so John and Richard could perform proxy baptisms for the dead. Howard and his sons also enjoyed building model trains, going camping, and doing other outdoor activities together.

Howard was both working full time and going to law school when John and Richard were born, and he was called to be a bishop when they were very young—ages four and two—so building a strong family required an extra measure of devotion from Claire. She gave that devotion gladly. "My desire and my greatest ambition . . . has been to be a good wife, to be a good homemaker, and to be a really good mother," she said. "We have worked hard to keep our boys close to the Church; the boys and I have had wonderful times together."[44] Howard often paid tribute to Claire for her influence and sacrifices in raising their sons.

During the years of raising a family and serving in Church leadership callings, Howard also built a thriving law practice. Working mostly with business and corporate clients, he became a highly respected attorney in Southern California. He was elected to serve on the board of directors of more than two dozen companies.

In his profession, Howard was known for his integrity, precise thinking, clear communications, and sense of fairness. He was also known as a "people lawyer"—someone who "always seemed to have time and the interest to help people with their problems."[45] One attorney said that Howard "was much more concerned about

Howard and Claire Hunter with their sons John and Richard

seeing that people got the help they needed than that he got compensated for it."[46]

President of the Pasadena California Stake

In February 1950, Elder Stephen L Richards and Elder Harold B. Lee of the Quorum of the Twelve traveled to California to divide the rapidly growing Pasadena Stake. They interviewed many brethren in the stake, including Howard. After prayerfully considering whom the Lord would have serve as stake president, at nearly midnight they sent for Howard and extended the calling to him. Elder Richards and Elder Lee told him to get a good night's sleep and call them early the next morning with his recommendation for counselors. "I went home that night, but I didn't sleep," Howard said. "The calling was overwhelming. Claire and I talked for a long time."[47]

After President Hunter and his counselors were sustained, they began assessing needs in the stake. A high priority for the new stake presidency was helping members build spiritual strength. One concern was that families were becoming fragmented, partly because they were involved in so many activities. After leaders prayed and counseled together, they felt impressed to emphasize family home evening and to reserve Monday nights for families. All Church buildings in the stake were closed on Monday nights, and "no other

Leaders in the Pasadena Stake, 1950. Left to right: *Daken K. Broadhead,*
first counselor in the stake presidency; Howard W. Hunter, president;
A. Kay Berry, second counselor; and Emron "Jack" Jones, clerk.

events were held which would conflict with that sacred evening,"
explained President Hunter.[48]

Early in his service, President Hunter and other stake presidents
in Southern California met with Elder Stephen L Richards to discuss
a seminary program for high school students. President Hunter recalled, "[Elder Richards] explained that they would like to try an
experiment with early-morning seminary classes in an area where
the law did not provide for released time [from school] for religious
education."[49] President Hunter was appointed chairman of a committee that studied the feasibility of the idea. After completing the
study, the committee recommended introducing early-morning seminary for the students in three high schools. As a youth, President
Hunter's son Richard was part of the early-morning seminary experiment. He recalled, "We wondered whether someone had lost
their mind to have a class at 6:00 a.m., but it became our favorite
time of the day, where we could be together as Church friends and
learn."[50] This program was soon expanded to other students and
was the forerunner of the early-morning seminary program for the
youth of the Church.

At the October 1951 general conference, the First Presidency met
with the stake presidents from Southern California to announce

their desire to build a temple in Los Angeles. The prospect of having a temple nearby brought great joy—and would require great sacrifice, as Church members were asked to contribute $1 million toward its construction. When President Hunter returned to California, he met with stake and ward leaders and said, "Give the people the opportunity of receiving great blessings by contributing generously to the temple."[51] Within six months, members in Southern California had pledged $1.6 million toward building the temple, which was dedicated in 1956.

In addition to contributing funds for the temple and other Church buildings, members provided volunteer labor. When meetinghouses were built, President Hunter spent many hours assisting with a shovel, hammer, or paintbrush. Additionally, members provided volunteer labor for Church welfare projects, which included poultry farms, citrus groves, and canneries. For eight years, President Hunter had the assignment of coordinating the work of 12 stakes on these projects, and he often assisted in the work himself. "He never asked anyone to do something or take an assignment that he wouldn't do himself," a friend observed.[52] Years later, as a member of the Quorum of the Twelve, Elder Hunter said:

"I have never been on a gloomy welfare project. I have climbed trees and picked lemons, peeled fruit, tended boiler, carried boxes, unloaded trucks, cleaned the cannery, and a thousand and one other things, but the things I remember most are the laughing and the singing and the good fellowship of people engaged in the service of the Lord."[53]

In November 1953, President and Sister Hunter and other members of the Pasadena Stake traveled to the Mesa Arizona Temple to do ordinance work. November 14 was President Hunter's 46th birthday, and before a session began that day, the temple president asked him to address those who were assembled in the chapel. He later wrote of this experience:

"While I was speaking to the congregation, . . . my father and mother came into the chapel dressed in white. I had no idea my father was prepared for his temple blessings, although Mother had been anxious about it for some time. I was so overcome with emotion that I was unable to continue to speak. President Pierce [the temple president] came to my side and explained the reason for the interruption. When my father and mother came to the temple that morning they asked the president not to mention to me that they were there because they wanted it to be a birthday surprise. This was a birthday I have never forgotten because on that day they were endowed and I had the privilege of witnessing their sealing, following which I was sealed to them."[54]

About three years later, the eternal bonds of President Hunter's family were completed when Dorothy was sealed to her parents in the newly dedicated Los Angeles California Temple.

As a stake president, Howard led with love. A woman who served in a stake calling said, "You felt appreciated and wanted and needed. . . . He made people responsible when they received a calling, but if they needed his opinion or counsel, he was always there. We knew that we had his complete support and interest."[55] One of his counselors noted, "He praised people for their accomplishments and let them rise to high expectations."[56] A stake member who said President Hunter was her most influential teacher explained, "This man loved others by putting them in high priority, by listening to understand, and by sharing his experiences with others."[57]

By the fall of 1959, Howard W. Hunter had presided over the Pasadena Stake for more than nine years, giving service that had blessed the lives of thousands of Latter-day Saints in Southern California. His ministry was about to expand to bless the lives of Church members throughout the world.

Quorum of the Twelve

"Thou shalt bear record of my name, . . . and thou shalt send forth my word unto the ends of the earth" (D&C 112:4).

On October 9, 1959, between sessions of general conference in Salt Lake City, Howard learned that President David O. McKay wanted to meet with him. He immediately went to the Church Administration Building, where President McKay greeted him warmly and said, "President Hunter, . . . the Lord has spoken. You are called to be one of his special witnesses, and tomorrow you will be

The Quorum of the Twelve Apostles, 1965. Seated left to right: *Ezra Taft Benson, Mark E. Petersen (on arm of chair), Joseph Fielding Smith (quorum president), and LeGrand Richards.* Standing left to right: *Gordon B. Hinckley, Delbert L. Stapley, Thomas S. Monson, Spencer W. Kimball, Harold B. Lee, Marion G. Romney, Richard L. Evans, and Howard W. Hunter.*

sustained as a member of the Council of the Twelve."[58] Regarding that experience, Howard wrote:

"I cannot attempt to explain the feeling that came over me. Tears came to my eyes and I could not speak. I have never felt so completely humbled as when I sat in the presence of this great, sweet, kindly man—the prophet of the Lord. He told me what a great joy this would bring into my life, the wonderful association with the brethren, and that hereafter my life and time would be devoted as a servant of the Lord and that I would hereafter belong to the Church and the whole world. . . . He put his arms around me and assured me that the Lord would love me and I would have the sustaining confidence of the First Presidency and Council of the Twelve. . . . I [told him] I would gladly give my time, my life, and all that I possessed to this service."[59]

As soon as Howard left President McKay's office, he went to his hotel room and called Claire, who was in Provo visiting their son John and his wife and their baby. At first Howard could hardly speak. When he finally told Claire of the calling, they were both overcome with emotion.

The next day, at the Saturday morning session of general conference, Howard William Hunter was sustained as a member of the Quorum of the Twelve Apostles. "I felt . . . the weight of the world on my shoulders," he said of that time. "As the conference proceeded I was most uncomfortable and wondered if I could ever feel that this was my proper place."[60]

President McKay called on Elder Hunter to speak in the Sunday afternoon session of the conference. After briefly reviewing his life and bearing his testimony, he said:

"I do not apologize for the tears that come to my eyes on this occasion because I believe that I face friends, my brethren and sisters in the Church, whose hearts beat the same as mine today, in the thrill of the gospel and in service to others.

"President McKay, . . . I accept, without reservation, the call which you have made of me, and I am willing to devote my life and all that I have to this service. Sister Hunter joins me in this pledge."[61]

Elder Hunter was ordained an Apostle on October 15, 1959. At age 51, he was the youngest member of the Twelve, whose average age at the time was nearly 66.

For the next 18 months, Elder Hunter commuted between California and Utah as he completed the necessary work in his law practice and prepared to move. One of his clients said that "the Church must have made a very attractive offer" to entice him to leave such a successful law practice. Regarding that, Elder Hunter wrote in his journal:

"Most people do not understand why persons of our religious faith respond to calls made to serve or the commitment we make to give our all. . . . I have thoroughly enjoyed the practice of law, but this call that has come to me will far overshadow the pursuit of the profession or monetary gain."[62]

Elder Hunter's apostolic ministry would span more than 35 years, and during that time he would travel to nearly every country in the world to fulfill his charge as a special witness of Jesus Christ (see D&C 107:23).

The Genealogical Society of Utah

"Let us . . . offer unto the Lord . . . a book containing the records of our dead, which shall be worthy of all acceptation" (D&C 128:24).

In 1964 the First Presidency appointed Elder Hunter to be president of the Church's Genealogical Society, which was then known as the Genealogical Society of Utah. That organization was the forerunner of the Church's Family History Department. Its purpose was to gather, preserve, and share genealogical information throughout the world. Elder Hunter presided over the society for eight years, and during that time he oversaw far-reaching changes in expediting, refining, and expanding family history work.

By 1969 the organization had amassed "more than 670,000 rolls of microfilm, representing the equivalent of three million volumes of 300 pages each." It had also collected "six million completed records of family groups, a card file index of 36 million individuals, and a book collection of more than 90,000 volumes."[63] Each week, about 1,000 rolls of microfilm were being added from around the world. Processing those records and making them accessible—both for research and for temple work—was an enormous task. Under Elder Hunter's leadership, the Genealogical Society began using the latest computer technologies to assist with the work. One writer noted that the society became "world famous among professional organizations for its progressive record-keeping activities."[64]

Elder Hunter was released as president of the Genealogical Society in 1972. Summarizing the impact of his efforts, Elder Richard G. Scott said, "He dedicated a significant portion of his life to that work and laid the foundations and the direction from which the Church is still reaping the benefits."[65]

The Polynesian Cultural Center

"Hearken ye people from afar; and ye that are upon the islands of the sea, listen together" (D&C 1:1).

In 1965 the First Presidency appointed Elder Hunter to be president and chairman of the board of the Polynesian Cultural Center in Laie, Hawaii. At the time, the center had been open for only 15 months and was facing many challenges. Tourist attendance was low, and people had different points of view about the center's objectives and programs. A week after Elder Hunter was appointed, he went to Laie and began a careful study of the center's strengths and needs.

Under Elder Hunter's leadership, the Polynesian Cultural Center became one of the most popular tourist attractions in Hawaii, drawing nearly one million visitors in 1971. Elder Hunter also oversaw a large expansion of the center and its programs. Also important, in Elder Hunter's words, was that the center provided employment that allowed "thousands of students from the South Pacific [to be] assisted in getting their education, most of whom would not have been able to leave their islands to go to school [otherwise]."[66]

After presiding over the Polynesian Cultural Center for 12 years, Elder Hunter was released in 1976. His service as president helped fulfill the words of President David O. McKay, who said in 1955 that the small village of Laie had the potential to become "a missionary factor, influencing not thousands, not tens of thousands, but millions of people who will come seeking to know what this town and its significance are."[67]

Church Historian

"It is the duty of the Lord's clerk, whom he has appointed,
to keep a history, and a general church record of all things
that transpire in Zion" (D&C 85:1).

In January 1970, President David O. McKay passed away, and Joseph Fielding Smith was set apart as the new President of the Church. Joseph Fielding Smith had been serving as Church Historian for the previous 49 years, and when he became President of the Church, Elder Hunter was called to succeed him in that assignment. "President Smith had been the Church Historian for so many years that I could hardly visualize myself in that position," he said.[68]

Elder Hunter approached this new responsibility with his usual zeal. "The assignment as given by the Lord through revelation is tremendously challenging—both in fulfilling the task of collection and writing and in making the material of use to the members of

The Brigham Young University Jerusalem Center for Near Eastern Studies

the Church," he said.[69] The *Church News* reported that the Church Historian was "responsible for all the record keeping of the Church, including minutes, temple records, all ordinations, patriarchal blessings, and . . . a current compilation of Church history."[70]

In 1972, members of the Twelve were relieved of some of their heavy administrative duties so they could devote more time to their apostolic ministry. As part of that change, Elder Hunter was released as Church Historian but maintained an advisory role over the Church's Historical Department. "This will leave me in a position of direction but relieved of the operational function," he wrote.[71] He continued in an advisory role until 1978.

Service in the Holy Land

Howard W. Hunter developed a special love for the Holy Land when he traveled there with his family in 1958 and 1960. During his service as an Apostle, he returned more than two dozen times. "His desire to be where the Savior walked and taught seemed insatiable," said Elder James E. Faust of the Quorum of the Twelve.[72]

Keenly aware of the conflicts in the region, Elder Hunter carried a message of love and peace. "Both the Jews and the Arabs are children of our Father," he said. "They are both children of promise, and as a church we do not take sides. We have love for and an interest in each. The purpose of the gospel of Jesus Christ is to bring about love, unity, and brotherhood of the highest order."[73]

Between 1972 and 1989, Elder Hunter fulfilled key assignments for two special projects in Jerusalem: the Orson Hyde Memorial Garden and the Brigham Young University (BYU) Jerusalem Center for Near Eastern Studies. Early in the Church's history—in 1841—Elder Orson Hyde of the Quorum of the Twelve offered a dedicatory prayer on the Mount of Olives, east of Jerusalem. In 1972 the First Presidency asked Elder Hunter to begin looking for possible sites to construct an Orson Hyde memorial in Jerusalem. In 1975 the city of Jerusalem opened the way for what would eventually become the Orson Hyde Memorial Garden, built on the Mount of Olives.

During the next few years, Elder Hunter traveled to Jerusalem many times to negotiate contracts for the memorial and to oversee its design and construction. The project was completed in 1979 and was dedicated that year by President Spencer W. Kimball. After conducting the dedicatory services, Elder Hunter expressed his belief that the memorial "will have a great impact for good in extending a favorable image of the Church."[74]

Even before the Orson Hyde Memorial Garden was completed, Elder Hunter had been looking for a site where the Church could build a center for BYU's study abroad program. The center would also provide a meeting place for members of the Jerusalem Branch. Overseeing this project would be one of the most complex, sensitive assignments of Elder Hunter's ministry.

Church leaders selected a site, but obtaining approval for the land lease and building plans required nearly five years of what Elder Hunter described as "endless work."[75] After extensive debate and negotiations, the Israeli government allowed construction of the center to proceed.

*President Hunter at the Brigham Young University Jerusalem Center
for Near Eastern Studies, before dedicating the center*

By May 1988 the construction was mostly completed and the lease was ready to sign. By that time, Howard W. Hunter was serving as Acting President of the Twelve. He had undergone serious back surgery the previous year and was unable to walk, but nevertheless he flew to Jerusalem to sign the lease. While he was there, BYU students and members of the Jerusalem Branch held a small reception to express their gratitude. A history of the branch tells of this poignant scene as the reception began: "Still recovering from back surgery, President Hunter was wheeled through the main entrance by President [Jeffrey R.] Holland [of Brigham Young University] as the choir greeted them by singing 'The Holy City.'"[76] Tears were rolling down President Hunter's cheeks.

In May 1989, President Hunter returned to Jerusalem to dedicate the center. This dedicatory service culminated a decade of extraordinary effort by him and others to bring the Jerusalem Center from a hope to a reality. "President Howard W. Hunter . . . was the constant thread and the loving watchman on the tower over that project from the time it was only a dream," said Elder Jeffrey R. Holland.[77] In the dedicatory prayer, President Hunter said:

"This building . . . has been constructed for the housing of those who love thee and seek to learn of thee and follow in the footsteps of thy Son, our Savior and Redeemer. It is beautiful in every respect, exemplifying the beauty of what it represents. O Father, we thank thee for the privilege of building this house to thee for the benefit and learning of thy sons and daughters."[78]

The Expanding Church

"Zion must increase in beauty, and in holiness; her borders must be enlarged; her stakes must be strengthened" (D&C 82:14).

When Howard W. Hunter was called as an Apostle in 1959, there were about 1.6 million members of the Church. During the following decades, he played a key role in the Church's unprecedented worldwide growth. On hundreds of weekends, he traveled to stakes to strengthen members and call new leaders. He also met with government officials in many nations, helping open doors for missionary work.

By 1975, Church membership had increased to about 3.4 million and was growing especially fast in Latin America. Late that year, Elder Hunter and Elder J. Thomas Fyans, an Assistant to the Twelve, were assigned to divide 5 stakes in Mexico City. After meeting with leaders in the area and reviewing information from the stake presidents, Elder Hunter directed the organization of 15 stakes from those 5 stakes—all in one weekend.[79] With typical understatement, he wrote, "I doubt there has ever been such a mass organization in the Church, and we were tired by the time we got home."[80]

Claire, a Devoted Companion

"My wife has been a sweet and loving companion," Elder Hunter said when he was called to the Quorum of the Twelve in 1959.[81] For many years, Claire usually accompanied Elder Hunter in his travels as an Apostle. President Thomas S. Monson recalled a time when he observed Claire showing her love for the children in Tonga: "She would take those sweet little Tongan children in her arms and put one on each knee as she spoke to them . . . and then explained to the teachers of the Primary how blessed and privileged they were

Howard and Claire Hunter

to have the opportunity of teaching such precious little children. She knew the worth of a human soul."[82]

In a 1974 interview, Elder Hunter said of Claire: "Throughout our whole marriage, . . . she has always been standing by with love, consideration, and encouragement. . . . She's been a great support."[83]

By the time of that interview, Claire had begun to experience serious health challenges. At first she had severe headaches and occasional memory loss and disorientation. Later she suffered several small strokes that made it difficult for her to talk or use her hands. When she reached the point of needing constant care, Elder Hunter was determined to provide as much as he could while also fulfilling his responsibilities as a member of the Quorum of the Twelve. He arranged for someone to stay with Claire during the day, but he cared for her at night. Elder Hunter endured some health problems of his own during these years, including a heart attack in 1980.

Claire suffered a cerebral hemorrhage in 1981 and another in 1982. The second one left her so incapacitated that doctors insisted she be placed in a care center so she could receive proper medical attention. She remained in the center for the last 18 months of her life. During that time, President Hunter visited her at least once a day except when he was traveling on Church assignments. Although

Claire did not recognize him much of the time, he continued to tell her of his love and to make sure that she was comfortable. A grandson said, "He was always in a hurry to see her, to be by her side, and take care of her."[84] Recalling his father's care for his mother, Richard Hunter wrote:

"My mother had the best care possible in her declining years because Dad took care of her. All the family watched with great awe and respect as he switched into the role of a caregiver. . . . I remember the weight he felt when the doctor warned him [that] it may be the worst thing that could happen to her if she stayed at home and didn't enter a skilled nursing facility. If she stayed at home, he would likely die in his attempt to care for her because of his own physical limitation. Then she would be left alone in her care. His devotion to her is one of the things that will always be tender for our family."[85]

Claire passed away on October 9, 1983. Having observed Elder Hunter's caring as Claire suffered through more than 10 years of illness, Elder James E. Faust said, "[The] tenderness which was evident in their communication was heartrending and touching. I have never seen such an example of devotion of a husband to his wife."[86]

President of the Quorum of the Twelve

President Spencer W. Kimball passed away in November 1985, and Ezra Taft Benson succeeded him as President of the Church. Marion G. Romney became President of the Quorum of the Twelve by virtue of being the senior member of the quorum. Because of President Romney's poor health, Elder Hunter, who was next in seniority, was set apart as Acting President of the Twelve. He became President of the Twelve in June 1988, about two weeks after the death of President Romney.

President Hunter served as Acting President or President of the Quorum of the Twelve for eight and a half years. During that time, the worldwide ministry of the Twelve continued to expand as the Church grew from 5.9 million members to 8.7 million, with wards or branches in 149 nations and territories. "It's an exciting time in Church history," President Hunter said in 1988. "Today, walking isn't fast enough. We have to be on the run to keep up and move the work forward."[87] In fulfilling the responsibility to bear witness of Jesus Christ and build up the Church throughout the world, President Hunter led by example. He traveled throughout the United States and to more than 25 other nations during his service as President of the Twelve.

President Hunter pressed forward despite many setbacks with his health. In 1986 he underwent open-heart surgery, and in 1987 he underwent back surgery. Although his back healed, he was unable to walk because of nerve damage and other complications. That October, he sat in a wheelchair while giving his general conference address. "Forgive me if I remain seated while I present these few remarks," he began. "It is not by choice that I speak from a wheelchair. I notice that the rest of you seem to enjoy the conference sitting down, so I will follow your example."[88]

Determined to regain the use of his legs, President Hunter went through a strenuous regimen of physical therapy. At the next general conference, in April 1988, he slowly walked to the pulpit with a walker. In December he used a walker to attend the weekly temple meeting of the First Presidency and Twelve, the first time in more than a year that he had not come in a wheelchair. "When I came into the council room, the brethren stood and clapped," he said. "This is the first time I have heard clapping in the temple. . . . Most of the doctors have told me that I would never be able to stand or walk, but they have failed to take into consideration the power of prayer."[89]

In April 1990, as a meeting of the Quorum of the Twelve was concluding, President Hunter asked, "Does anyone have anything that is not on the agenda?" When no one spoke, he announced, "Well, then, . . . if no one else has anything to say, I thought I'd just let you know that I'm going to be married this afternoon." One member of the Twelve said the announcement was such a surprise that "everyone wondered if they had heard correctly." President Hunter explained to his brethren, "Inis Stanton is an old acquaintance from California. I've been visiting with her for some time, and I've decided to be married."[90] Inis had been a member of the El Sereno Ward when President Hunter was bishop. Their paths

Howard and Inis Hunter

crossed later when Inis moved to Utah and was a receptionist in the Church Office Building. They were married in the Salt Lake Temple on April 12, 1990, by President Gordon B. Hinckley.

Nearly seven years had passed since Claire's death. Inis was a source of great comfort and strength to President Hunter during his service as President of the Quorum of the Twelve and President of the Church. She accompanied him on most of his travels to meet with the Saints all over the world.

On February 7, 1993, President Hunter went to Brigham Young University to speak at a fireside that was attended by 17,000 people. He was just beginning his address when a man rushed onto the stand, carrying a briefcase in one hand and a black object in the other. "Stop right there!" the man shouted. He threatened to detonate what he claimed was a bomb unless President Hunter read a prepared statement. President Hunter refused and stood resolutely at the pulpit the entire time the man was threatening him. As fear and commotion spread through the building, the audience began to sing "We Thank Thee, O God, for a Prophet." After a few minutes of suspense, two security personnel restrained the man, and President Hunter was lowered to the floor for safety. When order was restored, he rested briefly and then continued with his remarks. "Life has a fair number of challenges in it," he began, and then added, "as demonstrated."[91]

During the previous 20 years, President Hunter had endured numerous trials, including the failing health and eventual death of Claire, multiple hospitalizations for his own health problems, and great pain and physical disability. His teachings through those years often focused on adversity and bore testimony of the Savior Jesus Christ as the source for peace and help in times of trial. In one sermon he taught:

"Prophets and Apostles of the Church have faced . . . personal difficulties. I acknowledge that I have faced a few, and you will undoubtedly face some of your own now and later in your life. When these experiences humble us and refine us and teach us and bless us, they can be powerful instruments in the hands of God to make us better people, to make us more grateful, more loving, and more considerate of other people in their own times of difficulty."[92]

Such teachings were like a loving embrace to those who were suffering. The inspired words of President Howard W. Hunter encouraged many to turn to the Savior, as he had done himself.

President of the Church

"President Hunter is one of the most loving, Christlike men we have ever known. His spiritual depth is so profound as to be unfathomable. Having been under the guiding influence of the Lord Jesus Christ as His special witness for so many years, President Hunter's spirituality has been honed in a remarkable way. It is the wellspring of his whole being" (James E. Faust).[93]

On May 30, 1994, President Ezra Taft Benson passed away after an extended illness. Six days later, the Quorum of the Twelve Apostles met in the Salt Lake Temple to reorganize the First Presidency. As the senior Apostle, Howard W. Hunter was set apart as President of the Church. He called Gordon B. Hinckley and Thomas S. Monson, who had been serving as counselors to President Benson, to be his counselors.

President Hunter with his counselors in the First Presidency: President Gordon B. Hinckley (left) and President Thomas S. Monson (right)

In a press conference the next day, President Hunter made his first public statements as President of the Church. "Our hearts have been very tender since the death of our friend and brother Ezra Taft Benson," he began. "I have felt his loss in a particularly personal way in light of the new responsibility that has come to me since his passing. I have shed many tears and have sought my Father in Heaven in earnest prayer with a desire to be equal to the high and holy calling which is now mine.

"My greatest strength through these past hours and recent days has been my abiding testimony that this is the work of God and not men, that Jesus Christ is the authorized and living head of this church and He leads it in word and deed. I pledge my life, my strength, and the full measure of my soul to serving Him fully."[94]

After expressions of love, President Hunter issued two invitations to Church members. The first was to be more diligent in following the example of Jesus Christ, and the second was to partake more fully of the blessings of the temple (see pages 1–3). He also invited those who were hurt, struggling, or afraid to "come back [and] let us stand with you and dry your tears."[95]

Despite fragile health, President Hunter was determined to do all he could to meet with and strengthen the Saints. Two weeks after becoming President, he gave his first major addresses, speaking to new mission presidents and then to more than 2,200 missionaries. Later that month he went to Carthage and Nauvoo, Illinois, to commemorate the 150th anniversary of the martyrdom of Joseph and Hyrum Smith. "Wherever we went, people crowded around him," President Gordon B. Hinckley said. "He shook hands with thousands, with a particular smile when children gathered about to look into his eyes and grasp his hand."[96]

On October 1, 1994, in the Saturday morning session of general conference, Church members formally sustained Howard W. Hunter as President of The Church of Jesus Christ of Latter-day Saints and as prophet, seer, and revelator. In his opening address, President Hunter repeated his invitations for Church members to follow the Savior's example and to "look to the temple of the Lord as the great symbol of your membership."[97] He emphasized temples again the next week, when he traveled to Florida to dedicate the Orlando Florida Temple. "The gospel plan that the Lord revealed is not complete without a temple," he taught, "for it is herein that the ordinances necessary for His plan of life and salvation are administered."[98]

In November, President Hunter spoke at a satellite broadcast commemorating the 100th anniversary of the Genealogical Society— an event that had special meaning for him, since he had presided over the organization from 1964 to 1972. "I look back in wonder at the tapestry woven by the Lord in the furthering of temple and family history work," he said. He then declared, "I have one overriding message: This work must hasten."[99]

President Hunter continued to labor vigorously through the end of the year. At the First Presidency Christmas devotional, he testified of the Savior and again emphasized the importance of following His example:

"The Savior dedicated His life to blessing other people. . . . Never did [He] give in expectation of receiving. He gave freely and lovingly, and His gifts were of inestimable value. He gave eyes to the blind, ears to the deaf, and legs to the lame; cleanliness to the unclean, wholeness to the infirm, and breath to the lifeless. His gifts were opportunity to the downtrodden, freedom to the oppressed, forgiveness to the repentant, hope to the despairing, and light in the darkness. He gave us His love, His service, and His life. And most important, He gave us and all mortals resurrection, salvation, and eternal life.

"We should strive to give as He gave. To give of oneself is a holy gift. We give as a remembrance of all the Savior has given."[100]

As part of his address, he also adapted a message that had been published in a magazine the same year he was called as an Apostle:

"This Christmas, mend a quarrel. Seek out a forgotten friend. Dismiss suspicion and replace it with trust. Write a letter. Give a soft answer. Encourage youth. Manifest your loyalty in word and deed. Keep a promise. Forgo a grudge. Forgive an enemy. Apologize. Try to understand. Examine your demands on others. Think first of someone else. Be kind. Be gentle. Laugh a little more. Express your gratitude. Welcome a stranger. Gladden the heart of a child. Take pleasure in the beauty and wonder of the earth. Speak your love and then speak it again."[101]

The next week President Hunter traveled to Mexico City to organize the Church's 2,000th stake. Nineteen years earlier in Mexico City, he had directed the organization of 15 stakes from what were 5 stakes in a single weekend. President Gordon B. Hinckley described the creation of the 2,000th stake as "a significant milestone in the history of the Church."[102]

One night during those months, President Hunter's son Richard was in the Joseph Smith Memorial Building and saw that one of the hostesses was in a wheelchair. "I could tell it was new for her," he said. "I went to talk with her and said my father had a wheelchair just like hers. She said to me that the prophet of her Church also had a wheelchair just like hers. She said that if he can do it, then maybe she could as well. That gave her hope. I think that Dad was beloved by many. Perhaps one of the reasons for that is they could see he suffered just like they do, and he bore up under that load of suffering, and that gave them hope." [103]

To begin the year 1995, President Hunter dedicated the Bountiful Utah Temple. He presided over six dedicatory sessions before becoming so fatigued that he was admitted to a hospital. After he was released a few days later, the Church issued a statement saying that he had prostate cancer that had spread to his bones. President Hunter did not make another public appearance during the final six weeks of his life, although he continued to meet with his counselors and conduct Church business at his residence. "I am grateful that he had the opportunity to dedicate [that temple]," President Gordon B. Hinckley said, "particularly in light of his earlier plea that members of the Church 'look to the temple of the Lord as the great symbol of [their] membership.'" [104]

President Howard W. Hunter passed away on March 3, 1995, at the age of 87. His final words, spoken in "a very quiet, sweet voice" to those at his bedside, were simply, "Thank you." [105] Although he had been President of the Church for only nine months, his influence had been profound. "Members of the Church all over the world have become bonded to him in a special way as their prophet, seer, and revelator," said Elder James E. Faust. "They have seen in him the personification of the attributes of the Savior himself. They have responded in a remarkable way to his prophetic messages of making our lives more Christlike and of making our temples the center of our worship." [106]

At President Hunter's funeral, President Gordon B. Hinckley said in tribute:

"A majestic tree in the forest has fallen, leaving a place of emptiness. A great and quiet strength has departed from our midst.

"Much has been said about his suffering. I believe that it went on longer and was more sharp and deep than any of us really knew.

33

He developed a high tolerance for pain and did not complain about it. That he lived so long is a miracle in and of itself. His suffering has comforted and mitigated the pain of many others who suffer. They know that he understood the heaviness of their burdens. He reached out to these with a special kind of love.

"Much has been said about his kindness, his thoughtfulness, his courtesy to others. It is all true. He surrendered himself to the pattern of the Lord whom he loved. He was a quiet and thoughtful man. But he also could be aroused to voice strong and wise opinions. . . .

"Brother Hunter was kind and gentle. But he also could be strong and persuasive in his statements. . . . He was trained in the law. He knew how to present a matter. He laid out the various premises in orderly fashion. He moved from these to his conclusion. When he spoke, we all listened. His suggestions most often prevailed. But when they were not accepted, he had the flexibility to withdraw his advocacy. . . .

"For thirty-six years now, wearing the mantle of the holy apostleship, his has been a leading and powerful voice in declaring the teachings of the gospel of Jesus Christ and moving forward the work of the Church. He has traveled widely over the earth as a true and able minister in the service of the Master. . . .

"Howard W. Hunter, prophet, seer, and revelator, had a sure and certain testimony of the living reality of God, our Eternal Father. He voiced with great conviction his witness of the divinity of the Lord Jesus Christ, the Redeemer of mankind. He spoke with love for the Prophet Joseph Smith, and for all of those who succeeded him in [the] line of succession until President Hunter's own time. . . .

"May God bless his memory to our great good."[107]

Notes

1. In Jay M. Todd, "President Howard W. Hunter: Fourteenth President of the Church," *Ensign,* July 1994, 4.

2. Howard W. Hunter, "Fear Not, Little Flock" (address given at Brigham Young University, Mar. 14, 1989), 2; speeches.byu.edu.

3. In Todd, "President Howard W. Hunter," 5.

4. In J M. Heslop, "He Found Pleasure in Work," *Church News,* Nov. 16, 1974, 4.

5. In Heslop, "He Found Pleasure in Work," 4, 12.

6. In Heslop, "He Found Pleasure in Work," 4.

7. In Kellene Ricks, "Friend to Friend: From an Interview with Howard W. Hunter, President of the Quorum of the Twelve Apostles," *Friend,* Apr. 1990, 6.

8. In Gerry Avant, "Elder Hunter—Packed Away Musician's Career for Marriage," *Church News,* May 19, 1985, 4.

9. In Ricks, "Friend to Friend," 6.

10. In Heslop, "He Found Pleasure in Work," 4.

11. In Ricks, "Friend to Friend," 6.

12. In Avant, "Elder Hunter," 4.

13. See "Eagle Scout Qualifies," *Idaho Statesman,* May 12, 1923; quoted in Eleanor Knowles, *Howard W. Hunter* (1994), 41.

14. In Don L. Searle, "President Howard W. Hunter: Acting President of the Quorum of the Twelve Apostles," *Ensign,* Apr. 1986, 22.

15. In James E. Faust, "The Way of an Eagle," *Ensign,* Aug. 1994, 4.

16. In Knowles, *Howard W. Hunter,* 22.

17. In James E. Faust, "The Way of an Eagle," 4, 6.

18. In Knowles, *Howard W. Hunter,* 22.

19. Historical Sketch of the Boise Stake of The Church of Jesus Christ of Latter-day Saints (1924), 6, Church History Library, Salt Lake City.

20. In Knowles, *Howard W. Hunter,* 41.

21. The Boise Tabernacle was torn down in 1992 by the Boise School District, which had purchased it from the Church several years earlier (see "Preservationists Protest Demolition Work on Tabernacle in Boise," *Deseret News,* Sept. 9, 1992, B3).

22. In Knowles, *Howard W. Hunter,* 55.

23. In Heslop, "He Found Pleasure in Work," 4; see also Knowles, *Howard W. Hunter,* 57.

24. In Knowles, *Howard W. Hunter,* 64.

25. In Knowles, *Howard W. Hunter,* 65.

26. In Knowles, *Howard W. Hunter,* 71.

27. In Gerry Avant, "She Made Home a Happy Place," *Church News,* Nov. 16, 1974, 5.

28. In Knowles, *Howard W. Hunter,* 79–80.

29. In Knowles, *Howard W. Hunter,* 81.

30. Unpublished manuscript by Richard A. Hunter. This book includes a few quotations from President Hunter's son Richard because he was available to provide information and insights while the book was being prepared. President Hunter's son John was not available for consultation because he passed away in 2007.

31. In Knowles, *Howard W. Hunter,* 87.

32. In Knowles, *Howard W. Hunter,* 88.

33. In Heslop, "He Found Pleasure in Work," 4.

34. In Knowles, *Howard W. Hunter,* 91.

35. In Knowles, *Howard W. Hunter,* 90.

36. See Knowles, *Howard W. Hunter,* 94.

37. In Heslop, "He Found Pleasure in Work," 4.

38. In Knowles, *Howard W. Hunter,* 97.

39. In Knowles, *Howard W. Hunter,* 98.

40. In Knowles, *Howard W. Hunter,* 98.

41. In Knowles, *Howard W. Hunter,* 100–101.

42. Charles C. Pulsipher, "My Most Influential Teacher," *Church News,* Jan. 10, 1981, 2.

43. Unpublished manuscript by Richard A. Hunter.

44. In Doyle L. Green, "Howard William Hunter: Apostle from California," *Improvement Era,* Jan. 1960, 37.

45. Cree-L Kofford, in Knowles, *Howard W. Hunter,* 120.

46. John S. Welch, in Knowles, *Howard W. Hunter,* 119.

47. In Knowles, *Howard W. Hunter,* 123.

48. In Knowles, *Howard W. Hunter,* 125.

49. In Knowles, *Howard W. Hunter,* 131.

50. Unpublished manuscript by Richard A. Hunter.

51. In Knowles, *Howard W. Hunter,* 127.

52. Charles C. Pulsipher, "My Most Influential Teacher," 2.

53. Howard W. Hunter, "Welfare and the Relief Society," *Relief Society Magazine,* Apr. 1962, 238.

54. In Knowles, *Howard W. Hunter,* 135. Concerning his grandfather, Richard A. Hunter wrote: "I always knew him as a faithful Church member. He was always found doing some good deed. You would call him 'Mr. Mormon.' Many of his neighbors and ward members would tell stories of the kind and thoughtful things he did. He was beloved in the Church community" (unpublished manuscript).

55. In Knowles, *Howard W. Hunter,* 137.

56. In Knowles, *Howard W. Hunter,* 139.

57. Betty C. McEwan, "My Most Influential Teacher," *Church News,* June 21, 1980, 2.

58. In Knowles, *Howard W. Hunter,* 144.

59. In Knowles, *Howard W. Hunter,* 144.

60. In Knowles, *Howard W. Hunter,* 145–46.

61. In Conference Report, Oct. 1959, 121.

62. In Knowles, *Howard W. Hunter,* 151.

63. Douglas D. Palmer, "The World Conference on Records," *Improvement Era,* July 1969, 7.

64. Jay M. Todd, "Elder Howard W. Hunter, Church Historian," *Improvement Era,* Apr. 1970, 27.

65. In Knowles, *Howard W. Hunter,* 194.

66. In Knowles, *Howard W. Hunter,* 208.

67. In Knowles, *Howard W. Hunter,* 205.

68. In Todd, "Elder Howard W. Hunter, Church Historian," 27.

69. In Todd, "Elder Howard W. Hunter, Church Historian," 27.

70. "New Church Historian Called," *Church News,* Feb. 14, 1970, 3.

71. In Knowles, *Howard W. Hunter,* 197.

72. James E. Faust, "Howard W. Hunter: Man of God," *Ensign,* Apr. 1995, 27.

73. Howard W. Hunter, "All Are Alike unto God," *Ensign,* June 1979, 74.

74. In Knowles, *Howard W. Hunter,* 215.

75. In Knowles, *Howard W. Hunter,* 218.

76. In Knowles, *Howard W. Hunter,* 222; abbreviations spelled out.

77. In Gerry Avant, "He Wanted to Visit the Holy Land 'Just One More Time,'" *Church News,* Mar. 11, 1995, 9.

78. In Francis M. Gibbons, *Howard W. Hunter: Man of Thought and Independence, Prophet of God* (2011), 119.

79. See "Growth in Mexican Cities Explodes into 16 Stakes," *Church News,* Nov. 22, 1975, 3.

80. In Knowles, *Howard W. Hunter,* 202.

81. In Conference Report, Oct. 1959, 121.

82. In Knowles, *Howard W. Hunter,* 168–69.

83. In Avant, "She Made Home a Happy Place," 5.

84. In Searle, "President Howard W. Hunter," 25.

85. Unpublished manuscript by Richard A. Hunter.

86. James E. Faust, in "President Howard W. Hunter: The Lord's 'Good and Faithful Servant,'" *Ensign,* Apr. 1995, 15.

87. In Dell Van Orden, "Exciting Time in Church History," *Church News,* June 25, 1988, 6.

88. Howard W. Hunter, "The Opening and Closing of Doors," *Ensign,* Nov. 1987, 54.

89. In Knowles, *Howard W. Hunter,* 284.

90. In Knowles, *Howard W. Hunter,* 291.

91. In Knowles, *Howard W. Hunter,* 305–6.

92. Howard W. Hunter, "An Anchor to the Souls of Men," *Ensign,* Oct. 1993, 71.

93. James E. Faust, "The Way of an Eagle," 13.

94. In Todd, "President Howard W. Hunter," 4.

95. In Todd, "President Howard W. Hunter," 5; see also Howard W. Hunter, "Exceeding Great and Precious Promises," *Ensign,* Nov. 1994, 8.

96. Gordon B. Hinckley, "A Prophet Polished and Refined," *Ensign,* Apr. 1995, 34.

97. Howard W. Hunter, "Exceeding Great and Precious Promises," *Ensign,* Nov. 1994, 8.

98. In Gerry Avant, "Temple Is Dedicated in Sunshine State," *Church News,* Oct. 15, 1994, 3.

99. Howard W. Hunter, "We Have a Work to Do," *Ensign,* Mar. 1995, 64.

100. Howard W. Hunter, "The Gifts of Christmas," *Ensign,* Dec. 2002, 18.

101. Howard W. Hunter, "The Gifts of Christmas," 18–19; adapted from "What We Think Christmas Is," *McCall's,* Dec. 1959, 82–83.

102. Gordon B. Hinckley, "A Prophet Polished and Refined," 34.

103. Unpublished manuscript by Richard A. Hunter.

104. Gordon B. Hinckley, "A Prophet Polished and Refined," 34.

105. In Dell Van Orden, "14th President of the Church Dies at Age 87; He Touched Millions of Lives across the World," *Church News,* Mar. 11, 1995, 3.

106. James E. Faust, "Howard W. Hunter: Man of God," 26.

107. Gordon B. Hinckley, "A Prophet Polished and Refined," 33–35.

*"How often do we think of the Savior? How deeply and
how gratefully and how adoringly do we reflect on his life?
How central to our lives do we know him to be?"*

Jesus Christ—Our Only Way to Hope and Joy

"If our lives and our faith are centered upon Jesus Christ and his restored gospel, nothing can ever go permanently wrong."

From the Life of Howard W. Hunter

A prominent theme in President Howard W. Hunter's teachings is that true peace, healing, and happiness come only as a person strives to know and follow Jesus Christ. President Hunter taught that "Christ's way is not only the *right* way, but ultimately the *only* way to hope and joy."[1]

President Hunter was likewise bold in testifying of the Savior's divine mission. "As an ordained Apostle and special witness of Christ, I give to you my solemn witness that Jesus Christ is in fact the Son of God," he declared. "He is the Messiah prophetically anticipated by Old Testament prophets. He is the Hope of Israel, for whose coming the children of Abraham, Isaac, and Jacob had prayed during the long centuries of prescribed worship. . . .

"It is by the power of the Holy Ghost that I bear my witness. I know of Christ's reality as if I had seen with my eyes and heard with my ears. I know also that the Holy Spirit will confirm the truthfulness of my witness in the hearts of all those who listen with an ear of faith."[2]

Feeling drawn to the places where Jesus ministered, President Hunter traveled to the Holy Land more than two dozen times. Elder James E. Faust of the Quorum of the Twelve said that "Jerusalem was like a magnet to him. . . . His desire to be where the Savior walked and taught seemed insatiable. He loved all the sights and the sounds. He especially loved the Galilee. But he loved one place most of all. He would *always* say, 'Let's go to the Garden Tomb just once more, for old time's sake.' There he would sit and meditate as though he were piercing the veil between himself and the Savior."³

Teachings of Howard W. Hunter

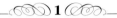 **1**

⭐ **We must know Christ better than we know Him and remember Him more often than we remember Him.**

Members of The Church of Jesus Christ of Latter-day Saints sing reverently:

Jesus, the very thought of thee
With sweetness fills my breast;
But sweeter far thy face to see
And in thy presence rest. . . .

. . . How often do we think of the Savior? How deeply and how gratefully and how adoringly do we reflect on his life? How central to our lives do we know him to be?

For example, how much of a normal day, a working week, or a fleeting month is devoted to "Jesus, the very thought of thee"? Perhaps for some of us, not enough.

Surely life would be more peaceful, surely marriages and families would be stronger, certainly neighborhoods and nations would be safer and kinder and more constructive if more of the gospel of Jesus Christ "with sweetness" could fill our breasts.

Unless we pay more attention to the thoughts of our hearts, I wonder what hope we have to claim that greater joy, that sweeter prize: someday his loving "face to see / And in [his] presence rest."

Every day of our lives and in every season of the year . . . , Jesus asks each of us, as he did following his triumphant entry into Jerusalem those many years ago, "What think ye of Christ? whose son is he?" (Matt. 22:42.)

We declare that he is the Son of God, and the reality of that fact should stir our souls more frequently.⁴

*"May we be more devoted and disciplined followers of Christ.
May we cherish him in our thoughts and speak his name with love."*

We must know Christ better than we know him; we must remember him more often than we remember him; we must serve him more valiantly than we serve him. Then we will drink water springing up unto eternal life and will eat the bread of life.[5]

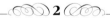

2

Jesus is our only true source of hope and lasting joy.

*O hope of ev'ry contrite heart,
O joy of all the meek,
To those who fall, how kind thou art!
How good to those who seek!*

What a lovely verse of music, and what a message of hope anchored in the gospel of Christ! Is there one among us, in any walk of life, who does not need hope and seek for greater joy? These are the universal needs and longings of the human soul, and they are the promises of Christ to his followers. Hope is extended to "ev'ry contrite heart" and joy comes to "all the meek."

Contrition is costly—it costs us our pride and our insensitivity, but it especially costs us our sins. For, as King Lamoni's father knew twenty centuries ago, this is the price of true hope. "O God," he cried, "wilt thou make thyself known unto me, and I will give away all my sins to know thee . . . that I may be raised from the dead, and be saved at the last day." (Alma 22:18.) When we, too, are willing to give away all our sins to know him and follow him, we, too, will be filled with the joy of eternal life.

And what of the meek? In a world too preoccupied with winning through intimidation and seeking to be number one, no large crowd of folk is standing in line to buy books that call for mere meekness. But the meek shall inherit the earth, a pretty impressive corporate takeover—and done *without* intimidation! Sooner or later, and we pray sooner *than* later, everyone will acknowledge that Christ's way is not only the *right* way, but ultimately the *only* way to hope and joy. Every knee shall bow and every tongue will confess that gentleness is better than brutality, that kindness is greater than coercion, that the soft voice turneth away wrath. In the end, and sooner than that whenever possible, we must be more like him. . . .

Jesus, our only joy be thou,
As thou our prize wilt be;
Jesus, be thou our glory now,
And thru eternity.

That is my personal prayer and my wish for all the world. . . . I testify that Jesus is the only true source of lasting joy, that our only lasting peace is in him. I do wish him to be "our glory now," the glory each of us yearns for individually and the only prize men and nations can permanently hold dear. He is our prize in time and in eternity. Every other prize is finally fruitless. Every other grandeur fades with time and dissolves with the elements. In the end, . . . we will know no true joy save it be in Christ.

. . . May we be more devoted and disciplined followers of Christ. May we cherish him in our thoughts and speak his name with love. May we kneel before him with meekness and mercy. May we bless and serve others that they may do the same.[6]

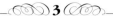

The greatest need in all the world is an active and sincere faith in the Savior and His teachings.

There are those who declare it is old-fashioned to believe in the Bible. Is it old-fashioned to believe in God, in Jesus Christ, the Son of the Living God? Is it old-fashioned to believe in his atoning sacrifice and the resurrection? If it is, I declare myself to be old-fashioned and the Church is old-fashioned. In great simplicity the Master taught the principles of life eternal and lessons that bring happiness to those with the faith to believe. It doesn't seem reasonable to assume the necessity of modernizing these teachings of the Master. His message concerned principles that are eternal.[7]

In this age, as in every age before us and in every age that will follow, the greatest need in all the world is an active and sincere faith in the basic teachings of Jesus of Nazareth, the living Son of the living God. Because many reject those teachings, that is all the more reason why sincere believers in the gospel of Jesus Christ should proclaim its truth and show by example the power and peace of a righteous, gentle life. . . .

How are we supposed to act when we are offended, misunderstood, unfairly or unkindly treated, or sinned against? What are we supposed to do if we are hurt by those we love, or passed over for promotion, or are falsely accused, or have our motives unfairly assailed?

Do we fight back? Do we send in an ever-larger battalion? Do we revert to an eye for an eye and a tooth for a tooth, or . . . do we come to the realization that this finally leaves us blind and toothless? . . .

In the majesty of his life and the example of his teachings, Christ gave us much counsel with secure promises always attached. He taught with a grandeur and authority that filled with hope the educated and the ignorant, the wealthy and the poor, the well and the diseased.[8]

Strive to build a personal testimony of Jesus Christ and the atonement. A study of the life of Christ and a testimony of his reality is

The Savior can calm the storms in our lives.

something each of us should seek. As we come to understand his mission, and the atonement which he wrought, we will desire to live more like him.[9]

4

As we exercise faith in the Savior, He will calm the troubled waters of our lives.

All of us have seen some sudden storms in our lives. A few of them . . . can be violent and frightening and potentially destructive. As individuals, as families, as communities, as nations, even as a church, we have had sudden squalls arise which have made us ask one way or another, "Master, carest thou not that we perish?" [Mark 4:38.] And one way or another we always hear in the stillness after the storm, "Why are ye so fearful? how is it that ye have no faith?" [Mark 4:40.]

None of us would like to think we have *no* faith, but I suppose the Lord's gentle rebuke here is largely deserved. This great Jehovah, in whom we say we trust and whose name we have taken upon us, is he who said, "Let there be a firmament in the midst of the waters, and let it divide the waters from the waters." (Gen. 1:6.) And he is also the one who said, "Let the waters under the heaven be gathered together unto one place, and let the dry land appear." (Gen. 1:9.) Furthermore, it was he who parted the Red Sea, allowing the Israelites to pass through on dry ground. (See Ex. 14:21–22.) Certainly it should be no surprise that he could command a few elements acting up on the Sea of Galilee. And our faith should remind us that he can calm the troubled waters of our lives. . . .

We will all have some adversity in our lives. I think we can be reasonably sure of that. Some of it will have the potential to be violent and damaging and destructive. Some of it may even strain our faith in a loving God who has the power to administer relief in our behalf.

To those anxieties I think the Father of us all would say, "Why are ye so fearful? how is it that ye have no faith?" And of course that has to be faith for the whole journey, the entire experience, the fulness of our life, not simply around the bits and pieces and tempestuous moments. . . .

Jesus said, "In the world ye shall have tribulation: but be of good cheer; I have overcome the world." (John 16:33.)[10]

5

As we center our lives on the Savior, we need not fear, and our worries will be turned to joys.

I know enough about your busy and hectic lives to know that you sometimes get frustrated. You might even worry a little bit from time to time. I know all about that. . . .

My message to you today is to "fear not, little flock." It is to encourage you to rejoice in the great blessings of life. It is to invite you to feel the great thrill of gospel living and our Father in Heaven's love. Life is wonderful, even in the hard times, and there is happiness, joy, and peace at stops all along the way, and endless portions of them at the end of the road.

Sure, there are plenty of things to worry about—some of them very serious things—but that is why we speak in gospel terms of faith, and hope, and charity. As Latter-day Saints, ours is "the abundant life," and we try to emphasize our blessings and opportunities while we minimize our disappointments and worries. "Search diligently, pray always, and be believing," the scripture says, "and all things shall work together for your good" (D&C 90:24). I want to remind you of that promise. . . .

Please remember this one thing. If our lives and our faith are centered upon Jesus Christ and his restored gospel, nothing can ever go permanently wrong. On the other hand, if our lives are not centered on the Savior and his teachings, no other success can ever be permanently right. . . .

We all struggle with health problems occasionally—others do so constantly. Illness and disease are part of the burden of mortality. Have faith and be positive. The power of the priesthood is real, and there is so much that is good in life, even if we struggle physically. It is a joy to know that there will be no injury or disease in the Resurrection.

Some of our concerns may come in the form of temptations. Others may be difficult decisions pertaining to education or career or money or marriage. Whatever your burden is, you will find the strength you need in Christ. Jesus Christ is Alpha and Omega, literally the beginning and the end. He is with us from start to finish, and as such is more than a spectator in our lives. . . .

If the yoke under which we struggle is sin itself, the message is the same. Christ knows the full weight of our sins, for he carried it first. If our burden is not sin nor temptation, but illness or poverty or rejection, it's the same. He knows. . . .

He suffered so much more than our sins. He whom Isaiah called the "man of sorrows" (Isaiah 53:3; Mosiah 14:3) knows perfectly every problem through which we pass because he chose to bear the full weight of all our troubles and our pains. . . .

Brothers and sisters, you have and will have worries and challenges of many kinds, but embrace life joyfully and full of faith. Study the scriptures regularly. Pray fervently. Obey the voice of the

Spirit and the prophets. Do all that you can to help others. You will find great happiness in such a course. Some glorious day all your worries will be turned to joys.

As Joseph Smith wrote to the struggling Saints from his cell in Liberty Jail:

Let us cheerfully do all things that lie in our power; and then may we stand still, with the utmost assurance, to see the salvation of God, and for his arm to be revealed [D&C 123:17; emphasis added].

[In the words of the Lord to the Prophet Joseph Smith:]

Fear not, little flock; do good; let earth and hell combine against you, for if ye are built upon my rock, they cannot prevail. . . .

Look unto me in every thought; doubt not, fear not.

Behold the wounds which pierced my side, and also the prints of the nails in my hands and feet; be faithful, keep my commandments, and ye shall inherit the kingdom of heaven [D&C 6:34–37].[11]

Suggestions for Study and Teaching

Questions
- Consider how you would answer President Hunter's questions in section 1. How can we make Jesus Christ more central in our lives? How can we make Him more central in our homes? How can we come to know Christ better than we know Him?

- What does it "cost us" to receive the hope, joy, and peace that Christ offers? (See section 2.) When have you felt the hope, peace, and joy that come from the Savior?

- Why do you think "the greatest need in all the world is an active and sincere faith in the basic teachings of Jesus of Nazareth"? (See section 3.) How can you show your faith in Christ's teachings when you feel "offended, misunderstood, unfairly or unkindly treated, or sinned against"?

- What can we learn from President Hunter's teachings about fear and faith? (See section 4.) How can faith help us overcome fear? Reflect on occasions when the Savior has calmed the storms in your life as you have exercised faith in Him.

• How can President Hunter's counsel in section 5 help us "embrace life joyfully," even when we experience sorrows, disappointments, and illnesses? How can we develop an eternal perspective? How has the Savior helped you have a more abundant life?

Related Scriptures

Matthew 11:28–30; John 14:6; 2 Nephi 31:19–21; Alma 5:14–16; 7:10–14; 23:6; Helaman 3:35; 5:9–12; D&C 50:40–46; 93:1

Study Help

"As you study, pay careful attention to ideas that come to your mind and feelings that come to your heart" (*Preach My Gospel* [2004], 18). Consider recording the impressions you receive, even if they seem unrelated to the words you are reading. They may be the very things the Lord wants to reveal to you.

Notes

1. "Jesus, the Very Thought of Thee," *Ensign,* May 1993, 65.
2. "An Apostle's Witness of Christ," *Ensign,* Jan. 1984, 70.
3. James E. Faust, "Howard W. Hunter: Man of God," *Ensign,* Apr. 1995, 27.
4. "Jesus, the Very Thought of Thee," 63–64.
5. "What Manner of Men Ought Ye to Be?" *Ensign,* May 1994, 64; see also "He Invites Us to Follow Him," *Ensign,* Sept. 1994, 5.
6. "Jesus, the Very Thought of Thee," 64–65.
7. In Eleanor Knowles, *Howard W. Hunter* (1994), 318.
8. "The Beacon in the Harbor of Peace," *Ensign,* Nov. 1992, 18.
9. *The Teachings of Howard W. Hunter,* ed. Clyde J. Williams (1997), 30.
10. "Master, the Tempest Is Raging," *Ensign,* Nov. 1984, 33–35.
11. "Fear Not, Little Flock" (address given at Brigham Young University, Mar. 14, 1989), 1–2, 4–5; speeches.byu.edu.

"My Peace I Give unto You"

"Peace can come to an individual only by an unconditional surrender—surrender to him who is the Prince of peace, who has the power to confer peace."

From the Life of Howard W. Hunter

One of President Howard W. Hunter's associates in the Quorum of the Twelve described him as a man of "extraordinary patience that comes from great inner peace."[1] President Hunter spoke often about inner peace, teaching that a person can receive it only by turning to God—by trusting Him, exercising faith, and striving to do His will. Such peace helped sustain him through many difficult times.

In late 1975 a doctor recommended brain surgery for President Hunter's wife, Claire. President Hunter agonized over whether the surgery was in Claire's best interest, since it would strain her fragile body and might not improve her condition. He went to the temple, counseled with family members, and soon felt that the surgery offered the best hope for giving Claire some relief. Describing his feelings on the day of the operation, he wrote:

"I went with her as far as the doors to the operating room, gave her a kiss, and she was taken on through the doors. As time went by, I waited and wondered. . . . Suddenly the tense anxiety turned into a feeling of peace. I knew the right decision had been made and that my prayers had been answered."[2]

In 1989, President Hunter had another experience during which he felt peace in a troubling time. He was in Jerusalem to dedicate the Brigham Young University Jerusalem Center for Near Eastern Studies. Several groups had protested the Church's presence in Jerusalem, and some had threatened violence. One of the speakers at the dedication was Elder Boyd K. Packer of the Quorum of the Twelve, who later related this incident:

We must "fix our eyes on Jesus" and never "turn away
our eyes from him in whom we must believe."

"As I was speaking, there was some excitement in the back of the hall. Men in military uniforms had entered the room. They sent a note to President Hunter. I turned and asked for instructions. He said, 'There's been a bomb threat. Are you afraid?' I said, 'No.' He said, 'Neither am I; finish your talk.'"[3] The dedication services proceeded without incident; there was no bomb.

In situations like these, President Hunter trusted in this promise of peace from the Savior, which he often quoted: "Peace I leave with you, my peace I give unto you: not as the world giveth, give I unto you. Let not your heart be troubled, neither let it be afraid" (John 14:27).

Teachings of Howard W. Hunter

Jesus Christ is our source of true peace.

In foretelling the birth of Christ more than 700 years before it occurred, the prophet Isaiah used titles expressing great admiration. . . . One of these titles that is of particular interest in our present world is "Prince of Peace" (Isa. 9:6). "Of the increase of his government and peace there shall be no end," Isaiah declared (v. 7). What a thrilling hope for a war-weary, sin-laden world![4]

The peace for which the world longs is a time of suspended hostilities; but men do not realize that peace is a state of existence that comes to man only upon the terms and conditions set by God, and in no other way.

In a psalm in the Book of Isaiah are these words: "Thou wilt keep him in perfect peace, whose mind is stayed on thee: because he trusteth in thee." (Isa. 26:3.) This perfect peace mentioned by Isaiah comes to one only through a belief in God. This is not understood by an unbelieving world.

On the last occasion that Jesus had supper with the Twelve, he washed their feet, broke bread for them, and passed them the cup; then, after Judas had left their midst, the Master spoke to them at some length. Among other things, he told of his impending death and of the legacy he left for each of them. He had accumulated no goods, property, nor wealth. The record tells us of no possessions other than the clothing he wore, and on the next day after the crucifixion this would be divided by the soldiers, who would cast lots for his coat. His bequest was given to his disciples in these simple yet profound words: "Peace I leave with you, my peace I give unto you: not as the world giveth, give I unto you. Let not your heart be troubled, neither let it be afraid." (John 14:27.)

He used the Jewish form of salutation and benediction: "My peace I give unto you." This salutation and bequest was not to be taken by them in the usual sense, for he said, ". . . not as the world giveth, give I unto you." Not empty wishes, not just polite ceremony, as the people of the world use the words as matters of custom; but as the author and Prince of peace, he gave it to them. He bestowed it upon them and said, "Let not your heart be troubled, neither let it be afraid." Within a few hours they would be subjected to trouble, but with his peace they could overcome fear and stand firm.

His last statement to them before the closing prayer on that memorable evening was this: ". . . in the world ye shall have tribulation: but be of good cheer; I have overcome the world." (John 16:33.)[5]

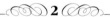 **2**

We cultivate peace as we live the principles of the gospel.

There is but one guiding hand in the universe, only one truly infallible light, one unfailing beacon to the world. That light is Jesus Christ, the light and life of the world, the light which one Book of Mormon prophet described as "a light that is endless, that can never be darkened." (Mosiah 16:9.)

As we search for the shore of safety and peace, whether we be individual women and men, families, communities, or nations, Christ is the only beacon on which we can ultimately rely. He is the one who said of his mission, "I am the way, the truth, and the life." (John 14:6.) . . .

Consider, for example, this instruction from Christ to his disciples. He said, "Love your enemies, bless them that curse you, do good to them that hate you, and pray for them which despitefully use you, and persecute you." (Matt. 5:44.)

Think of what this admonition alone would do in your neighborhood and mine, in the communities in which you and your children live, in the nations which make up our great global family. I realize this doctrine poses a significant challenge, but surely it is a more agreeable challenge than the terrible tasks posed for us by the war and poverty and pain the world continues to face.[6]

When we try to help those who have offended us, when we pray for those who have unrighteously used us, our lives can be beautiful. We can have peace when we come into a unity with the Spirit and with each other as we serve the Lord and keep his commandments.[7]

The world in which we live, whether close to home or far away, needs the gospel of Jesus Christ. It provides the only way the world will ever know peace. . . . We need a more peaceful world, growing out of more peaceful families and neighborhoods and communities. To secure and cultivate such peace, "we must love others, even our enemies as well as our friends" [*Teachings of Presidents of the Church: Joseph Smith* (2007), 393]. . . . We need to extend the hand of friendship. We need to be kinder, more gentle, more forgiving, and slower to anger.[8]

God's chief way of acting is by persuasion and patience and long-suffering, not by coercion and stark confrontation. He acts by gentle solicitation and by sweet enticement.[9]

There is no promise of peace to those who reject God, to those who will not keep his commandments, or to those who violate his laws. The Prophet Isaiah spoke of the decadence and corruption of leaders and then continued in his admonitions by saying: "But the wicked are like the troubled sea, when it cannot rest, whose waters cast up mire and dirt. There is no peace, saith my God, to the wicked." (Isa. 57:20–21.) . . .

. . . Indifference to the Savior or failure to keep the commandments of God brings about insecurity, inner turmoil, and contention. These are the opposite of peace. Peace can come to an individual only by an unconditional surrender—surrender to him who is the Prince of peace, who has the power to confer peace.[10]

The troubles of the world often expressed in screaming headlines should remind us to seek for the peace that comes from living the simple principles of the gospel of Christ. The vociferous minorities will not unsettle our peace of soul if we love our fellowmen and have faith in the atoning sacrifice of the Savior and the quiet assurance he gives of life everlasting. Where do we find such faith in a troubled world? The Lord said, "Ask, and it shall be given you; seek, and ye shall find; knock, and it shall be opened unto you. For every one that asketh receiveth; and he that seeketh findeth; and to him that knocketh it shall be opened." (Luke 11:9–10.)[11]

It seems that two eternal truths must be accepted by all if we are to find peace in this world and eternal life in the world to come. (1) That Jesus is the Christ, the very eternal son of our Heavenly Father, who came to earth for the express purpose of redeeming mankind from sin and the grave, and that he lives to bring us back to the presence of the Father. (2) That Joseph Smith was his prophet, raised up in this latter-day to restore the truth which had been lost to mankind because of transgression. If all men would accept and live these two fundamental truths, peace would be brought to the world.[12]

If you, yourself, resist . . . temptations and determine to pay the daily price, to live the Law of the Harvest by clean, moral thoughts and practices, by upright, honest dealings, by integrity and conscientiousness in your studies, by fasting, prayer, and worship, you will reap the harvest of freedom and inner peace and prosperity.[13]

A life filled with unselfish service will also be filled with peace that surpasses understanding. . . . This peace can come only through living the principles of the gospel. These principles constitute the program of the Prince of Peace.[14]

So much in our world is calculated to destroy . . . personal peace through sins and temptations of a thousand kinds. We pray that the lives of the Saints will be lived in harmony with the ideal set before us by Jesus of Nazareth.

We pray that Satan's efforts will be thwarted, that personal lives can be peaceful and calm, that families can be close and concerned with every member, that wards and stakes, branches and districts

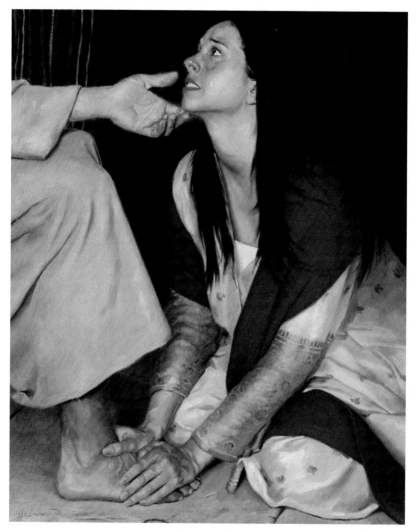

"A life filled with unselfish service will also be filled
with peace that surpasses understanding."

can form the great body of Christ, meeting every need, soothing every hurt, healing every wound until the whole world, as Nephi pleaded, will "press forward with a steadfastness in Christ, having a perfect brightness of hope, and a love of God and of all men. . . .

"My beloved brethren," continued Nephi, "this is the way; and there is none other way." (2 Nephi 31:20–21.)[15]

⟨⟨⟩⟩ 3 ⟨⟨⟩⟩

The Savior can help us find peace
regardless of the turmoil around us.

Jesus was not spared grief and pain and anguish and buffeting. No tongue can speak the unutterable burden he carried, nor have we the wisdom to understand the prophet Isaiah's description of him as "a man of sorrows." (Isa. 53:3.) His ship was tossed most of his life, and, at least to mortal eyes, it crashed fatally on the rocky coast of Calvary. We are asked not to look on life with mortal eyes; with spiritual vision we know something quite different was happening upon the cross.

Peace was on the lips and in the heart of the Savior no matter how fiercely the tempest was raging. May it so be with us—in our own hearts, in our own homes, in our nations of the world, and even in the buffetings faced from time to time by the Church. We should not expect to get through life individually or collectively without some opposition.[16]

One may live in beautiful and peaceful surroundings but, because of inner dissension and discord, be in a state of constant turmoil. On the other hand, one may be in the midst of utter destruction and the bloodshed of war and yet have the serenity of unspeakable peace. If we look to man and the ways of the world, we will find turmoil and confusion. If we will but turn to God, we will find peace for the restless soul. This was made clear by the words of the Savior: "In the world ye shall have tribulation" (John 16:33); and in his bequest to the Twelve and to all mankind, he said, "Peace I leave with you, my peace I give unto you: not as the world giveth. . . ." (John 14:27.)

We can find this peace now in a world of conflict if we will but accept his great gift and his further invitation: "Come unto me, all ye that labour and are heavy laden, and I will give you rest.

"Take my yoke upon you, and learn of me; for I am meek and lowly in heart: and ye shall find rest unto your souls." (Matt. 11:28–29.)

This peace shelters us from the worldly turmoil. The knowledge that God lives, that we are his children, and that he loves us soothes the troubled heart. The answer to the quest lies in faith in God and in his Son, Jesus Christ. This will bring peace to us now and in the eternity to follow.[17]

In this world of confusion and rushing, temporal progress, we need to return to the simplicity of Christ. . . . We need to study the simple fundamentals of the truths taught by the Master and eliminate the controversial. Our faith in God needs to be real and not speculative. The restored gospel of Jesus Christ can be a dynamic, moving influence, and true acceptance gives us a meaningful, religious experience. One of the great strengths of the Mormon religion is this translation of belief into daily thinking and conduct. This replaces turmoil and confusion with peace and tranquility.[18]

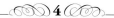 **4**

By fixing our eyes on Jesus, we can triumph over elements that would destroy peace.

Let me recall one of the great stories of Christ's triumph over that which seems to test us and try us and bring fear to our hearts. As Christ's disciples had set out on one of their frequent journeys across the Sea of Galilee, the night was dark and the elements were strong and contrary. The waves were boisterous and the wind was bold, and these mortal, frail men were frightened. Unfortunately there was no one with them to calm and save them, for Jesus had been left alone upon the shore.

As always, he was watching over them. He loved them and cared for them. In their moment of greatest extremity they looked and saw in the darkness an image in a fluttering robe, walking toward them on the ridges of the sea. They cried out in terror at the sight, thinking that it was a phantom that walked upon the waves. And through the storm and darkness to them—as so often to us, when, amid the darknesses of life, the ocean seems so great and our little boats so small—there came the ultimate and reassuring voice of peace with this simple declaration, "It is I; be not afraid." Peter exclaimed, "Lord, if it be thou, bid me come unto thee on the water." And Christ's answer to him was the same as to all of us: "Come."

Peter sprang over the vessel's side and into the troubled waves, and while his eyes were fixed upon the Lord, the wind might toss his hair and the spray might drench his robes, but all was well. Only when with wavering faith he removed his glance from the Master to look at the furious waves and the black gulf beneath him, only then did he begin to sink. Again, like most of us, he cried, "Lord, save me." Nor did Jesus fail him. He stretched out his hand and grasped the drowning disciple with the gentle rebuke, "O thou of little faith, [why] didst thou doubt?"

Then safely aboard their little craft, they saw the wind fall and the crash of the waves become a ripple. Soon they were at their haven, their safe port, where all would one day hope to be. The crew as well as his disciples were filled with deep amazement. Some of them addressed him by a title which I declare today: "Truly thou art the Son of God." (Adapted from Farrar, *The Life of Christ,* pp. 310–13; see Matt. 14:22–33.)

It is my firm belief that if as individual people, as families, communities, and nations, we could, like Peter, fix our eyes on Jesus, we too might walk triumphantly over "the swelling waves of disbelief" and remain "unterrified amid the rising winds of doubt." But if we turn away our eyes from him in whom we must believe, as it is so easy to do and the world is so much tempted to do, if we look to the power and fury of those terrible and destructive elements around us rather than to him who can help and save us, then we shall inevitably sink in a sea of conflict and sorrow and despair.

At such times when we feel the floods are threatening to drown us and the deep is going to swallow up the tossed vessel of our faith, I pray we may always hear amid the storm and the darkness that sweet utterance of the Savior of the world: "Be of good cheer; it is I; be not afraid." (Matt. 14:27.)[19]

Suggestions for Study and Teaching

Questions
- President Hunter teaches that Jesus Christ is the source of true peace (see section 1). What experiences have helped you come to know this truth? How can we receive the peace that Jesus offers?

- How does loving others bring us peace? (See section 2.) How does living the gospel help us have peace? Why is "unconditional surrender" to the Savior necessary for us to have peace?

- Review President Hunter's teachings in section 3. How have you experienced the fulfillment of the Savior's promise to "give you rest" from your burdens as you come unto Him?

- Reflect on President Hunter's account of Peter walking on water (see section 4). What can you learn from this account about how to find peace in times of trouble? How has the Savior helped you to "be of good cheer" and "be not afraid" in difficult times?

Related Scriptures

Psalms 46:10; 85:8; Isaiah 32:17; Mark 4:36–40; Romans 8:6; Galatians 5:22–23; Philippians 4:9; Mosiah 4:3; D&C 19:23; 59:23; 88:125

Teaching Help

Invite class members to select one of the sections in the chapter they would like to discuss and to form a group with others who chose the same section. Encourage each group to discuss the related question at the end of the chapter.

Notes

1. In Eleanor Knowles, *Howard W. Hunter* (1994), 185.

2. In Knowles, *Howard W. Hunter,* 266.

3. Boyd K. Packer, "President Howard W. Hunter—He Endured to the End," *Ensign,* Apr. 1995, 29.

4. "The Gifts of Christmas," *Ensign,* Dec. 2002, 16.

5. In Conference Report, Oct. 1966, 15–16.

6. "The Beacon in the Harbor of Peace," *Ensign,* Nov. 1992, 18.

7. *The Teachings of Howard W. Hunter,* ed. Clyde J. Williams (1997), 40.

8. "A More Excellent Way," *Ensign,* May 1992, 61, 63.

9. "The Golden Thread of Choice," *Ensign,* Nov. 1989, 18.

10. In Conference Report, Oct. 1966, 16.

11. In Conference Report, Oct. 1969, 113.

12. *The Teachings of Howard W. Hunter,* 172–73.

13. *The Teachings of Howard W. Hunter,* 73–74.

14. "The Gifts of Christmas," 19.

15. In Conference Report, Apr. 1976, 157.

16. "Master, the Tempest Is Raging," *Ensign,* Nov. 1984, 35.

17. In Conference Report, Oct. 1966, 16–17.

18. In Conference Report, Oct. 1970, 131–32.

19. "The Beacon in the Harbor of Peace," 19.

In our trials, the Savior extends to each of us the invitation He extended to the man at the pool of Bethesda: "Wilt thou be made whole?" (John 5:6).

Adversity—Part of God's Plan for Our Eternal Progress

"When [the difficulties of mortality] humble us
and refine us and teach us and bless us,
they can be powerful instruments in the
hands of God to make us better people."

From the Life of Howard W. Hunter

At the April 1980 general conference, Elder Howard W. Hunter, then a member of the Quorum of the Twelve Apostles, told of joining a large crowd to watch the long-boat races in Samoa. "The crowd was restless," he said, "and most eyes were turned toward the sea, watching for the first glimpse of the [boats]. Suddenly there was a roar from the crowd as the boats came into sight in the distance. Each of them had a crew of fifty powerful oarsmen dipping and pulling the oars with a rhythm that forced the crafts through the waves and foaming water—a beautiful sight.

"The boats and men were soon in full view as they raced toward the finish. Even though these powerful men pulled with their might, the weight of a boat with fifty men moved against a powerful adverse force—the resistance of the water.

"The cheering of the crowd reached a crescendo when the first long-boat crossed the finish line."

After the race, Elder Hunter walked to where the boats were docked and spoke with one of the oarsmen, who explained that the prow of the long-boat "is so constructed that it cuts through and divides the water to help overcome the resistance that retards the speed of the boat. He further explained that the pulling of the oars against the resistance of the water creates the force that causes the boat to move forward. Resistance creates both the opposition and the forward movement."[1]

Elder Hunter used the boat race in Samoa to introduce a talk about the purposes of adversity. During his ministry as an Apostle, he spoke about adversity many times, offering counsel, hope, and encouragement. He spoke from personal experience, having endured life-threatening illnesses and other trials. He testified with firm conviction that in times of trouble, "Jesus Christ possesses the power to ease our burdens and lighten our loads."[2]

Teachings of Howard W. Hunter

1

Adversity is part of God's plan for our eternal progress.

I have observed that life—every life—has a full share of ups and downs. Indeed, we see many joys and sorrows in the world, many changed plans and new directions, many blessings that do not always look or feel like blessings, and much that humbles us and improves our patience and our faith. We have all had those experiences from time to time, and I suppose we always will. . . .

. . . President Spencer W. Kimball, who knew a good deal about suffering, disappointment, and circumstances beyond his control, once wrote:

"Being human, we would expel from our lives physical pain and mental anguish and assure ourselves of continual ease and comfort, but if we were to close the doors upon sorrow and distress, we might be excluding our greatest friends and benefactors. Suffering can make saints of people as they learn patience, long-suffering, and self-mastery" [*Faith Precedes the Miracle* (1972), 98].

In that statement, President Kimball refers to closing doors upon certain experiences in life. . . . Doors close regularly in our lives, and some of those closings cause genuine pain and heartache. But I *do* believe that where one such door closes, another opens (and perhaps more than one), with hope and blessings in other areas of our lives that we might not have discovered otherwise.

. . . A few years ago, [President Marion G. Romney] said that all men and women, including the most faithful and loyal, would find adversity and affliction in their lives because, in the words of Joseph Smith, "Men have to suffer that they may come upon Mount Zion and be exalted above the heavens" [*Teachings of Presidents of the Church: Joseph Smith* (2007), 230; see Conference Report, Oct. 1969, 57].

President Romney then said:

"This does not mean that we crave suffering. We avoid all we can. However, we now know, and we all knew when we elected to come into mortality, that we would here be proved in the crucible of adversity and affliction. . . .

"[Furthermore,] the Father's plan for proving [and refining] his children did not exempt the Savior himself. The suffering he undertook to endure, and which he did endure, equaled the combined suffering of all men [and women everywhere. Trembling and bleeding and wishing to shrink from the cup, he said,] 'I partook and finished my preparations unto the children of men' (D&C 19:18–19)" (in Conference Report, Oct. 1969, p. 57).

All of us must finish our "preparations unto the children of men" [D&C 19:19]. Christ's preparations were quite different from our own, but we all have preparations to make, doors to open. To make such important preparations often will require some pain, some unexpected changes in life's path, and some submitting, "even as a child doth submit to his father" [Mosiah 3:19]. Finishing divine preparations and opening celestial doors may take us—indeed, undoubtedly will take us—right up to the concluding hours of our mortal lives.[3]

We came to mortal life to encounter resistance. It was part of the plan for our eternal progress. Without temptation, sickness, pain, and sorrow, there could be no goodness, virtue, appreciation for well-being, or joy. . . . We must remember that the same forces of resistance which prevent our progress afford us also opportunities to overcome.[4]

Our mortal tribulations are for our growth and experience.

When [the difficulties of mortality] humble us and refine us and teach us and bless us, they can be powerful instruments in the hands of God to make us better people, to make us more grateful, more loving, and more considerate of other people in their own times of difficulty.

Yes, we all have difficult moments, individually and collectively, but even in the most severe of times, anciently or in modern times, those problems and prophecies were never intended to do anything but bless the righteous and help those who are less righteous move toward repentance. God loves us, and the scriptures tell us he "gave his only begotten Son, that whosoever believeth in him should not perish, but have everlasting life" [John 3:16].[5]

The great Book of Mormon patriarch, Lehi, spoke encouragingly to his son Jacob, a son born in the wilderness in a time of travail and opposition. Jacob's life was not as he might have expected it to be and not as the ideal course of experience might have outlined. He had suffered afflictions and setbacks, but Lehi promised that such afflictions would be consecrated for his son's gain (see 2 Nephi 2:2).

Then Lehi added these words that have become classic:

"For it must needs be, that there is an opposition in all things. If not so, . . . righteousness could not be brought to pass, neither wickedness, neither holiness nor misery, neither good nor bad" (2 Nephi 2:11).

I have taken great comfort over the years in this explanation of some of life's pain and disappointment. I take even greater comfort that the greatest of men and women, including the Son of God, have faced such opposition in order to better understand the contrast between righteousness and wickedness, holiness and misery, good and bad. From out of the dark, damp confinement of Liberty Jail, the Prophet Joseph Smith learned that if we are called to pass through tribulation, it is for our growth and experience and will ultimately be counted for our good (see D&C 122:5–8).

*When Joseph Smith was in Liberty Jail, the Lord revealed to him
that adversity can give us experience and be for our good.*

Where one door shuts, another opens, even for a prophet in prison. We are not always wise enough nor experienced enough to judge adequately all of the possible entries and exits. The mansion that God prepares for each of his beloved children may have only certain hallways and banisters, special carpets and curtains that he would have us pass on our way to possess it. . . .

At various times in our lives, probably at repeated times in our lives, we do have to acknowledge that God knows what we do not know and sees what we do not see. "For my thoughts are not your thoughts, neither are your ways my ways, saith the Lord" (Isaiah 55:8).

If you have troubles at home with children who stray, if you suffer financial reverses and emotional strain that threaten your homes and your happiness, if you must face the loss of life or health, may peace be unto your soul. We will not be tempted beyond our ability to withstand [see 1 Corinthians 10:13; Alma 13:28; 34:39]. Our detours and disappointments are the straight and narrow path to Him.[6]

3

We have every reason to be optimistic and confident even in times of difficulty.

There have always been some difficulties in mortal life, and there always will be. But knowing what we know, and living as we are supposed to live, there really is no place, no excuse, for pessimism and despair.

In my lifetime I have seen two world wars, plus Korea, plus Vietnam and [more]. I have worked my way through the Depression and managed to go to law school while starting a young family at the same time. I have seen stock markets and world economics go crazy, and I have seen a few despots and tyrants go crazy, all of which caused quite a bit of trouble around the world in the process.

So I hope you won't believe all the world's difficulties have been wedged into your decade, or that things have never been worse than they are for you personally, or that they will never get better. I reassure you that things have been worse and they *will* always get better. They always do—especially when we live and love the gospel of Jesus Christ and give it a chance to flourish in our lives. . . .

Contrary to what some might say, you have every reason in this world to be happy and to be optimistic and to be confident. Every generation since time began has had some things to overcome and some problems to work out.[7]

4

When we come to the Savior, He will ease our burdens and lighten our loads.

"Come unto me, all ye that labour and are heavy laden, and I will give you rest.

"Take my yoke upon you, and learn of me; for I am meek and lowly in heart: and ye shall find rest unto your souls.

"For my yoke is easy, and my burden is light." (Matt. 11:28–30.) . . .

. . . This marvelous offer of assistance extended by the Son of God himself was not restricted to the Galileans of his day. This call to shoulder his easy yoke and accept his light burden is not limited to bygone generations. It was and is a universal appeal to all people, to all cities and nations, to every man, woman, and child everywhere.

In our own great times of need we must not leave unrecognized this unfailing answer to the cares and worries of our world. Here is the promise of personal peace and protection. Here is the power to remit sin in all periods of time. We, too, must believe that Jesus Christ possesses the power to ease our burdens and lighten our loads. We, too, must come unto him and there receive rest from our labors.

Of course, obligations go with such promises. "Take my yoke upon you," he pleads. In biblical times the yoke was a device of great assistance to those who tilled the field. It allowed the strength of a second animal to be linked and coupled with the effort of a single animal, sharing and reducing the heavy labor of the plow or wagon. A burden that was overwhelming or perhaps impossible for one to bear could be equitably and comfortably borne by two bound together with a common yoke. His yoke requires a great and earnest effort, but for those who truly are converted, the yoke is easy and the burden becomes light.

Why face life's burdens alone, Christ asks, or why face them with temporal support that will quickly falter? To the heavy laden it is Christ's yoke, it is the power and peace of standing side by side with a God that will provide the support, balance, and the strength to meet our challenges and endure our tasks here in the hardpan field of mortality.

Obviously, the personal burdens of life vary from person to person, but every one of us has them. . . . Of course, some sorrows are brought on by the sins of a world not following the counsel of [our] Father in Heaven. Whatever the reason, none of us seems to be completely free from life's challenges. To one and all, Christ said, in effect: As long as we all must bear some burden and shoulder some yoke, why not let it be mine? My promise to you is that my yoke is easy, and my burden is light. (See Matt. 11:28–30.)[8]

"Disciples of Christ in every generation are invited, indeed commanded, to be filled with a perfect brightness of hope."

5

Latter-day Saints need not fear the tribulations of the last days.

The scriptures . . . indicate that there will be seasons of time when the whole world will have some difficulty. We know that in our dispensation unrighteousness will, unfortunately, be quite evident, and it will bring its inevitable difficulties and pain and punishment. God will cut short that unrighteousness in his own due time, but our task is to live fully and faithfully and not worry ourselves sick about the woes of the world or when it will end. Our task is to have the gospel in our lives and to be a bright light, a city set on the hill, which reflects the beauty of the gospel of Jesus Christ and the joy and happiness that will always come to every people in every age who keep the commandments.

In this last dispensation there will be great tribulation. (See Matt. 24:21.) We know that there will be wars and rumors of wars (see D&C 45:26) and that the whole earth will be in commotion (see D&C

45:26). All dispensations have had their perilous times, but our day will include genuine peril. (See 2 Tim. 3:1.) Evil men will flourish (see 2 Tim. 3:13), but then evil men have very often flourished. Calamities will come and iniquity will abound. (See D&C 45:27.)

Inevitably the natural result of some of these kinds of prophecies is fear, and that is not fear limited to a younger generation. It is fear shared by those of any age who don't understand what we understand.

But I want to stress that these feelings are not necessary for faithful Latter-day Saints, and they do not come from God. To ancient Israel, the great Jehovah said:

"Be strong and of a good courage, fear not, nor be afraid of them: for the Lord thy God, he it is that doth go with thee; he will not fail thee, nor forsake thee. . . .

"And the Lord, he it is that doth go before thee; he will be with thee, he will not fail thee, neither forsake thee: fear not, neither be dismayed." (Deut. 31:6, 8.)

And to you, our marvelous generation in modern Israel, the Lord has said:

"Therefore, fear not, little flock; do good; let earth and hell combine against you, for if ye are built upon my rock, they cannot prevail. . . .

"Look unto me in every thought; doubt not, fear not." (D&C 6:34, 36.)

Such counsel is laced throughout our modern scriptures. Listen to this wonderful reassurance: "Fear not, little children, for you are mine, and I have overcome the world, and you are of them that my Father hath given me." (D&C 50:41.) "Verily I say unto you my friends, fear not, let your hearts be comforted; yea, rejoice evermore, and in everything give thanks." (D&C 98:1.)

In light of such wonderful counsel, I think it is incumbent upon us to rejoice a little more and despair a little less, to give thanks for what we have and for the magnitude of God's blessings to us, and to talk a little less about what we may not have or what anxiety may accompany difficult times in this or any generation.

A time of great hope and excitement

For Latter-day Saints this is a time of great hope and excitement—one of the greatest eras in the Restoration and therefore one of the greatest eras in any dispensation, inasmuch as ours is the greatest of all dispensations. We need to have faith and hope, two of the great fundamental virtues of any discipleship of Christ. We must continue to exercise confidence in God, inasmuch as that is the first principle in our code of belief. We must believe that God has all power, that he loves us, and that his work will not be stopped or frustrated in our individual lives or in the world generally. . . .

I promise you in the name of the Lord whose servant I am that God will always protect and care for his people. We will have our difficulties the way every generation and people have had difficulties. But with the gospel of Jesus Christ, you have every hope and promise and reassurance. The Lord has power over his Saints and will always prepare places of peace, defense, and safety for his people. When we have faith in God we can hope for a better world—for us personally, and for all mankind. The prophet Ether taught anciently (and he knew something about troubles): "Wherefore, whoso believeth in God might with surety hope for a better world, yea, even a place at the right hand of God, which hope cometh of faith, maketh an anchor to the souls of men, which would make them sure and steadfast, always abounding in good works, being led to glorify God." (Ether 12:4.)

Disciples of Christ in every generation are invited, indeed commanded, to be filled with a perfect brightness of hope. (See 2 Ne. 31:20.)

Seeking to dispel fear

. . . If our faith and hope are anchored in Christ, in his teachings, commandments, and promises, then we are able to count on something truly remarkable, genuinely miraculous, which can part the Red Sea and lead modern Israel to a place "where none shall come to hurt or make afraid." (*Hymns,* 1985, no. 30.) Fear, which can come upon people in difficult days, is a principal weapon in the arsenal which Satan uses to make mankind unhappy. He who fears loses strength for the combat of life in the fight against evil.

Therefore the power of the evil one always tries to generate fear in human hearts. In every age and in every era, mankind has faced fear.

As children of God and descendants of Abraham, Isaac, and Jacob, we must seek to dispel fear from among people. A timid, fearing people cannot do their work well, and they cannot do God's work at all. The Latter-day Saints have a divinely assigned mission to fulfill which simply must not be dissipated in fear and anxiety.

An Apostle of the Lord in an earlier day said this: "The key to the conquest of fear has been given through the Prophet Joseph Smith. 'If ye are prepared ye shall not fear.' (D&C 38:30.) That divine message needs repeating today in every stake and ward." (Elder John A. Widtsoe, in Conference Report, Apr. 1942, p. 33.)

Are we prepared to surrender to God's commandments? Are we prepared to achieve victory over our appetites? Are we prepared to obey righteous law? If we can honestly answer yes to those questions, we can bid fear to depart from our lives. Surely the degree of fear in our hearts may well be measured by our preparation to live righteously—living in a way that should characterize every Latter-day Saint in every age and time.

The privilege, honor, and responsibility of living in the latter days

Let me close with one of the greatest statements I have ever read from the Prophet Joseph Smith, who faced such immense difficulties in his life and who, of course, paid the ultimate price for his victory. But he *was* victorious, and he was a happy, robust, optimistic man. Those who knew him felt his strength and courage, even in the darkest of times. He did not sag in spirits, or long remain in any despondency.

He said about our time—yours and mine—that ours is the moment "upon which prophets, priests and kings [in ages past] have dwelt with peculiar delight; [all these ancient witnesses for God] have looked forward with joyful anticipation to the day in which we live; and fired with heavenly and joyful anticipations they have sung and written and prophesied of this our day; . . . we are the favored people that God has [chosen] to bring about the Latter-day glory" [*Teachings of Presidents of the Church: Joseph Smith*, 186].

What a privilege! What an honor! What a responsibility! And what joy! We have every reason in time and eternity to rejoice and give thanks for the quality of our lives and the promises we have been given.[9]

Suggestions for Study and Teaching

Questions

- How can it help us to know that adversity is part of God's plan for our eternal progress? (See section 1.) Why do you think adversity is a necessary part of mortality?

- Review President Hunter's teachings in section 2 about some of the purposes of adversity. How have you seen that adversity can be for our benefit? How can we come to see adversity from the Lord's eternal perspective?

- Why, as President Hunter teaches, do we have reason to be happy and optimistic even in times of difficulty? (See section 3.) How can we develop greater optimism during such times? What are some blessings we continue to have even during the most severe adversity?

- How do we accept the Savior's invitation to let Him carry our burdens and lighten our loads? (See section 4.) What does it mean to take His yoke upon us? How has the Savior helped you in times of difficulty?

- President Hunter teaches that feelings of fear about the tribulations of the last days do not come from God (see section 5). How is living by fear harmful? How can we live with hope and faith rather than by fear?

Related Scriptures

John 14:27; 16:33; Hebrews 4:14–16; 5:8–9; 1 Nephi 1:20; Alma 36:3; D&C 58:2–4; 101:4–5; 121:7–8; 122:7–9

Study Help

"Many find that the best time to study is in the morning after a night's rest. . . . Others prefer to study in the quiet hours after the work and worries of the day are over. . . . Perhaps what is more important than the hour of the day is that a regular time be set aside for study" (Howard W. Hunter, "Reading the Scriptures," *Ensign,* Nov. 1979, 64).

Notes

1. "God Will Have a Tried People," *Ensign,* May 1980, 24.

2. "Come unto Me," *Ensign,* Nov. 1990, 17–18.

3. "The Opening and Closing of Doors," *Ensign,* Nov. 1987, 54, 59.

4. "God Will Have a Tried People," 25–26.

5. "An Anchor to the Souls of Men," *Ensign,* Oct. 1993, 71.

6. "The Opening and Closing of Doors," 59–60.

7. "An Anchor to the Souls of Men," 70.

8. "Come unto Me," 17–18.

9. "An Anchor to the Souls of Men," 71–73.

*"The Lord promised that if we would be humble in . . . times of need
and turn to him for aid, we would 'be made strong, and [be] blessed
from on high'" (D&C 1:28).*

Help from on High

"Perhaps no promise in life is more reassuring
than that promise of divine assistance and
spiritual guidance in times of need."

From the Life of Howard W. Hunter

Howard W. Hunter learned to pray when he was a young boy. "My mother had taught me to pray and to thank Heavenly Father for all the things that I enjoyed," he said. "I often thanked Him for the beauty of the earth and for the wonderful times that I had at the ranch and by the river and with the Scouts. I also learned to ask Him for the things that I wanted or needed. . . . I knew that God loved me and listened to me."[1]

Throughout his life, President Hunter turned to prayer as a source of divine assistance, and he taught others to do the same. For example, when he was serving as a bishop, a man in his ward expressed bitterness toward another man. President Hunter's counsel reflected his testimony of the help that comes through prayer:

"I said to him, 'My brother, if you will go home and pray for him every morning and every night, I'll meet you two weeks from today at this same time and then we will decide what should be done.'"

After following this counsel, the man returned and humbly said of the other man, "He needs some help."

"Are you willing to help him?" President Hunter asked.

"Yes, of course," the man said.

"All the venom was gone and all the bitterness was gone," President Hunter later recalled. "This is the way it is when we pray for one another."[2]

Teachings of Howard W. Hunter

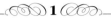 1

Our Heavenly Father promises to give us assistance and guidance in times of need.

All of us face times in our lives when we need heavenly help in a special and urgent way. We all have moments when we are overwhelmed by circumstances or confused by the counsel we get from others, and we feel a great need to receive spiritual guidance, a great need to find the right path and do the right thing. In the scriptural preface to this latter-day dispensation, the Lord promised that if we would be humble in such times of need and turn to him for aid, we would "be made strong, and [be] blessed from on high, and receive knowledge from time to time." (D&C 1:28.) That help is ours if we will but seek it, trust in it, and follow what King Benjamin, in the Book of Mormon, called "the enticings of the Holy Spirit." (Mosiah 3:19.)

Perhaps no promise in life is more reassuring than that promise of divine assistance and spiritual guidance in times of need. It is a gift freely given from heaven, a gift that we need from our earliest youth through the very latest days of our lives. . . .

In the gospel of Jesus Christ, we have help from on high. "Be of good cheer," the Lord says, "for I will lead you along." (D&C 78:18.) "I will impart unto you of my Spirit, which shall enlighten your mind, which shall fill your soul with joy." (D&C 11:13.)

I testify of the divinity of Jesus Christ. God does live and imparts to us his Spirit. In facing life's problems and meeting life's tasks, may we all claim that gift from God, our Father, and find spiritual joy.[3]

 2

Like Joseph Smith, we can turn to the scriptures and prayer to be taught from on high.

The boy-prophet Joseph Smith . . . sought to know the mind and will of the Lord at a time of confusion and concern in his life. . . . The area near Palmyra, New York, had become a place of "unusual excitement on the subject of religion" during young Joseph's boyhood years there. Indeed, the entire district appeared to him to be affected by it, with "great multitudes," he wrote, uniting themselves to the different religious parties and causing no small "stir and division" among the people [Joseph Smith—History 1:5].

For a boy who had barely turned fourteen, his search for the truth was made even more difficult and confusing because members of the Smith family differed in their religious preferences at the time.

Now, with that familiar background and setting, I invite you to consider these rather remarkable thoughts and feelings from a boy of such a tender age. He wrote:

"During this time of great excitement my mind was called up to serious reflection and great uneasiness; but though my feelings were deep and often poignant, still I kept myself aloof from all these [factions] . . . ; so great were the confusion and strife among the different denominations, that it was impossible for a person young as I was, and so unacquainted with men and things, to come to any certain conclusion who was right and who was wrong.

"My mind at times was greatly excited, the cry and tumult were so great and incessant. . . .

"In the midst of this war of words and tumult of opinions, I often said to myself: What is to be done? Who of all these parties are right; or, are they all wrong together? If any one of them be right, which is it, and how shall I know it?

"While I was laboring under the extreme difficulties caused by the contests of these parties of religionists, I was one day reading the Epistle of James, first chapter and fifth verse, which reads: *If any of you lack wisdom, let him ask of God, that giveth to all men liberally, and upbraideth not; and it shall be given him.*

"Never did any passage of scripture come with more power to the heart of man than this did at this time to mine. It seemed to enter with great force into every feeling of my heart. I reflected on it again and again, knowing that if any person needed wisdom from God, I did; for how to act I did not know, and unless I could get more wisdom than I then had, I would never know" [Joseph Smith—History 1:8–12].

We can follow Joseph Smith's example in seeking wisdom from God.

Of course, what happened next changed the course of human history. Determining to "ask of God," young Joseph retired to a grove near his rural home. There, in answer to his fervent prayer, God, the Eternal Father, and his Son, Jesus Christ visited Joseph and counseled him. That great manifestation, of which I humbly testify, answered many more questions for our dispensation than simply which church young Joseph should or should not join.

But my purpose . . . is not to outline the first moments of the Restoration, though it is one of the most sacred stories in the scriptures. I wish, rather, simply to emphasize the impressive degree of spiritual sensitivity demonstrated by this very young and untutored boy.

How many of us, at fourteen or any age, could keep our heads steady and our wits calm with so many forces tugging and pulling on us, especially on such an important subject as our eternal salvation? How many of us could withstand the emotional conflict that might come when parents differ in their religious persuasions? How many of us, at fourteen or fifty, would search within our souls and search within holy writ to find answers to what the Apostle Paul called "the deep things of God"? (1 Cor. 2:10.)

How remarkable . . . that this lad would turn profoundly to the scriptures and then to private prayer, perhaps the two greatest sources of spiritual insight and spiritual impression that are available universally to mankind. Certainly he was torn by differing opinions, but he was determined to do the right thing and determined to find the right way. He believed, as you and I must believe, that he could be taught and blessed from on high, as he was.

But, we may say, Joseph Smith was a very special spirit, and his was a special case. What about the rest of us who may now be older—at least older than fourteen—and have not been destined to open a dispensation of the gospel? We also must make decisions and sort out confusion and cut through a war of words in a whole host of subjects that affect our lives. The world is full of such difficult decisions, and sometimes as we face them, we may feel our age or our infirmities.

Sometimes we may feel that our spiritual edge has grown dull. On some very trying days, we may even feel that God has forgotten us, has left us alone in our confusion and concern. But that feeling is no more justified for the older ones among us than it is for the younger and less experienced. God knows and loves us all. We are, every one of us, his daughters and his sons, and whatever life's lessons may have brought us, the promise is still true: "If any of you lack wisdom, let him ask of God, that giveth to all men liberally, and upbraideth not; and it shall be given him." (James 1:5.)[4]

 **3**

Prayer is one way to receive spiritual knowledge and guidance.

The learning and wisdom of the earth and all that is temporal comes to us through our physical senses in earthly, temporal ways. We touch, we see, we hear and taste and smell and learn. However, spiritual knowledge, as Paul has said, comes to us in a spiritual way from its spiritual source. Paul continues:

"But the natural man receiveth not the things of the Spirit of God: for they are foolishness unto him: neither can he know them, because they are spiritually discerned." (1 Cor. 2:14.)

We have found, and know, that the only way to gain spiritual knowledge is to approach our Father in Heaven through the Holy Spirit in the name of Jesus Christ. When we do this, and if we are spiritually prepared, we see things our eyes have not previously seen, and we hear things we may not have previously heard—"the things which God hath prepared," using Paul's words. (1 Cor. 2:9.) These things we receive through the Spirit.

We believe, and testify to the world, that communication with our Father in Heaven and direction from the Lord are available today. We testify that God speaks to man as he did in the days of the Savior and in Old Testament times.[5]

We can pray always, not just in desperate times.

Our modern times seem to suggest that prayerful devotion and reverence for holiness is unreasonable or undesirable, or both. And yet, skeptical "modern" men have need for prayer. Perilous moments, great responsibility, deep anxiety, overwhelming grief—these challenges that shake us out of old complacencies and established routines will bring to the surface our native impulses. If we let them, they will humble us, soften us, and turn us to respectful prayer.

If prayer is only a spasmodic cry at the time of crisis, then it is utterly selfish, and we come to think of God as a repairman or a service agency to help us only in our emergencies. We should remember the Most High day and night—always—not only at times when all other assistance has failed and we desperately need help. If there is any element in human life on which we have a record of miraculous success and inestimable worth to the human soul, it is prayerful, reverential, devout communication with our Heavenly Father.

"Give ear to my words, O Lord, consider my meditation," the Psalmist sang.

"Hearken unto the voice of my cry, my King, and my God: for unto thee will I pray.

"My voice shalt thou hear in the morning, O Lord; in the morning will I direct my prayer unto thee, and will look up." (Ps. 5:1–3.)

Perhaps what this world needs, as much as anything, is to "look up" as the Psalmist said—to look up in our joys as well as our afflictions, in our abundance as well as in our need. We must continually

"Prayer is the utterance of the soul to God the Father."

look up and acknowledge God as the giver of every good thing and the source of our salvation. . . .

There are wide areas of our society from which the spirit of prayer and reverence and worship has vanished. Men and women in many circles are clever, interesting, or brilliant, but they lack one crucial element in a complete life. They do not look up. They do not offer up vows in righteousness [see D&C 59:11]. Their conversation sparkles, but it is not sacred. Their talk is witty, but it is not wise. Whether it be in the office, the locker room, or the laboratory, they have come too far down the scale of dignity who display their own limited powers and then find it necessary to blaspheme those unlimited powers that come from above.

Unfortunately we sometimes find this lack of reverence even within the Church. Occasionally we visit too loudly, enter and leave meetings too disrespectfully in what should be an hour of prayer and purifying worship. Reverence is the atmosphere of heaven.

Prayer is the utterance of the soul to God the Father. We do well to become more like our Father by looking up to him, by remembering him always, and by caring greatly about his world and his work.[6]

5

We develop our ability to receive spiritual knowledge as we take time to meditate, ponder, and pray.

Developing spirituality and attuning ourselves to the highest influences of godliness is not an easy matter. It takes time and frequently involves a struggle. It will not happen by chance, but is accomplished only through deliberate effort and by calling upon God and keeping his commandments. . . .

The Prophet Joseph Smith . . . has given us perhaps the clearest statement of all on the need to become spiritual as well as the time and patience which we must recognize are part of the process. [He] said: "We consider that God has created man with a mind capable of instruction, and a faculty which may be enlarged in proportion to the heed and diligence given to the light communicated from heaven to the intellect; and that the nearer man approaches perfection, the clearer are his views, and the greater his enjoyments, till he has overcome the evils of his life and lost every desire for sin; and like the ancients, arrives at that point of faith where he is wrapped in the power and glory of his Maker, and is caught up to dwell with Him. But we consider that this is a station to which no man ever arrived in a moment" [*Teachings of Presidents of the Church: Joseph Smith* (2007), 210–11].[7]

We must take time to prepare our minds for spiritual things. The development of spiritual capacity does not come with the conferral of authority. There must be desire, effort, and personal preparation. This requires, of course, . . . fasting, prayer, searching the scriptures, experience, meditation, and a hungering and thirsting after the righteous life.

I find it helpful to review these admonitions from Almighty God:

"If thou shalt ask, thou shalt receive revelation upon revelation, knowledge upon knowledge, that thou mayest know the mysteries and peaceable things—that which bringeth joy, that which bringeth life eternal" (D&C 42:61).

"Ask the Father in my name in faith, believing that you shall receive, and you shall have the Holy Ghost, which manifesteth all things which are expedient unto the children of men" (D&C 18:18).

"Let the solemnities of eternity rest upon your minds" (D&C 43:34).

"Treasure up in your minds continually the words of life, and it shall be given you in the very hour that portion that shall be meted unto every man" (D&C 84:85).

"Search diligently; pray always, and be believing, and all things shall work together for your good, if ye walk uprightly and remember the covenant wherewith ye have covenanted one with another" (D&C 90:24).

"God shall give unto you knowledge by his Holy Spirit, yea, by the unspeakable gift of the Holy Ghost" (D&C 121:26).

These are promises that the Lord will surely fulfill if we prepare ourselves.

Take time to meditate, ponder, and pray on spiritual matters.[8]

 **6**

God will help us progress spiritually one step at a time.

Part of our difficulty as we strive to acquire spirituality is the feeling that there is much to do and that we are falling far short. Perfection is something yet ahead for every one of us; but we can capitalize on our strengths, begin where we are, and seek after the happiness that can be found in pursuing the things of God. We should remember the Lord's counsel:

"Wherefore, be not weary in well-doing, for ye are laying the foundation of a great work. And out of small things proceedeth that which is great.

"Behold, the Lord requireth the heart and a willing mind; and the willing and obedient shall eat the good of the land of Zion in these last days." (D&C 64:33–34.)

It has always been encouraging to me that the Lord said it is the "willing and obedient [who] shall eat the good of the land of Zion in these last days." All of us can be willing and obedient. If the Lord had said the perfect shall eat the good of the land of Zion in these last days, I suppose some of us would be discouraged and give up. . . .

The place to begin is here. The time to start is now. The length of our stride needs be but one step at a time. God, who has "designed our happiness," will lead us along even as little children, and we will by that process approach perfection.

None of us has attained perfection or the zenith of spiritual growth that is possible in mortality. Every person can and must make spiritual progress. The gospel of Jesus Christ is the divine plan for that spiritual growth eternally. It is more than a code of ethics. It is more than an ideal social order. It is more than positive thinking about self-improvement and determination. The gospel is the saving power of the Lord Jesus Christ with his priesthood and sustenance and with the Holy Spirit. With faith in the Lord Jesus Christ and obedience to his gospel, a step at a time improving as we go, pleading for strength, improving our attitudes and our ambitions, we will find ourselves successfully in the fold of the Good Shepherd. That will require discipline and training and exertion and strength. But as the Apostle Paul said, "I can do all things through Christ which strengtheneth me." (Philip. 4:13.)

A modern-day revelation makes this promise: "Put your trust in that Spirit which leadeth to do good—yea, to do justly, to walk humbly, to judge righteously; and this is my Spirit.

"Verily, verily, I say unto you, I will impart unto you of my Spirit, which shall enlighten your mind, which shall fill your soul with joy;

"And then shall ye know, or by this shall you know, all things whatsoever you desire of me, which are pertaining unto things of righteousness, in faith believing in me that you shall receive." (D&C 11:12–14.)[9]

Suggestions for Study and Teaching

Questions

- After reading section 1, reflect on times when you have needed heavenly help. How has the promise of divine help in times of need blessed your life?

- In section 2, what can we learn from Joseph Smith's example that could help us when we face confusion? How can we develop greater spiritual sensitivity like Joseph's?

- Ponder President Hunter's teachings about how we receive spiritual knowledge (see section 3). How can we increase our desire and ability to gain spiritual knowledge? What are some ways that spiritual knowledge has helped you?

- What are the dangers of viewing God "as a repairman or a service agency to help us only in our emergencies"? (See section 4.) How has prayer been a blessing to you?

- In section 5, President Hunter teaches us how to develop spirituality. Why is effort necessary to develop spiritual strength? What can we learn from the scriptures that President Hunter cites in this section?

- Review President Hunter's teachings in section 6 about spiritual growth. How has spiritual growth been a step-by-step process for you? How can President Hunter's teachings in this section be helpful if you feel that you are falling short in your spiritual growth?

Related Scriptures

Psalm 25:5; Proverbs 3:6; 2 Nephi 32:8–9; Alma 5:46; 34:17–27; 37:36–37; D&C 8:2–3; 88:63; 112:10; Joseph Smith—History 1:13–17

Teaching Help

Invite class members to search the chapter, looking for sentences or paragraphs that are important to them. Ask them to share these sentences or paragraphs and to explain why they are meaningful.

Notes

1. In Kellene Ricks, "Friend to Friend: From an Interview with Howard W. Hunter, President of the Quorum of the Twelve Apostles," *Friend,* Apr. 1990, 6.

2. *The Teachings of Howard W. Hunter,* ed. Clyde J. Williams (1997), 39–40.

3. "Blessed from on High," *Ensign,* Nov. 1988, 59, 61.

4. "Blessed from on High," 59–60.

5. "Conference Time," *Ensign,* Nov. 1981, 13.

6. "Hallowed Be Thy Name," *Ensign,* Nov. 1977, 52–53.

7. "Developing Spirituality," *Ensign,* May 1979, 25.

8. *The Teachings of Howard W. Hunter,* 36–37.

9. "Developing Spirituality," 25–26.

Joseph Smith, Prophet of the Restoration

"I bear solemn testimony of the Prophet Joseph Smith as the Lord's anointed servant in these the latter days."

From the Life of Howard W. Hunter

Nancy Nowell, who was one of Howard W. Hunter's paternal great-great-grandmothers, moved to Lapeer, Michigan, in the mid-1830s. In 1842 a missionary of The Church of Jesus Christ of Latter-day Saints came to Lapeer from Nauvoo, Illinois. Nancy listened to his message, prayed about it, and received a testimony that he was teaching the truth. She went to Nauvoo to learn more about the Church, and in her journal she made this record of her experience:

"I went to hear the Mormon preacher [Joseph Smith] with great caution, hoping not to be deceived. His subject was the second coming of Christ. I had a testimony that he spoke the truth, and that Joseph Smith was a true prophet, called and ordained of God to do a great work, because he had brought forth the truth as it was taught by Jesus Christ. I asked to be baptized."[1]

Like his great-great-grandmother Nancy Nowell, Howard W. Hunter had a sure testimony of Joseph Smith's prophetic mission. Three weeks after becoming President of the Church, he traveled to Nauvoo to commemorate the 150th anniversary of the martyrdom of Joseph and Hyrum Smith. In a meeting held at the Nauvoo Temple site, President Hunter said:

"The responsibility I feel for the work the Prophet Joseph inaugurated fills me with a determination to do all I can in the time and season allotted to me. Surely Joseph was faithful and true to his time and season! . . . I bear solemn testimony of the Prophet Joseph

"Joseph Smith was not only a great man, but he was an
inspired servant of the Lord, a prophet of God."

Smith as the Lord's anointed servant in these the latter days. To his testimony of the divinity and reality of Jesus Christ I add my own."[2]

Later that day, in a meeting held beside the Carthage Jail, President Hunter testified, "Joseph Smith, who gave his life at this place, was the instrument the Lord used to restore the fulness of His gospel and the authority of His priesthood."[3]

Teachings of Howard W. Hunter

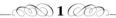

God the Father and Jesus Christ appeared to Joseph Smith to initiate the Restoration.

Many times the gospel [has] been given to the world through the prophets, and each time [it has been] lost because of disobedience. In the year 1820 the silence was broken, and the Lord again appeared to a prophet. This prophet, Joseph Smith, could testify of his own positive knowledge that God lives, that Jesus is the Christ, the Son of God, a Resurrected Being, separate and distinct from the Father. He did not testify as to what he believed or what he or others thought or conjectured, but of what he knew. This knowledge came to him because God the Father and the Son appeared to him in person and spoke to him.[4]

God . . . revealed himself [to Joseph Smith] as a personal being. Furthermore, the Father and the Son demonstrated the undeniable truth that they are separate and distinct personages. Indeed, the relationship of the Father and the Son was reaffirmed by the divine introduction to the boy prophet, "This is My Beloved Son. Hear Him!" [Joseph Smith—History 1:17].[5]

When men heard that young Joseph Smith was claiming God had manifested Himself to the boy, they mocked him and turned away from him, just as in the Christian era wise and able men in Athens turned away from a singular man ministering in their midst. Yet the fact remains that Paul, in that earlier experience, was the only man in that great city of learning who knew that a person may pass through the portals of death and live. He was the only man in Athens who could clearly delineate the difference between the formality of idolatry and the heartfelt worship of the only true and living God. [See Acts 17:19–20, 22–23.][6]

Those who rejected the Savior when he came to earth with the declaration that he was the Son of God said of him: "Is not this the carpenter's son?" (Matthew 13:55.) When Joseph announced that he had seen a vision and had seen the Father and the Son, the query came to the minds and lips of the neighbors, the ministers, and the townspeople: "Is not this the farmer's son?" Christ was persecuted and put to death, but time has been his vindicator. As with the carpenter's son, so it has been with the farmer's son.[7]

Joseph Smith was not only a great man, but he was an inspired servant of the Lord, a prophet of God. His greatness consists in one thing—the truthfulness of his declaration that he saw the Father and the Son and that he responded to the reality of that divine revelation. . . .

I testify . . . that the Father and the Son did appear to the Prophet Joseph Smith to initiate this great rolling forth of the latter-day work in our time.

I testify that the boy prophet, who in so many ways remains the central miracle . . . of this church's experience, is living proof that, within God's hands and under the direction of the Savior of the world, weak and simple things should come forth and break down the mighty and strong ones.[8]

Jesus Christ reestablished His Church through the Prophet Joseph Smith.

On the sixth of April, 1830, . . . a group of men and women, acting in obedience to a commandment of God, assembled in the house of Mr. Peter Whitmer [Sr.] to organize The Church of Jesus Christ of Latter-day Saints. . . . None of them laid any claim to special learning or significant leadership. They were honorable people and respectable citizens, but were virtually unknown outside of their own immediate neighborhood. . . .

These humble, ordinary men gathered because one of them, Joseph Smith, Jr., a very young man, had set forth a most remarkable claim. He declared to them and all others who would listen that he had received profound and repeated heavenly communications, including an open vision of God the Father and his Beloved Son, Jesus Christ. As a result of these revelatory experiences, Joseph Smith had already published the Book of Mormon, a record of Christ's dealings with the ancient inhabitants of America. Furthermore, the Lord had commanded this young man, by now only twenty-four years of age, to reinstitute the Church that had existed in New Testament times and that in its restored purity should again be designated by the name of its chief cornerstone and eternal head, the Lord Jesus Christ himself.

Thus, humbly but most significantly was opened the first scene in the great Church drama that eventually would affect not only that generation of men but the entire human family. . . . A humble beginning, yes, but the claim that God had spoken, that Christ's Church was again organized and its doctrines reaffirmed by divine revelation, was the most outstanding declaration made to the world since the days of the Savior himself when he walked the paths of Judea and the hills of Galilee.[9]

Part of the divine revelation [Joseph Smith received] was instruction to reestablish the true and living Church, restored in these modern times as it existed in the day of the Savior's own mortal ministry. The Prophet Joseph Smith said the Church of Jesus Christ was "organized in accordance with commandments and revelations given by Him to ourselves in these last days, as well as according to the order of the Church as recorded in the New Testament" [*Teachings of Presidents of the Church: Joseph Smith* (2007), 138]. . . .

. . . Those who were baptized into the Church on the sixth of April, 1830, believed in the existence of a personal God; they believed that his reality and the reality of his Son, Jesus Christ, constitute the eternal foundation upon which this church is built.[10]

Through [Joseph Smith] and by subsequent events, the priesthood and the gospel in its fulness were once more restored to the earth, never again to be removed [see D&C 65:2]. The Church of Christ, the kingdom of God on earth, was reestablished and destined, according to scripture, to roll forth and fill the whole earth [see Daniel 2:35].[11]

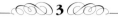

3

Joseph Smith was a prophet, seer, and revelator.

The coming of the Prophet Joseph into the world was the fulfillment of a prophecy uttered many centuries ago by Joseph who was sold into Egypt:

"A seer shall the Lord my God raise up, who shall be a choice seer unto the fruit of my loins. . . . And his name shall be called after me; and it shall be after the name of his father" (2 Nephi 3:6, 15).

Joseph Smith, Jr., was called after the name of Joseph of old who was carried captive into Egypt, and also after the name of his father, Joseph Smith, Sr., thus fulfilling this prophecy. He is known as the Prophet Joseph Smith and is called "Joseph the Seer." He is often referred to as "prophet, seer, and revelator."

The terms "Prophet" and "Seer" and "Revelator" are often used interchangeably and are thought by many to be one and the same thing. They are not the same, however, and these three terms have separate and distinct meanings.

[Elder] John A. Widtsoe defines a prophet as a teacher—one who expounds truth. He teaches truth as revealed by the Lord to man, and under inspiration explains it to the understanding of the people. The word "prophet" is often used to designate one who receives revelation and direction from the Lord. Many have thought that a prophet is essentially a foreteller of future events and happenings, but this is only one of the many functions of a prophet. He is a spokesman for the Lord.

A seer is one who sees. This does not mean that he sees through his natural eyes but rather through spiritual eyes. The seeric gift is a supernatural endowment. Joseph was like unto Moses, the ancient seer, and Moses saw God face to face, but he explains how he saw him in these words:

"But now mine own eyes have beheld God; but not my natural, but my spiritual eyes, for my natural eyes could not have beheld; for I should have withered and died in his presence; but his glory was upon me; and I beheld his face, for I was transfigured before him" (Moses 1:11).

The Prophet Joseph Smith's life "was led by revelation."

We should not suppose that to see spiritually is not to see literally. Such vision is not fancy or imagination. The object is actually beheld but not with the natural eyes. Each of us has spiritual eyes which are the counterpart of our natural eyes. We were first created spiritually and then our bodies were created as the covering of our spirit. We are told that in our first estate we walked by sight. This was through the vision of our spiritual eyes because we had not yet been given bodies with natural eyes. All men have spiritual sight but are not always privileged to use such sight unless quickened by the Spirit of the Lord. . . .

By the power of the Holy Ghost, certain persons, sent to the earth for that purpose, are able to see and behold the things which pertain to God. A seer is one who sees and knows of things which are past, and also of things which are to come, and by them shall all things be revealed (see Mosiah 8:15–17). In short, he is one who sees, who walks in the light of the Lord with spiritual eyes open and quickened by the power of the Holy Ghost. Moses, Samuel, Isaiah, Ezekiel, and many others were seers, because they were privileged to have a nearer view of the divine glory and power than other mortals have.

A revelation makes known something unknown or which has been previously known by man and taken from his memory. Always the revelation deals with truth, and always it comes with the divine stamp of approval. Revelation is received in various ways, but it always presupposes that the revelator has so lived and conducted himself as to be in tune or harmony with the divine spirit of revelation, the spirit of truth, and therefore capable of receiving divine messages.

To summarize we may say a prophet is a teacher of divine truth, a seer in every sense of the word. [Joseph Smith's] sense of spiritual sight was quickened to a remarkable degree and spiritualized by the Holy Ghost. It was by this gift that he beheld the Father and the Son when he went into the woods to pray. As we follow his life and works from that point, we find that he did not attempt to proceed on his own powers. He was dependent upon the Lord and thereby received his help and was given his instruction. His life was led by revelation.[12]

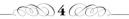

Praise to the man who communed with Jehovah.

When we sing of Joseph Smith, "Praise to the Man" (*Hymns,* 1985, no. 27), we remember so many praiseworthy things about him.

We praise him for his capacity to commune not only with Jehovah but also with other personages of heaven. So many visited, gave keys, and tutored that "choice seer" raised up in the latter days (2 Ne. 3:6–7). When Father Smith blessed young Joseph in 1834, he declared that ancient Joseph in Egypt saw this latter-day seer. Ancient

Joseph wept when he realized how the work of the Prophet Joseph would bless the earlier Joseph's numerous posterity.

We praise Joseph Smith, too, for his diligence and capacity to translate and to receive hundreds of pages of revealed scripture. He was the revealing conduit. Through him, it has been estimated, more marvelous pages of scripture passed than through any other human in history.

We praise Joseph not only for his capacity to endure but to "endure it well" (D&C 121:8). Early on, as a boy, there was the painful operation on his leg—without which surgery he could not have made the later arduous Zion's Camp march from Ohio to Missouri. During the march Joseph "walked most of the time and had a full proportion of blistered, bloody, and sore feet" [*Teachings of Presidents of the Church: Joseph Smith,* 287]. Likewise, we praise him and Emma for enduring the sorrowful loss of six of their natural and adopted children to early death. Parents who have lost even one child are filled with empathy.

We praise Joseph for the capacity to endure persecution, including the long and severe deprivations in Liberty Jail. To so many, everything then seemed hopeless. Yet the Lord of heaven reassured imprisoned Joseph that "the ends of the earth shall inquire after thy name" (D&C 122:1). We live in a day where there is increased inquiry about Joseph Smith and the restored gospel.

Joseph has long since fulfilled his wish that he might hold "an even weight in the balance with" the ancients [*Teachings of Presidents of the Church: Joseph Smith,* 230]. We can now sing of how Joseph has been "crowned in the midst of the prophets of old" (*Hymns,* 1985, no. 27).

We praise Joseph for enduring bitter and repeated betrayals and disappointments. Thus, he went to Carthage "like a lamb to the slaughter," "calm as a summer's morning," and "void of offense towards . . . all men" (D&C 135:4). He did not go to Carthage bitterly. He did not go to Carthage complainingly. What a marvelous capacity to endure well!

Joseph knew which way he faced. It was toward the Savior Jesus Christ to whom he listened ever since our Heavenly Father first instructed young Joseph, saying, "This is My Beloved Son. Hear Him!" [Joseph Smith—History 1:17].[13]

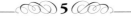

The life and mission of the Prophet Joseph Smith help us turn to the paths that lead to eternal life.

I am grateful for this man, for his teachings, for his revelations, for what he has left for us, for it was through him that the gospel was restored to the earth. I think there is no more beautiful story in all of history than the simple, sweet story of the lad who went into the woods near his home, kneeling in prayer and receiving heavenly visitors.

Now we look into his life and into his works. Many have pried into them to find the mystery of it all behind the written word, but there is no mystery. . . . There was a simple faith, the faith of a young boy who was to be trained in the things that pertained to God. And as time went by, this young man, without scholarly achievements and without education, was educated by the Lord for the things which should come.

Now we have been given intelligence and a mind. We only need to train and cultivate it as the Lord instructed Joseph and have a simple faith as he had and be willing to follow simple instructions. When we do so and follow the path that [the Lord] would have us follow and learn the lessons that He would have us learn, we find that our lives are purged of all things which are contrary to the purposes of God, and so it was with Joseph. He came to be a man nearer perfection, for he had cleansed his soul and his mind and lived close to the Lord and could talk with Him and hear Him speak the things which he has left for us through his revelations. Through his spiritual eyes he has been able to see that which has passed and that which lies ahead, and we have had proof of the truthfulness of that which he has seen. . . .

I am grateful for my membership in the Church, and my testimony of its divinity hinges upon the simple story of the lad under the trees kneeling and receiving heavenly visitors—not one God, but two separate individual personages, the Father and the Son, revealing again to the earth the personages of the Godhead. My faith and testimony hinges upon this simple story, for if it is not true, Mormonism falls. If it is true—and I bear witness that it is—it's one of the greatest single events in all history.

It is my prayer [that] as we commemorate this great prophet and reflect upon his life, that we have gratitude in our hearts for the things which have come into our lives by reason of his seership and his revelation to us—a choice seer, raised up by the Lord to guide us in these latter days, that we might turn our footsteps back to those paths which will lead us to exaltation and eternal life.[14]

Suggestions for Study and Teaching

Questions

- Ponder President Hunter's teachings about Joseph Smith's First Vision (see section 1). How has your testimony of the First Vision influenced you? Why is it vital for Latter-day Saints to have a testimony that Joseph Smith was a prophet of God?

- What are your impressions as you review President Hunter's teachings about the organization of the Church? (See section 2.) What blessings have come to you and your family through the restored Church of Jesus Christ?

- Why is it helpful to understand the meanings of the titles *prophet, seer,* and *revelator*? (See section 3.) How have you been blessed by prophets, seers, and revelators?

- In section 4, President Hunter outlines some of the reasons we praise Joseph Smith. How do these teachings increase your appreciation for the Prophet Joseph? What can you learn from Joseph Smith's example?

- Review President Hunter's teachings about Joseph Smith's faith, spiritual education, and obedience (see section 5). How do these teachings apply to us? How can we show gratitude for the blessings that have come to us through the Prophet Joseph Smith?

Related Scriptures

Joseph Smith Translation, Genesis 50:25–33; Daniel 2:44; Ephesians 2:19–22; 4:11–14; D&C 1:17–32; 5:9–10; 122:1–2; 135; Joseph Smith—History

Study Help

"As you feel the joy that comes from understanding the gospel, you will want to apply what you learn. Strive to live in harmony with your understanding. Doing so will strengthen your faith, knowledge, and testimony" (*Preach My Gospel* [2004], 19).

Notes

1. In Eleanor Knowles, *Howard W. Hunter* (1994), 7; see also page 6.
2. "The Temple of Nauvoo," *Ensign,* Sept. 1994, 63–64.
3. "Come to the God of All Truth," *Ensign,* Sept. 1994, 73.
4. In Conference Report, Oct. 1963, 100–101.
5. "The Sixth Day of April, 1830," *Ensign,* May 1991, 64.
6. "The Sixth Day of April, 1830," 63.
7. *The Teachings of Howard W. Hunter,* ed. Clyde J. Williams (1997), 228.
8. "The Sixth Day of April, 1830," 64–65.
9. "The Sixth Day of April, 1830," 63.
10. "The Sixth Day of April, 1830," 64.
11. In Conference Report, Oct. 1963, 101.
12. "Joseph Smith the Seer," in *The Annual Joseph Smith Memorial Sermons,* 2 vols. (1966), 2:193–94.
13. "The Temple of Nauvoo," 63–64.
14. "Joseph Smith the Seer," 2:197–98.

The Atonement and Resurrection of Jesus Christ

"We shall rise from mortal death to have life everlasting, because of the atoning sacrifice and resurrection of the Savior."

From the Life of Howard W. Hunter

On March 20, 1934, Howard and Claire Hunter's first child was born, a son they named Howard William Hunter Jr. and called Billy. During the summer they noticed that Billy seemed lethargic. Doctors diagnosed him with anemia, and Howard twice gave blood for transfusions, but Billy's condition did not improve. Further tests revealed a severe intestinal problem that was causing Billy to lose blood. Doctors performed surgery, with Howard lying beside his son to give blood, but the results were not encouraging. Three days later, on October 11, 1934, little Billy died quietly as his parents sat beside his bed. "We were grief-stricken and numb as we left the hospital into the night," Howard wrote.[1]

Through the experiences of Billy's death and the deaths of other loved ones, President Hunter was sustained by his testimony of the Savior's Atonement and Resurrection. "It is our firm belief that [the Atonement] is a reality," he testified, "and nothing is more important in the entire divine plan of salvation than the atoning sacrifice of Jesus Christ. We believe that salvation comes because of the atonement. In its absence the whole plan of creation would come to naught. . . . Without this atoning sacrifice, temporal death would be the end, and there would be no resurrection and no purpose in our spiritual lives. There would be no hope of eternal life."[2]

During the April general conferences, which are held around the time of Easter, President Hunter often spoke about the Resurrection of Jesus Christ. In the April 1983 general conference he said:

*The Savior's empty tomb "proclaims to all the world,
'He is not here, but is risen'" (Luke 24:6).*

"At this Easter season, I feel strongly the importance of my commission to testify of the reality of the Savior's resurrection. My brothers and sisters, there is a God in the heavens who loves and cares about you and me. We have a Father in Heaven, who sent his Firstborn of spirit children, his Only Begotten in the flesh, to be an earthly example for us, to take upon himself the sins of the world, and subsequently to be crucified for the sins of the world and be resurrected. . . .

"It is truly a beautiful message—there will be life after death; we can return to live with our Father in Heaven once again, because of the sacrifice the Savior has made for us, and because of our own repentance and obedience to the commandments.

"In the glorious dawn of Easter morning, when the thoughts of the Christian world are turned to the resurrection of Jesus for a few fleeting moments, let us express appreciation to our Heavenly Father for the great plan of salvation that has been provided for us."[3]

Teachings of Howard W. Hunter

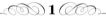 1

The Atonement was a supreme act of love by our Heavenly Father and His Beloved Son, Jesus Christ.

The Atonement of Jesus Christ was a foreordained assignment by our Heavenly Father to redeem his children after their fallen state. It was an act of love by our Heavenly Father to permit his Only Begotten to make an atoning sacrifice. And it was a supreme act of love by his beloved Son to carry out the Atonement.

I have stood in the garden of Gethsemane on many occasions. I've contemplated in my mind the suffering, the agony of the Savior—that agony that was experienced when our Heavenly Father permitted him, in a way our minds cannot even comprehend, to take upon himself the pain and sins of all mankind. My soul was filled with sorrow as I've thought of his great sacrifice for mankind.

I've stood beneath Golgotha, the place of the skull, and contemplated the humiliation of the crucifixion which led to our Savior's mortal death, but which brought to pass his and all mankind's immortality. And again my soul has been subdued.

And I've stood in front of the garden tomb and imagined that glorious day of resurrection when the Savior emerged from the tomb alive, resurrected, immortal. In that contemplation my heart has swelled with joy.

Through these experiences I've felt to pour out my soul in thanksgiving and appreciation to our Heavenly Father for the love which he and his Son have given to us through the glorious atoning sacrifice. In the words of Charles Gabriel, "I stand all amazed at the love Jesus offers me, confused at the grace that so fully he proffers me. I tremble to know that for me he was crucified, that for me, a sinner, he suffered, he bled and died. Oh, it is wonderful that he should care for me enough to die for me. Oh, it is wonderful, wonderful to me." . . .

I bear you my testimony, my brethren and sisters, that our Heavenly Father sent his beloved Son, Jesus Christ, into the world to fulfill the conditions upon which the plan of salvation would be operated. The Atonement represents his great love for us.[4]

 2

The Savior took upon Himself all of our sins, infirmities, grief, and pain.

As they met to celebrate the Passover, Jesus and his Apostles partook of the sacramental emblems that he initiated in this last supper together, and then walked to the Mount of Olives.

Always the teacher to the very end, he continued his discourse on the theme of the sacrificial lamb. He told them he would be smitten, and that they would be scattered as sheep without a shepherd (see Matthew 26:31). "But after I am risen again," he said, "I will go before you into Galilee" (Matthew 26:32).

In the hours that followed, he sweat drops of blood, was scourged by the very leaders who claimed to be custodians of his law, and was crucified in the company of thieves. It was as King Benjamin in the Book of Mormon prophesied: "He shall suffer temptations, and pain of body, hunger, thirst, and fatigue, even more than man can suffer, except it be unto death; for behold, blood cometh from every pore, so great shall be his anguish for the wickedness and the abominations of his people. . . .

"He cometh unto his own, that salvation might come unto the children of men . . . ; and even after all this they shall consider him a man, and say that he hath a devil, and shall scourge him, and shall crucify him" (Mosiah 3:7, 9).

We are indebted to the prophet Alma for our knowledge of the full measure of his suffering: "He shall go forth, suffering pains and afflictions and temptations of every kind; and this that the word might be fulfilled which saith he will take upon him the pains and the sicknesses of his people.

"And he will take upon him death, that he may loose the bands of death which bind his people; and he will take upon him their infirmities, that his bowels may be filled with mercy, according to the flesh, that he may know according to the flesh how to succor his people according to their infirmities" (Alma 7:11–12).

Think of it! When his body was taken from the cross and hastily placed in a borrowed tomb, he, the sinless Son of God, had already taken upon him not only the sins and temptations of every human soul who will repent, but all of our sickness and grief and pain of every kind. He suffered these afflictions as we suffer them, according to the flesh. He suffered them all. He did this to perfect his mercy and his ability to lift us above every earthly trial.[5]

We may, in fact, make wrong choices, bad choices, hurtful choices. And sometimes we do just that, but that is where the mission and mercy of Jesus Christ comes into full force and glory. . . . He has provided a mediating atonement for the wrong choices we make. He is our advocate with the Father and has paid, in advance, for the faults and foolishness we often see in the exercise of our freedom. We must accept his gift, repent of those mistakes, and follow his commandments in order to take full advantage of this redemption. The offer is always there; the way is always open. We can always, even in our darkest hour and most disastrous errors, look to the Son of God and live.[6]

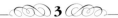

Jesus Christ arose from the grave and was the firstfruits of the Resurrection.

Go with me back in time to those final scenes in the Holy Land. The end of our Lord's mortal life was near. He had healed the sick, raised the dead, and expounded the scriptures, including those prophecies of his own death and resurrection. He said to his disciples:

"Behold, we go up to Jerusalem; and the Son of man shall be betrayed unto the chief priests and unto the scribes, and they shall condemn him to death,

"And shall deliver him to the Gentiles to mock, and to scourge, and to crucify him: and the third day he shall rise again" (Matthew 20:18–19). . . .

As the dawn of that third day was beginning, Mary Magdalene and "the other Mary" had come to the sepulchre in which his lifeless body had been laid [Matthew 28:1; see also Mark 16:1; Luke 24:10]. Earlier, the chief priests and the Pharisees had gone to Pilate and persuaded him to place a guard at the door of the sepulchre, "lest his disciples come by night, and steal him away, and say unto the people, He is risen from the dead" (Matthew 27:64). But two mighty angels had rolled the stone from the door of the tomb, and the would-be guards had fled in terror at the sight.

When the women came to the tomb, they found it open and empty. The angels had tarried to tell them the greatest news ever to fall on human ears: "He is not here: for he is risen, as he said" (Matthew 28:6).[7]

No doctrine in the Christian canon is more important to all mankind than the doctrine of the resurrection of the Son of God. Through him came the resurrection of all men, women, and children who have ever been—or ever will be—born into the world.

In spite of the great importance we place upon the resurrection in our doctrine, perhaps many of us may not yet have fully glimpsed its spiritual significance and eternal grandeur. If we had, we would marvel at its beauty as did Jacob, the brother of Nephi,

*Jesus Christ appeared to Mary Magdalene shortly after
He was resurrected (see John 20:1–18).*

and we would shudder at the alternative we would have faced had
we not received this divine gift. Jacob wrote:

"O the wisdom of God, his mercy and grace! For behold, if the
flesh should rise no more our spirits must become subject to that

angel who fell from before the presence of the Eternal God, and became the devil, to rise no more" (2 Nephi 9:8).

Surely the resurrection is the center of every Christian's faith; it is the greatest of all of the miracles performed by the Savior of the world. Without it, we are indeed left hopeless. Let me borrow the words of Paul: "If there be no resurrection of the dead, . . . then is our preaching vain, . . . and we are found false witnesses of God; because we have testified of God that he raised up Christ. . . . If Christ be not raised, your faith is vain; ye are yet in your sins" (1 Corinthians 15:13–15, 17).[8]

Without the Resurrection, the gospel of Jesus Christ becomes a litany of wise sayings and seemingly unexplainable miracles—but sayings and miracles with no ultimate triumph. No, the ultimate triumph is in the ultimate miracle: for the first time in the history of mankind, one who was dead raised himself into living immortality. He *was* the Son of God, the Son of our immortal Father in Heaven, and his triumph over physical and spiritual death is the good news every Christian tongue should speak.

The eternal truth is that Jesus Christ arose from the grave and was the firstfruits of the Resurrection. (See 1 Cor. 15:23.) The witnesses of this wonderful occurrence cannot be impeached.

Among the chosen witnesses are the Lord's Apostles. Indeed, the call to the holy apostleship is one of bearing witness to the world of the divinity of the Lord Jesus Christ. Joseph Smith said, "The fundamental principles of our religion are the testimony of the Apostles and Prophets, concerning Jesus Christ, that He died, was buried, and rose again the third day, and ascended into heaven; and all other things which pertain to our religion are only appendages to it." (*History of the Church,* 3:30.) . . .

In teaching his Apostles, Christ made known to them "that the Son of Man must suffer many things, and be rejected of the elders, and of the chief priests, and scribes, and be killed, and after three days rise again." (Mark 8:31.) So it was. He was crucified and placed in the tomb. On the third day, he did arise to live again—the Savior of all mankind and the firstfruits of the Resurrection. Through this atoning sacrifice, all men shall be saved from the grave and shall live again. This always has been the testimony of the Apostles, to which I add my witness.[9]

Jesus appeared to many after His Resurrection.

In the days that followed his resurrection, the Lord appeared unto many. He displayed his five special wounds to them. He walked and talked and ate with them, as if to prove beyond a doubt that <u>a resurrected body is indeed a physical body of tangible flesh and bones</u>. Later he ministered to the Nephites, whom he commanded to "arise and come forth unto me, that ye may thrust your hands into my side, and also that ye may feel the prints of the nails in my hands and in my feet, that ye may know that I am the God of Israel, and the God of the whole earth, and have been slain for the sins of the world.

"And . . . the multitude went forth, and thrust their hands into his side, and did feel the prints of the nails in his hands and in his feet; and this they did do, going forth one by one until they had all gone forth, and did see with their eyes and did feel with their hands, and did know of a surety and did bear record, that it was he, of whom it was written by the prophets, that should come" (3 Nephi 11:14–15).

It is the responsibility and joy of all men and women everywhere to "seek this Jesus of whom the prophets and apostles have [testified]" (Ether 12:41) and to have the spiritual witness of his divinity. It is the right and blessing of all who humbly seek, to hear the voice of the Holy Spirit, bearing witness of the Father and his resurrected Son.[10]

The testimony of those who saw [Jesus] as a living person after his death has never been contradicted. He appeared at least ten or eleven times: to Mary Magdalene and the other women in the garden, to the two disciples on the road to Emmaus, to Peter at Jerusalem, to the apostles when Thomas was absent and again when he was present, to the apostles at the Sea of Galilee, and on a mountain to over 500 brethren at once, to James the brother of the Lord, and to the apostles at the time of the ascension.[11]

As one called and ordained to bear witness of the name of Jesus Christ to all the world, I testify at this Easter season that he lives. He has a glorified, immortal body of flesh and bones. He is the Only Begotten Son of the Father in the flesh. He is the Savior, the Light and Life of the world. Following his crucifixion and death, he appeared as a resurrected being to Mary, to Peter, to Paul, and to many others. He showed himself to the Nephites. He has shown himself to Joseph Smith, the boy prophet, and to many others in our dispensation.[12]

5

We shall rise from death and have life everlasting.

Easter is the celebration of the free gift of immortality given to all men, restoring life and healing all wounds. Though all will die as part of the eternal plan of growth and development, nevertheless we can all find comfort in the Psalmist's statement, "Weeping may endure for a night, but joy cometh in the morning." (Ps. 30:5.)

It was Job who posed what might be called the question of the ages: "If a man die, shall he live again?" (Job 14:14.) Christ's answer rings down through time to this very hour: "Because I live, ye shall live also." (John 14:19.)[13]

There is a separation of the spirit and the body at the time of death. The resurrection will again unite the spirit with the body, and the body becomes a spiritual body, one of flesh and bones but quickened by the spirit instead of blood. Thus, our bodies after the resurrection, quickened by the spirit, shall become immortal and never die. This is the meaning of the statements of Paul that "there is a natural body, and there is a spiritual body" and "that flesh and blood cannot inherit the kingdom of God" [see 1 Corinthians 15:44, 50]. The natural body is flesh and blood, but quickened by the spirit instead of blood, it can and will enter the kingdom. . . .

I have a conviction that God lives and that Jesus is the Christ. As Paul bore testimony to the saints of Corinth by his letter at that Easter season many years ago, I add my witness that we shall rise from mortal death to have life everlasting, because of the atoning sacrifice and resurrection of the Savior. In my mind I picture him with arms outstretched to all who will hear:

". . . I am the resurrection, and the life: he that believeth in me, though he were dead, yet shall he live:

"And whosoever liveth and believeth in me shall never die." (John 11:25–26.)[14]

Christ's resurrection ushers in the blessing of immortality and the possibility of eternal life. His empty tomb proclaims to all the world, "He is not here, but is risen." (Luke 24:6.) These words contain all the hope, assurance, and belief necessary to sustain us in our challenging and sometimes grief-filled lives.[15]

Suggestions for Study and Teaching

Questions

- How does the Atonement demonstrate the love of Heavenly Father and Jesus Christ for us? (See section 1.) How can we show gratitude for this gift of love? (See D&C 42:29.)

- As you review section 2, look for the many ways the Atonement blesses us. How do President Hunter's teachings and use of the scriptures enhance your understanding of the Atonement? What experiences have strengthened your testimony of the Atonement? How can the power of the Atonement strengthen you during your trials?

- What are your impressions as you study President Hunter's teachings about the Resurrection? (See section 3.) How might we better appreciate the significance of the Resurrection?

- Review section 4, in which President Hunter details many witnesses of the Resurrection of Jesus Christ. Why is the testimony of these witnesses significant?

- Consider President Hunter's teaching that the Resurrection provides "all the hope, assurance, and belief necessary to sustain us in our challenging and sometimes grief-filled lives" (section 5). How is the Resurrection a source of hope and consolation for you? How has a testimony of the Resurrection enriched your life?

Related Scriptures

John 10:17–18; 2 Nephi 2:6–9, 22–27; 9:19–25; 3 Nephi 27:13–16; D&C 18:10–16; 19:15–20; Moses 6:59–60

Study Help

"Plan study activities that will build your faith in the Savior" (*Preach My Gospel* [2004], 22). For instance, as you study you might ask yourself questions such as the following: "How might these teachings help me increase my understanding of the Atonement of Jesus Christ? How can these teachings help me become more like the Savior?"

Notes

1. In Eleanor Knowles, *Howard W. Hunter* (1994), 88; see also 86–87.
2. In Conference Report, Oct. 1968, 139.
3. "Evidences of the Resurrection," *Ensign,* May 1983, 16.
4. "The Atonement of Jesus Christ" (address given at mission presidents' seminar, June 24, 1988), 2–3, 7, Church History Library, Salt Lake City; see also *The Teachings of Howard W. Hunter,* ed. Clyde J. Williams (1997), 8–9.
5. "He Is Risen," *Ensign,* May 1988, 16–17.
6. "The Golden Thread of Choice," *Ensign,* Nov. 1989, 18.
7. "He Is Risen," 16–17.
8. "He Is Risen," 16.
9. "An Apostle's Witness of the Resurrection," *Ensign,* May 1986, 16–17.
10. "He Is Risen," 17.
11. In Conference Report, Apr. 1963, 106.
12. "He Is Risen," 17.
13. "An Apostle's Witness of the Resurrection," 16.
14. In Conference Report, Apr. 1969, 138–39.
15. "An Apostle's Witness of the Resurrection," 15–16.

Continuous Revelation through Living Prophets

"We are guided by a living prophet of God—
one who receives revelation from the Lord."

From the Life of Howard W. Hunter

After being sustained as President of the Church in the October 1994 general conference, Howard W. Hunter expressed his feelings about his sacred responsibilities:

"My beloved brothers and sisters, thank you for your sustaining vote. I come before you humbly and meekly, saddened by the recent passing of our beloved prophet, President Ezra Taft Benson. My heart is tender upon the passing of my dear friend, particularly in light of the new responsibilities that have come to me.

"I have shed many tears and have sought my Father in Heaven in earnest prayer in the desire to be equal to this high and holy calling. I have prayed to be worthy to bear the assignment which thirteen other men in this dispensation have borne. Perhaps only they, watching from the other side of the veil, can fully understand the weight of responsibility and the deep dependence on the Lord that I feel in accepting this sacred calling."

President Hunter explained that he found strength and reassurance in his conviction that the Church is led not by men but by Jesus Christ Himself, who prepares and inspires those He calls to preside:

"My greatest strength through these past months has been my abiding testimony that this is the work of God and not of men. Jesus Christ is the head of this church. He leads it in word and deed. I am honored beyond expression to be called <u>for a season</u> to be an instrument in his hands to preside over his church. But without

*As a member of the Quorum of the Twelve Apostles, President Howard W.
Hunter counseled Latter-day Saints to follow the President of the Church.*

the knowledge that Christ is the head of the Church, neither I nor any other man could bear the weight of the calling that has come.

"In assuming this responsibility, I acknowledge God's miraculous hand in my life. He has repeatedly spared my life and restored my strength, has repeatedly brought me back from the edge of eternity, and has allowed me to continue in my mortal ministry for another season. I have wondered on occasion why my life has been spared. But now I have set that question aside and ask only for the faith and prayers of the members of the Church so we can work together, I laboring with you, to fulfill God's purposes in this season of our lives. . . .

"It has been thirty-five years since I was sustained as a member of the Quorum of the Twelve. Those years have been rich in preparation. . . . My walk is slower now, but my mind is clear, and my spirit is young. . . .

"Like my Brethren before me, I receive with this calling the assurance that God will direct his prophet. I humbly accept the call to serve and declare with the Psalmist, 'The Lord is my strength and my shield; my heart trusted in him, and I am helped' (Ps. 28:7)."[1]

Teachings of Howard W. Hunter

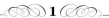

In each dispensation, God has raised up prophets as His spokesmen.

As one turns the pages of the Old Testament, there appear the writings of great men of ages past who are referred to as the prophets. The books of the New Testament contain, among other things, the writings, teachings, and history of men of a later dispensation, who have been designated as prophets. We also have the record of the prophets of the western part of the world, who raised their voices, proclaiming the word of the Lord, protesting unrighteousness, and teaching the principles of the gospel. All of these have left their witness.

A prophet is one who has been called and raised up by the Lord to further God's purposes among his children. He is one who has received the priesthood and speaks with authority. Prophets are

113

teachers and defenders of the gospel. They bear witness of the divinity of the Lord Jesus Christ. Prophets have foretold future happenings, but this is not the most important of their responsibilities, although it may be some evidence of prophetic power.

Righteous leadership has been needed in each dispensation of time, and God chose prophets for this purpose long before they came to this mortal existence [see Jeremiah 1:5; Abraham 3:23].[2]

A study of the revelations of the Lord in holy writ confirms the fact that it is continuous revelation that guides prophets and the Church in any age. Were it not for continuous revelation, Noah would not have been prepared for the deluge that encompassed the earth. Abraham would not have been guided from Haran to Hebron, the Land of Promise. Continuous revelation led the children of Israel from bondage back to their promised land. Revelation through prophets guided missionary efforts, directed the rebuilding of Solomon's temple, and denounced the infiltration of pagan practices among the Israelites.

Before the ascension of Christ, he promised the remaining eleven apostles, "Lo, I am with you alway, even unto the end of the world." (Matt. 28:20.) Following his ascension, he guided the Church by revelation until the death of the Apostles and subsequent apostasy of the Church of Jesus Christ.[3]

Down through its history, including this very day, the Church has had a prophet, seer, and revelator. At the head of the Church is Jesus Christ, who directs his prophet. . . . His counselors [and] the members of the Council of the Twelve . . . are also prophets, seers, and revelators. . . . Members of the Church do not have to listen to an uncertain trumpet. They can believe the voice of their leaders, knowing they are guided by the Lord.[4]

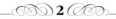 **2**

God provides guidance for His children through a living prophet today.

A distinctive sign of the last days that will precede the eventual second coming of the Lord was seen in vision by that same Apostle who recorded the book of Revelation. He said:

"I saw another angel fly in the midst of heaven, having the everlasting gospel to preach unto them that dwell on the earth, and to every nation, and kindred, and tongue, and people." (Rev. 14:6.) . . .

We testify to all the world that heavenly ministers have already appeared in our age, bringing authority from heaven and restoring truths lost through corrupted teachings and practices. God has spoken anew and continues to provide guidance for all his children through a living prophet today. We declare that he, as promised, is with his servants always and directs the affairs of his Church throughout the world. As in times past, revelation directs missionary labors, the building of temples, the calling of priesthood officers, and warns against the evils of society that may deny salvation to our Father's children.

In a revelation to a modern oracle, Joseph Smith, the Lord said:

"For I am no respecter of persons, and will that all men shall know that the day speedily cometh; the hour is not yet, but is nigh at hand, when peace shall be taken from the earth, and the devil shall have power over his own dominion.

"And also the Lord shall have power over his saints, and shall reign in their midst." (D&C 1:35–36.)

The Savior is reigning in the midst of the Saints today through continuous revelation. I testify that he is with his servants in this day and will be until the end of the earth.

May our vision not be so narrow that we would relegate revelation to only the ancients. God is merciful and loves his children in all ages and has revealed himself to this time in history.[5]

The Lord has revealed his mind and will to his anointed prophets. There is an unending stream of revelation flowing constantly from the headwaters of heaven to God's anointed servants on earth. Since the death of the Prophet Joseph Smith, the voice of the Lord to his prophets has continued as before.[6]

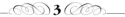

In this day of spiritual famine, we can find spiritual abundance by heeding the voice of the prophet.

Famine was one of the common scourges of Old Testament times, and people understood the devastating consequences of crop failure and starving people. Amos brought this understanding into sharp focus by his prediction of a spiritual famine. He said: ". . . not a famine of bread, nor a thirst for water, but of hearing the words of the Lord" [Amos 8:11]. . . .

Present-day reports of confusion and frustration of individuals and religious institutions, as they attempt to resolve their religious doubts and conflicts, remind us of these words of Amos: ". . . they shall run to and fro to seek the word of the Lord, and shall not find it" [Amos 8:12].

They seek to find the solution without building on the rock of revelation, as the Lord said must be done [see Matthew 16:17–18]. . . .

. . . The confusion and frustrations from which the world is suffering are not common to faithful members of the Church. . . . There is a believable voice to those who have faith and the will to believe. Certainly we live in a day of famine, as described by Amos. . . . Nevertheless, in what appears to be a spiritual famine, there are many who have found a spiritual abundance.

It is . . . my humble testimony that the gospel in its fullness has been restored in these latter days and that there is a prophet on the earth today who speaks the mind and will of the Lord to those who will hear and have the faith to follow.[7]

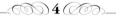

If we follow the teachings of the living prophets, we will not go amiss.

To peoples of past dispensations and ages, the most important prophet was the one then living, teaching, and revealing the will of the Lord in their time. In each of the past dispensations, prophets have been raised up by the Lord as his spokesmen to the people of that particular age and for the specific problems of that age.

It is the present living prophet who is our leader, our teacher. It is from him we take direction in the modern world. From all corners of the earth, we who sustain him as a prophet of the Lord express our appreciation for this source of divine guidance. . . .

As the prophets from the beginning to the present day pass in review before our memory, we become aware of the great blessing which comes to us from the influence of a living prophet. History should teach us that unless we are willing to heed the warnings and follow the teachings of a prophet of the Lord, we will be subject to the judgments of God.[8]

Only the President of the Church has the right to receive revelations for the entire Church or to give official interpretations of the scriptures or the doctrines of the Church:

"No one shall be appointed to receive commandments and revelations in this church excepting [the President of the Church], for he receiveth them even as Moses" (D&C 28:2).[9]

If we follow the advice, counsel, and teachings of the leaders of the Church in their instruction to us, we will not go amiss in that which is important for our own personal salvation and exaltation.[10]

I am overcome with gratitude for the revelations which have established the marvelous system by which his Church is governed. Each man who is ordained an Apostle and set apart as a member of the Quorum of the Twelve is sustained as a prophet, seer, and revelator. The First Presidency and the Quorum of the Twelve Apostles, called and ordained to hold the keys of the priesthood, have the authority and responsibility to govern the Church, to administer its ordinances, to teach its doctrine, and to establish and maintain its practices.

When a President of the Church is ill or not able to function fully in all of the duties of his office, his two Counselors, who, with him, comprise a Quorum of the First Presidency, carry on the work of the Presidency. Any major questions, policies, programs, or doctrines are prayerfully considered in council by the Counselors in the First Presidency and the Quorum of the Twelve Apostles. No decision emanates from the First Presidency and the Quorum of the Twelve without total unanimity among all concerned.

"Conference time is a season of spiritual revival when knowledge and testimony are increased and solidified."

Following this inspired pattern, the Church will move forward without interruption. The governance of the Church and the exercise of the prophetic gifts will always be vested in those apostolic authorities who hold and exercise all of the keys of the priesthood.[11]

 **5**

In general conference, we receive inspired counsel from prophets, seers, and revelators.

As I have pondered the messages of [general] conference, I have asked myself this question: How can I help others partake of the goodness and blessings of our Heavenly Father? The answer lies in following the direction received from those we sustain as prophets, seers, and revelators, and others of the General Authorities. Let us study their words, spoken under the Spirit of inspiration, and refer to them often. The Lord has revealed his will to the Saints in this conference.[12]

Much inspired counsel by prophets, seers, revelators, and other General Authorities of the Church is given during general conference. Our modern-day prophets have encouraged us to make the reading of the conference editions of our Church magazines an important and regular part of our personal study. Thus, general conference becomes, in a sense, a supplement to or an extension of the Doctrine and Covenants.[13]

Conference time is a season of spiritual revival when knowledge and testimony are increased and solidified that God lives and blesses those who are faithful. It is a time when an understanding that Jesus is the Christ, the Son of the living God, is burned into the hearts of those who have the determination to serve him and keep his commandments. Conference is the time when our leaders give us inspired direction in the conduct of our lives—a time when souls are stirred and resolutions are made to be better husbands and wives, fathers and mothers, more obedient sons and daughters, better friends and neighbors. . . .

We who are met here today [in general conference] claim a special, unique knowledge of the Savior's gospel. Most striking of all, to those who first became acquainted with us, is our declaration to the world that we are guided by a living prophet of God—one who communicates with, is inspired by, and receives revelation from the Lord.[14]

Suggestions for Study and Teaching

Questions

- Review President Hunter's teachings in section 1. Why has God provided prophets for each dispensation? What are some of the functions of prophets? How can we help children gain a testimony of prophets?

- How does having a living prophet bless us today? (See section 2.) Why is it important that there is "an unending stream of revelation" flowing from God to His living prophets?

- What are some evidences that we are living in a time of "spiritual famine"? (See section 3.) What blessings have you received by heeding the voice of the living prophet?

- President Hunter teaches that "only the President of the Church has the right to receive revelations for the entire Church" (section 4). Why is it helpful to know this? Why is it helpful to know that "we will not go amiss" as we follow the prophet?

- Consider the importance of general conference in your life. (See section 5.) What are some teachings from general conference that have blessed you? How can you make general conference a more powerful influence in your life and home?

Related Scriptures

Amos 3:7; Matthew 10:41; Luke 1:68–70; Joseph Smith Translation, 2 Peter 1:20–21; Mosiah 8:15–18; D&C 1:14–16, 37–38; 21:1, 4–6; 43:2–6; 107:91–92

Teaching Help

As a class, list on the board some questions that people of other faiths might have about the topic of the chapter. Invite class members to review the chapter, looking for answers to these questions, and then to share what they find.

Notes

1. "Exceeding Great and Precious Promises," *Ensign,* Nov. 1994, 7–8.
2. In Conference Report, Oct. 1963, 99.
3. "No Man Shall Add to or Take Away," *Ensign,* May 1981, 65.
4. "Spiritual Famine," *Ensign,* Jan. 1973, 65.
5. "No Man Shall Add to or Take Away," 65.
6. *The Teachings of Howard W. Hunter,* ed. Clyde J. Williams (1997), 196.
7. "Spiritual Famine," 64–65.
8. In Conference Report, Oct. 1963, 101.
9. *The Teachings of Howard W. Hunter,* 225.
10. *The Teachings of Howard W. Hunter,* 223.
11. "Exceeding Great and Precious Promises," 7. President Hunter spoke these important principles while he was President of the Church.
12. "Follow the Son of God," *Ensign,* Nov. 1994, 87.
13. *The Teachings of Howard W. Hunter,* 212.
14. "Conference Time," *Ensign,* Nov. 1981, 12–13.

Taking the Gospel
to All the World

"We are in the work of saving souls,
of inviting people to come unto Christ."

From the Life of Howard W. Hunter

In 1979, Elder Howard W. Hunter, then a member of the Quorum of the Twelve Apostles, said: "I fully believe that in the near future we will see some of the greatest advancements in spreading the gospel to all nations that have ever taken place in this dispensation or any previous dispensation. I am sure that we will be able to look back in retrospect . . . and record as Luke did, 'And the word of God increased' (Acts 6:7)."[1]

When Elder Hunter spoke those words, political restrictions prohibited missionaries from teaching the gospel in most countries of Eastern Europe and in the Soviet Union. Within 10 years, many of those restrictions began to be lifted. In 1989 and 1990 the Berlin Wall, which had separated West and East Germany for nearly 30 years, was torn down. President Hunter was serving as President of the Quorum of the Twelve at the time, and he expressed the following thoughts about that historic event and other changes that were occurring in the world:

"Much attention of late has been devoted to the Berlin Wall. Of course, we are all pleased to see that wall come down, representing as it does newfound freedoms. . . . As we try to understand the spirit of reconciliation sweeping the globe and to give it meaning within the gospel context, we have to ask ourselves: Could this not be the hand of the Lord removing political barriers and opening breaches in heretofore unassailable walls for the teaching of the gospel, all in accord with a divine plan and a divine timetable?"[2]

*"The gospel of Jesus Christ . . . is a global faith
with an all-embracing message."*

President Hunter felt that these changes placed an important responsibility on members of the Church. As more nations opened to missionary work, he said, more missionaries would be needed to fulfill the commission to take the gospel to all the world.[3]

President Hunter's eagerness to reach out to all of God's children, regardless of nationality or creed, was evident in his work in the Middle East. The First Presidency gave him significant assignments in Jerusalem, including oversight of the construction of the Orson Hyde Memorial Garden and the Brigham Young University Jerusalem Center for Near Eastern Studies. Although proselyting was not allowed in that region, President Hunter built lasting friendships among those with whom he worked, both Jewish and Arabic people. "The purpose of the gospel of Jesus Christ is to bring about love, unity, and brotherhood of the highest order," he said.[4]

In his work with God's children around the world, President Hunter's message was the same: "We are your brethren—we look upon no nation or nationality as second-class citizens. We invite all . . . to investigate our message and to receive our fellowship."[5]

Teachings of Howard W. Hunter

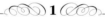 1

The restored gospel is for all people, based on the conviction that all are children of the same God.

The gospel of Jesus Christ, which gospel we teach and the ordinances of which we perform, is a global faith with an all-embracing message. It is neither confined nor partial nor subject to history or fashion. Its essence is universally and eternally true. Its message is for all the world, restored in these latter days to meet the fundamental needs of every nation, kindred, tongue, and people on the earth. It has been established again as it was in the beginning—to build brotherhood, to preserve truth, and to save souls. . . .

In the message of the gospel, the entire human race is one family descended from a single God. All men and women have not only a physical lineage leading back to Adam and Eve, their first earthly parents, but also a spiritual heritage leading back to God the Eternal

Father. Thus, all persons on earth are literally brothers and sisters in the family of God.

It is in understanding and accepting this universal fatherhood of God that all human beings can best appreciate God's concern for them and their relationship to each other. This is a message of life and love that strikes squarely against all stifling traditions based on race, language, economic or political standing, educational rank, or cultural background, for we are all of the same spiritual descent. We have a divine pedigree; every person is a spiritual child of God.

In this gospel view there is no room for a contracted, narrow, or prejudicial view. The Prophet Joseph Smith said: "Love is one of the chief characteristics of Deity, and ought to be manifested by those who aspire to be the sons of God. A man filled with the love of God, is not content with blessing his family alone, but ranges through the whole world, anxious to bless the whole human race" [*Teachings of Presidents of the Church: Joseph Smith* (2007), 330–31]. . . .

The restored gospel is a message of divine love for all people everywhere, based upon the conviction that all humans are children of the same God. This primary religious message was beautifully expressed in a statement of the First Presidency on February 15, 1978, as follows:

"Based upon ancient and modern revelation, The Church of Jesus Christ of Latter-day Saints gladly teaches and declares the Christian doctrine that all men and women are brothers and sisters, not only by blood relationship from common mortal progenitors but also as literal spirit children of an Eternal Father" [Statement of the First Presidency Regarding God's Love for All Mankind, Feb. 15, 1978].

Latter-day Saints have a positive and inclusive approach toward others who are not of our faith. We believe they are literally our brothers and sisters, that we are sons and daughters of the same Heavenly Father. We have a common genealogy leading back to God.[6]

2

The Church has a mission to teach
the gospel to all nations.

The Church, being the kingdom of God on earth, has a mission to all nations. "Go ye therefore, and teach all nations, baptizing them in the name of the Father, and of the Son, and of the Holy Ghost:

"Teaching them to observe all things whatsoever I have commanded you" (Matt. 28:19–20). These words from the lips of the Master know no national boundaries; they are not limited to any race or culture. One nation is not favored above another. The admonition is clear—"teach *all* nations." . . .

As members of the Lord's church, we need to lift our vision beyond personal prejudices. We need to discover the supreme truth that indeed our Father is no respecter of persons. Sometimes we unduly offend brothers and sisters of other nations by assigning exclusiveness to one nationality of people over another. . . .

Imagine a father with many sons, each having different temperaments, aptitudes, and spiritual traits. Does he love one son less than another? Perhaps the son who is least spiritually inclined has the father's attention, prayers, and pleadings more than the others. Does that mean he loves the others less? Do you imagine our Heavenly Father loving one nationality of his offspring more exclusively than others? As members of the Church, we need to be reminded of Nephi's challenging question: "Know ye not that there are more nations than one?" (2 Ne. 29:7). . . .

To our brothers and sisters of all nationalities: We bear solemn witness and testify that God has spoken in our day and time, that heavenly messengers have been sent, that God has revealed his mind and will to a prophet, Joseph Smith. . . .

As our Father loves all his children, we must love all people—of every race, culture, and nationality—and teach them the principles of the gospel that they might embrace it and come to a knowledge of the divinity of the Savior.[7]

"We are in the work of saving souls."

In our humble efforts to build brotherhood and to teach revealed truth, we say to the people of the world what President George Albert Smith so lovingly suggested:

"We have come not to take away from you the truth and virtue you possess. We have come not to find fault with you nor to criticize you. . . . Keep all the good that you have, and let us bring to you more good, in order that you may be happier and in order that you may be prepared to enter into the presence of our Heavenly Father."[8]

We are in the work of saving souls, of inviting people to come unto Christ, of bringing them into the waters of baptism so that they may continue to progress along the path that leads to eternal life. This world needs the gospel of Jesus Christ. The gospel provides the only way the world will ever know peace.[9]

As members of the Church of Jesus Christ, we seek to bring all truth together. We seek to enlarge the circle of love and understanding among all the people of the earth. Thus we strive to establish peace and happiness, not only within Christianity but among all mankind. . . .

That which Joseph [Smith] was instrumental in establishing, even The Church of Jesus Christ of Latter-day Saints, is now a world religion, not simply because its members are now found throughout the world, but chiefly because it has a comprehensive and inclusive message based upon the acceptance of all truth, restored to meet the needs of all mankind.

. . . We send this message of love and hope to all the world. Come to the God of all truth, who continues to speak to His children through prophets. Listen to the message of Him who continues to send His servants to preach the everlasting gospel to every nation, kindred, tongue, and people. Come and feast at the table laid before you by The Church of Jesus Christ of Latter-day Saints. Join us as we seek to follow the Good Shepherd who has provided it.[10]

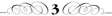

Those who have experienced the blessings of the Atonement of Jesus Christ are under obligation to bear testimony of Him.

What does the Atonement have to do with missionary work? Any time we experience the blessings of the Atonement in our lives, we cannot help but have a concern for the welfare of [others].

Examples abound in the Book of Mormon that illustrate this principle. When Lehi partook of the fruit of the tree, symbolic of partaking of the Atonement, he said, "I began to be desirous that my family should partake" (1 Nephi 8:12). When Enos experienced his conversion and received a forgiveness of his sins, because of his faith in Jesus Christ he said, "I began to feel a desire for the welfare of my brethren, the Nephites" (Enos 1:9). Then he prayed for the Lamanites, the implacable enemies to the Nephites. Then there is the example of the four sons of Mosiah—Ammon, Aaron, Omner, and Himni—who received a forgiveness of sins through the Atonement and then labored for years among the Lamanites to bring them to Christ. The record states that they could not bear the thought that any soul should perish (Mosiah 28:3).

This supernal example of the covenanted one desiring to share the gospel with others is best illustrated by the example of Alma the Younger. I would like to read to you his testimony. . . .

". . . From that time even until now, I have labored without ceasing, that I might bring souls unto repentance; that I might bring them to taste of the exceeding joy of which I did taste; that they might also be born of God, and be filled with the Holy Ghost" [Alma 36:24; see also Alma 36:12–23].

A great indicator of one's personal conversion is the desire to share the gospel with others. For this reason the Lord gave an obligation to every member of the Church to be missionaries.

Listen to the covenant one takes upon oneself when baptized into the Church:

"As ye are desirous to come into the fold of God, and to be called his people, and are willing to bear one another's burdens, that they may be light;

"Yea, and are willing to mourn with those that mourn; yea, and comfort those that stand in need of comfort, and to stand as witnesses of God at all times and in all things, and in all places that ye may be in, even until death, that ye may be redeemed of God, and be numbered with those of the first resurrection, that ye may have eternal life" (Mosiah 18:8–9).

We are to stand as witnesses of God at all times [and] in all places, even until death. We renew that covenant during the sacrament when we covenant to take the name of Christ upon us.

Missionary service is one important way we take upon ourselves his name. The Savior has said if we desire to take upon us his name, with full purpose of heart, we are called to go into all the world and preach his gospel to every creature (see D&C 18:28). . . .

Those of us who have partaken of the Atonement are under obligation to bear faithful testimony of our Lord and Savior. . . . The call to share the gospel with others represents our great love for our Heavenly Father's children as well as for the Savior and what he did for us.[11]

4

With the Lord's help, we can overcome all obstacles to sharing the gospel.

As the walls in Eastern Europe . . . and many other parts of the world come tumbling down, the corresponding need for more missionaries to fulfill the divine commission to take the gospel to all the earth will certainly go up! Are we ready to meet that contingency?

To satisfy the new demands being made upon us in this great missionary work of the last days, perhaps some of us (particularly the older generation whose families are raised) need to take stock to determine whether "walls" that we have built in our own minds need to come down.

For example, how about the "comfort wall" that seems to prevent many couples and singles from going on a mission? How about the "financial wall" of debt that interferes with some members' ability to go, or the "grandchildren wall," or the "health wall," or the "lack of self-confidence wall," or the "self-satisfied wall," or the "transgression wall," or the walls of fear, doubt, or complacency? Does anyone really doubt for a minute that with the help of the Lord he or she could bring those walls crashing down?

We have been privileged to be born in these last days, as opposed to some earlier dispensation, to help take the gospel to all the earth. There is no greater calling in this life. If we are content to hide behind self-made walls, we willingly forgo the blessings that are otherwise ours. The Lord in modern-day revelation explains the great need:

"For behold the field is white already to harvest; and lo, he that thrusteth in his sickle with his might, the same layeth up in store that he perisheth not, but bringeth salvation to his soul." (D&C 4:4.)

The Lord goes on to explain in that same revelation the qualifications that we need to be good missionaries. Knowing full well of our weaknesses and of our reservations as we stand before the huge gate of our self-made wall, he reassures us that divine help to overcome all obstacles will be forthcoming if we will only do our part, with the simple promise: "Ask, and ye shall receive; knock, and it shall be opened unto you." (D&C 4:7.)

129

May the Lord bless us that the walls of our minds may not obstruct us from the blessings that can be ours.[12]

Again and again during his mortal ministry, our Lord issued a call that was both an invitation and a challenge. To Peter and Andrew, Christ said, "Follow me, and I will make you fishers of men" (Matt. 4:19). . . .

Earlier prophets have taught that every able, worthy young man should serve a full-time mission. I emphasize this need today. We also have great need for our able, mature couples to serve in the mission field. Jesus told his disciples, "The harvest truly is great, but the labourers are few: pray ye therefore the Lord of the harvest, that he would send forth labourers into his harvest" (Luke 10:2).[13]

Suggestions for Study and Teaching

Questions

- Ponder President Hunter's teachings about the gospel being for all people, based on the truth that we are all children of God (see section 1). As we share the gospel, how can it help us to keep in mind that each person is literally our brother or sister?

- What do we learn from President Hunter's teachings in section 2 about how Heavenly Father feels about His children? What can you do to better love all people and share the gospel with them?

- How would you answer President Hunter's question "What does the Atonement have to do with missionary work?" (See section 3.) How can you increase your desire to share the gospel with others? What blessings have come as you have shared the gospel with someone—or as someone has shared it with you?

- After studying section 4, consider the "walls" that stop you from receiving the blessings of missionary work. Discuss ways to overcome those obstacles.

Related Scriptures

Amos 9:9; 2 Nephi 2:6–8; Mosiah 28:1–3; Alma 26:37; D&C 18:10–16; 58:64; 68:8; 88:81; 90:11; 123:12; Joseph Smith—Matthew 1:31

Teaching Help

"The Holy Ghost may prompt one or more of those you teach to contribute insights that others need to hear. Be open to promptings you receive to call on specific people. You may even feel impressed to ask a person who has not volunteered to express his or her views" (*Teaching, No Greater Call* [1999], 63).

Notes

1. "All Are Alike unto God," *Ensign,* June 1979, 74.

2. "Walls of the Mind," *Ensign,* Sept. 1990, 9–10.

3. See "Walls of the Mind," 10.

4. "All Are Alike unto God," 74.

5. "All Are Alike unto God," 74.

6. "The Gospel—A Global Faith," *Ensign,* Nov. 1991, 18–19.

7. "All Are Alike unto God," 72–74.

8. "The Gospel—A Global Faith," 19; the statement by George Albert Smith is found in *Teachings of Presidents of the Church: George Albert Smith* (2011), 152.

9. "Follow the Son of God," *Ensign,* Nov. 1994, 88.

10. "Come to the God of All Truth," *Ensign,* Sept. 1994, 73.

11. "The Atonement of Jesus Christ" (address given at the mission presidents' seminar, June 24, 1988), 4–7, Church History Library, Salt Lake City; see also *The Teachings of Howard W. Hunter,* ed. Clyde J. Williams (1997), 248–49.

12. "Walls of the Mind," 10.

13. "Follow the Son of God," 88.

"The payment of tithing strengthens faith, increases spirituality and spiritual capacity, and solidifies testimony."

The Law of Tithing

"A testimony of the law of tithing comes from living it."

Tithing is a way to help build Zion!

From the Life of Howard W. Hunter

Shortly before Howard W. Hunter and Claire Jeffs were to be married, Howard went to his bishop to obtain a temple recommend. He was surprised that during the interview, the bishop questioned whether he could support a wife and family on his income. Howard recalled, "When I told him how much I was making, he said the reason for his doubt as to my ability to support a wife was based on the amount of tithing I had paid."

Until that time, Howard had not been a full-tithe payer because he had not understood the importance of paying a full tithe. He explained, "Because my father had not been a member of the Church during my years at home, tithing had never been discussed in our family and I had never considered its importance."

Howard said that as he and the bishop continued to talk, the bishop "in his kindly way . . . taught me the importance of the law and when I told him I would henceforth be a full tithe payer, he continued the interview and relieved my anxiety by filling out and signing a recommendation form."

When Howard told Claire about this experience, he learned that she had always paid a full tithe. "We resolved that we would live this law throughout our marriage and tithing would come first," he said.[1]

Teachings of Howard W. Hunter

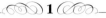

The Lord's definition of the law of tithing is simple.

The law [of tithing] is simply stated as "one-tenth of all their interest" (D&C 119:4). Interest means profit, compensation, increase. It is the wage of one employed, the profit from the operation of a business, the increase of one who grows or produces, or the income to a person from any other source. The Lord said it is a standing law "forever" as it has been in the past.[2]

Like all of the Lord's commandments and laws, [the law of tithing] is simple if we have a little faith. The Lord said in effect, "Take out the decimal point and move it over one place." That is the law of tithing. It's just that simple.[3]

The law of tithing existed from the beginning and continues today.

The first distinct mention of the word "tithe" in the Bible is in the very first book of the Old Testament. Abram . . . was met by Melchizedek, king of Salem and priest of the Most High God. Melchizedek blessed him, and Abram "gave him tithes of all." (Gen. 14:20.)

A few chapters later in the same book, Jacob, at Bethel made a vow in these words: . . . "Of all that thou shalt give me I will surely give the tenth unto thee." [Gen. 28:20–22.]

The third mention is in connection with the Levitical law. The Lord spoke through Moses:

"And all the tithe of the land, whether of the seed of the land, or of the fruit of the tree, is the Lord's: it is holy unto the Lord." (Lev. 27:30.)

Under the Levitical law the tithes were given to the Levites for their maintenance, and they in turn were charged with the paying of tithes on that which they received as shown by the words of the Lord as he instructed Moses:

"Thus speak unto the Levites, and say unto them, When ye take of the children of Israel the tithes which I have given you from them for your inheritance, then ye shall offer up an heave offering of it for the Lord, even a tenth part of the tithe." (Num. 18:26.)

This clearly indicates that the law of tithing was a part of the Levitical law and paid by all people—even the Levites themselves who were directed to pay tithing on the tithes which were received by them.

There are some who take the position that the law of the tithe was only a Levitical institution, but history confirms the fact that it has been and is a universal law. It was basic in the Mosaic law. It had existed from the beginning and is found in the ancient Egyptian law, in Babylonia, and can be traced throughout biblical history. It was mentioned by the Prophet Amos [see Amos 4:4] and by Nehemiah who was charged with the rebuilding of the walls of Jerusalem [see Nehemiah 10:37–38; 12:44; 13:5, 12]. Shortly thereafter Malachi began an even greater task of rebuilding the faith and the morale of a nation. In his supreme effort to strike out against the covetousness of those who were religious only in name, he lashed them with the accusation of a crime against God.

"Will a man rob God? Yet ye have robbed me. But ye say, Wherein have we robbed thee? In tithes and offerings.

"Ye are cursed with a curse: for ye have robbed me, even this whole nation.

"Bring ye all the tithes into the storehouse, that there may be meat in mine house, and prove me now herewith, saith the Lord of hosts, if I will not open you the windows of heaven and pour you out a blessing, that there shall not be room enough to receive it." (Mal. 3:8–10.) . . .

The words of Malachi close the Old Testament with a reiteration of the law of tithing, indicating there had been no abrogation of this law which had existed from the beginning. The New Testament dispensation, therefore, commenced under this admonition. . . .

Not long after the gospel was restored in this dispensation, the Lord gave a revelation to his people through a latter-day prophet defining the law . . . :

"And after that, those who have thus been tithed shall pay one tenth of all their interest annually; and this shall be a standing law unto them forever, for my holy priesthood, saith the Lord." (D&C 119:4.)[4]

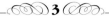

3

We make a gift and also pay an obligation with our tithes.

The tithe is God's law for his children, yet the payment is entirely voluntary. In this respect it does not differ from the law of the Sabbath or from any other of his laws. We may refuse to obey any or all of them. Our obedience is voluntary, but our refusal to pay does not abrogate or repeal the law.

If tithing is a voluntary matter, is it a gift or a payment of an obligation? There is a substantial difference between the two. A gift is a voluntary transfer of money or property without consideration. It is gratuitous. No one owes the obligation to make a gift. If tithing is a gift, we could give whatever we please, when we please, or make no gift at all. It would place our Heavenly Father in the very same category as the street beggar to whom we might toss a coin in passing.

The Lord has established the law of tithing, and because it is his law, it becomes our obligation to observe it if we love him and have a desire to keep his commandments and receive his blessings. In this way it becomes a debt. The man who doesn't pay his tithing because he is in debt should ask himself if he is not also in debt to the Lord. The Master said: "But seek ye first the kingdom of God, and his righteousness; and all these things shall be added unto you." (Matt. 6:33.)

We can't walk east and west at the same time. We can't serve both God and mammon. The man who rejects the law of the tithe is the man who has not given it a fair try. Of course it costs something. It takes work and thought and effort to live any of the laws of the gospel or any of its principles. . . .

It may be that we make a gift and also pay an obligation with our tithes. The payment of the obligation is to the Lord. The gift is to our fellow men for the upbuilding of God's kingdom. If one

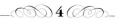
"It is not a burden to pay tithing, but a great privilege."

thoughtfully observes the proselyting done by the missionaries, the teaching program of the Church, the great educational system, and the building program to erect houses of worship, there will come a realization that it is not a burden to pay tithing, but a great privilege. The blessings of the gospel are shared with many through our tithes.[5]

4

An offering to the Lord should cost the giver something of value.

In 2 Samuel 24:18–25 we read that David would not make an offering unto the Lord of that which cost him nothing. He no doubt reasoned that unless the gift cost the giver something of value, it was not fit or appropriate to be an offering for the Lord.

Christ said it is more blessed to give than to receive [see Acts 20:35], yet there are some who will give only if it costs them nothing. This is not according to the teachings of the Master who said:

137

"If any man will come after me, let him deny himself" (Matthew 16:24).

There are some who will not live the law of tithing because of the cost. This is in contrast to the reasoning of David who would not make an offering unto the Lord unless it cost him something. The great moral principles encompassed in the law of tithing are overlooked by those who are not tithe payers, and they lack the understanding of the law and the reasons for it.[6]

5

Paying tithing brings great blessings.

The Lord gave the law [of tithing]. If we follow his law, we prosper, but when we find what we think is a better way, we meet failure. As I travel about the Church and see the results of the payment of tithes, I come to the conclusion that it is not a burden, but a great blessing.[7]

Pay an honest tithing. This eternal law, revealed by the Lord and practiced by the faithful from the ancient prophets down to the present, teaches us to put the Lord first in our lives. We may not be asked to sacrifice our homes or our lives, as was the case with the early Saints. We are challenged today to overcome our selfishness. We pay tithing because we love the Lord, not because we have the means to do so. We can expect that the Lord will open "the windows of heaven" (Malachi 3:10) and shower down blessings upon the faithful.[8]

We follow the principle of returning to the Lord a portion of his goodness to us, and this portion we refer to as tithing. Tithing . . . is entirely voluntary. We can pay tithing or not pay tithing. Those who do, receive blessings that are not known to others.[9]

Mary Fielding Smith [was an] indomitable pioneer mother who was the wife and widow of the Patriarch Hyrum Smith, brother of the Prophet. . . . One spring as the family opened their potato pits, she had her sons get a load of the best potatoes to take to the tithing office.

She was met at the steps of the office by one of the clerks, who [protested] as the boys began to unload the potatoes. "Widow Smith," he said, remembering no doubt her trials and sacrifices, "it's a shame that you should have to pay tithing." He . . . chided her for paying her tithing, and called her anything but wise and prudent. . . .

The little widow drew herself up to her full height and said, "William, you ought to be ashamed of yourself. Would you deny me a blessing? If I did not pay my tithing I should expect the Lord to withhold His blessings from me; I pay my tithing, not only because it is a law of God but because I expect a blessing by doing it. By keeping this and other laws, I expect to prosper and to be able to provide for my family." (Joseph Fielding Smith, *Life of Joseph F. Smith* [Salt Lake City, 1938], 158–59.)[10]

The principle of tithing should be more than a mathematical, mechanical compliance with the law. The Lord condemned the Pharisees for mechanically tithing herbs without coming into the circumference of spirituality [see Matthew 23:23]. If we pay our tithes because of our love for the Lord, in complete freedom and faith, we narrow our distance from him and our relationship to him becomes intimate. We are released from the bondage of legalism, and we are touched by the spirit and feel a oneness with God.

The payment of tithing strengthens faith, increases spirituality and spiritual capacity, and solidifies testimony. It gives the satisfaction of knowing one is complying with the will of the Lord. It brings the blessings that come from sharing with others through the purposes for which tithing is used. We cannot afford to deny ourselves these blessings. We cannot afford not to pay our tithing. We have a definite relationship to the future as well as to the present. What we give, and how we give, and the way we meet our obligations to the Lord has eternal significance.[1]

A testimony of the law of tithing comes from living it.[11]

Suggestions for Study and Teaching

Questions

• Review the definition of the law of tithing in section 1. What is tithing? What can we learn from President Hunter about the simplicity of the law of tithing?

• What insights have you gained from President Hunter's teachings about the history of tithing? (See section 2.) Why do you think President Hunter wanted us to understand that the law of tithing "has been and is a universal law"?

• How do we both "make a gift and also pay an obligation" with our tithing? (See section 3.) How does paying tithing show our love for the Lord? How can we come to feel that paying tithing is a privilege, not a burden?

• Why must an offering to the Lord cost the giver something of value? (See section 4.) How can any challenge or reluctance to pay tithing be overcome?

• Review the many blessings that President Hunter says come from paying tithing (see section 5). How have you seen these blessings in your life?

Related Scriptures

Alma 13:15; D&C 64:23; 104:14–18; 119; 120; Bible Dictionary, "Tithe"

Study Help

When first reading a chapter, you might want to read it quickly or review the headings to get an overview of the content. Then read the chapter additional times, going more slowly and studying it in depth. You might also want to read each section with the study questions in mind. As you do this, you may uncover profound insights and applications.

Notes

1. In Eleanor Knowles, *Howard W. Hunter* (1994), 80–81.

2. *The Teachings of Howard W. Hunter,* ed. Clyde J. Williams (1997), 105; see also Conference Report, Apr. 1964, 35.

3. *The Teachings of Howard W. Hunter,* 105.

4. In Conference Report, Apr. 1964, 33–35.

5. In Conference Report, Apr. 1964, 35–36.

6. *The Teachings of Howard W. Hunter,* 106; see also Conference Report, Apr. 1964, 33.

7. *The Teachings of Howard W. Hunter,* 105.

8. *The Teachings of Howard W. Hunter,* 105.

9. "Dedication of Goteborg Chapel" (address given in Goteborg, Sweden, on Sept. 10, 1967), 1, Church History Library, Salt Lake City.

10. Howard W. Hunter, *That We Might Have Joy* (1994), 136–37.

11. In Conference Report, Apr. 1964, 36.

*"We hope you are reading and studying the scriptures
on a daily basis as individuals and as families."*

The Scriptures—The Most Profitable of All Study

*"May each of us . . . draw closer to our Father
in Heaven and his Beloved Son through
consistent study of the holy scriptures."*

From the Life of Howard W. Hunter

President Howard W. Hunter had a great love for the scriptures and was a dedicated student of them. This love and study were reflected in his teachings, which were filled with stories and other passages from the standard works. Often when teaching a gospel principle, especially in general conference, he selected at least one story from the scriptures, told it in detail, and drew applications from it.

For example, when teaching about being committed to God, he recounted the stories of Joshua; of Shadrach, Meshach, and Abednego; and of others in the Old Testament who showed such commitment (see chapter 19). When teaching about service, he used examples from the Book of Mormon to show how some people who received little acclaim were "no less serviceable" than others whose service was more visible (see chapter 23). When teaching about how to have inner peace in times of turmoil, he again used extended passages from the scriptures, including the story of Peter walking on the water (see chapter 2). When teaching about the sacrament, he provided context by reviewing the story of the children of Israel and the Passover (see chapter 15).

President Hunter knew the importance of the scriptures in helping a person gain a testimony of Jesus Christ. Accordingly, he often taught from the scriptural accounts of the Savior's ministry, crucifixion, and resurrection. He declared:

"I am grateful for the library of scripture through which a greater knowledge of Jesus Christ can be learned by devoted study. I am grateful that in addition to the Old and New Testaments, the Lord, through prophets of The Church of Jesus Christ of Latter-day Saints, has added other revealed scripture as additional witnesses for Christ—the Book of Mormon, the Doctrine and Covenants, and the Pearl of Great Price—all of which I know to be the word of God. These bear witness that Jesus is the Christ, the Son of the living God."[1]

Teachings of Howard W. Hunter

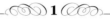

Studying the scriptures is the most profitable of all study in which we can engage.

Central to all truth is the testimony that Jesus of Nazareth is the Christ, the Great Jehovah, the Savior of the World, and the Only Begotten Son of the Living God. This is the message of the scriptures. Throughout each of these holy books there is an appeal to believe and have faith in God the Eternal Father and in his Son, Jesus Christ; and from the first to the last of these books of scripture is the call to do the will of God and keep his commandments.[2]

When we follow the counsel of our leaders to read and study the scriptures, benefits and blessings of many kinds come to us. This is the most profitable of all study in which we could engage. . . .

Scriptures contain the record of the self-revelation of God, and through them God speaks to man. Where could there be more profitable use of time than reading from the scriptural library the literature that teaches us to know God and understand our relationship to him? Time is always precious to busy people, and we are robbed of its worth when hours are wasted in reading or viewing that which is frivolous and of little value.[3]

We hope you are reading and studying the scriptures on a daily basis as individuals and as families. We should not take lightly the command of the Lord, "Search the scriptures; for in them ye think ye have eternal life: and they are they which testify of me" (John

5:39). The Spirit will come into your homes and your lives as you read the revealed word.[4]

We ought to have a Church full of women and men who know the scriptures thoroughly, who cross-reference and mark them, who develop lessons and talks from the Topical Guide, and who have mastered the maps, the Bible Dictionary, and the other helps that are contained in this wonderful set of standard works. There is obviously more there than we can master quickly. Certainly the scriptural field is "white already to harvest" [see D&C 4:4]. . . .

Not in this dispensation, surely not in any dispensation, have the scriptures—the enduring, enlightening word of God—been so readily available and so helpfully structured for the use of every man, woman, and child who will search them. The written word of God is in the most readable and accessible form ever provided to lay members in the history of the world. Surely we will be held accountable if we do not read them.[5]

Studying the scriptures helps us learn and obey God's will.

In order to be obedient to the law of the gospel and be obedient to the teachings of Jesus Christ, we must first understand the law and ascertain the will of the Lord. This is accomplished best by searching and studying the scriptures and the words of the proph- ets. In this way we become familiar with what God has revealed to man.

Among [the] Articles of Faith is one that declares, "We believe all that God has revealed, all that He does now reveal, and we believe that He will yet reveal many great and important things pertaining to the Kingdom of God" (Articles of Faith 1:9).

God's will has been revealed in the scriptures, and for this rea- son we have been commanded to read them to find the truth. The Lord explained to Oliver Cowdery how to ascertain these truths. He said, "Behold, I give unto you a commandment, that you rely upon the things which are written; for in them are all things written concerning the foundation of my church, my gospel, and my rock" (D&C 18:3–4).

Paul wrote to his good friend Timothy, urging him to read the scriptures, and in his letter said, "From a child thou hast known the holy scriptures, which are able to make thee wise unto salvation through faith which is in Christ Jesus." Then he added, "All scripture is given by inspiration of God, and is profitable for doctrine, for reproof, for correction, for instruction in righteousness" (2 Timothy 3:15–16). . . .

Our Church leaders have laid great stress on the matter of reading the scriptures and the words of the prophets, ancient and modern. Fathers and mothers have been asked to read the scriptures so that they may properly teach their children. Our children are reading the scriptures as the result of the example being set by parents. We are studying the scriptures at our family home evenings, and some families are reading scriptures together at an early morning hour. . . . This is the way we learn to know the will of the Lord, that we might be obedient.[6]

Consider the scriptural sequence that begins with giving diligence to the word of God and then proceeds to the promise that if we do, we may go into his very presence:

"And I now give unto you a commandment . . . to give diligent heed to the words of eternal life.

"For you shall live by every word that proceedeth forth from the mouth of God.

"For the word of the Lord is truth, and whatsoever is truth is light, and whatsoever is light is Spirit, even the Spirit of Jesus Christ. . . .

"And every one that hearkeneth to the voice of the Spirit cometh unto God, even the Father" (D&C 84:43–45, 47).

That is a wonderful journey initiated by the word of God and which will culminate in exaltation. "The words of Christ will tell you all things what ye should do" (2 Nephi 32:3).[7]

I commend to you the revelations of God as the standard by which we must live our lives and by which we must measure every decision and every deed. Accordingly, when you have worries and challenges, face them by turning to the scriptures and the prophets.[8]

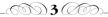

To understand the scriptures requires concentrated, consistent, prayerful study.

We urge each of you to carefully consider how much time you are currently giving to prayerful pondering of the scriptures.

As one of the Lord's servants, I challenge you to do the following:

1. Read, ponder, and pray over the scriptures daily as individual members of the Church.

2. Hold family scripture reading on a regular basis. We commend those of you who are already doing this and urge those of you who have not yet started to begin doing so without delay. . . .

May each of us go forth with a firm resolve to be more prayerful; to seek to live more fully by the Spirit; and to draw closer to our Father in Heaven and his Beloved Son through consistent study of the holy scriptures.[9]

Reading habits vary widely. There are rapid readers and slow readers, some who read only small snatches at a time and others who persist without stopping until the book is finished. Those who delve into the scriptural library, however, find that to understand requires more than casual reading or perusal—there must be concentrated study. It is certain that one who studies the scriptures every day accomplishes far more than one who devotes considerable time one day and then lets days go by before continuing. Not only should we study each day, but there should be a regular time set aside when we can concentrate without interference.

There is nothing more helpful than prayer to open our understanding of the scriptures. Through prayer we can attune our minds to seek the answers to our searchings. The Lord said: "Ask, and it shall be given you; seek, and ye shall find; knock, and it shall be opened unto you" (Luke 11:9). Herein is Christ's reassurance that if we will ask, seek, and knock, the Holy Spirit will guide our understanding if we are ready and eager to receive.

Many find that the best time to study is in the morning after a night's rest has cleared the mind of the many cares that interrupt

Scripture study "is the most profitable of all study in which we could engage."

thought. Others prefer to study in the quiet hours after the work and worries of the day are over and brushed aside, thus ending the day with a peace and tranquillity that comes by communion with the scriptures.

Perhaps what is more important than the hour of the day is that a regular time be set aside for study. It would be ideal if an hour could be spent each day; but if that much cannot be had, a half hour on a regular basis would result in substantial accomplishment. A quarter of an hour is little time, but it is surprising how much enlightenment and knowledge can be acquired in a subject so meaningful. The important thing is to allow nothing else to ever interfere with our study.

Some prefer to study alone, but companions can study together profitably. Families are greatly blessed when wise fathers and mothers bring their children about them, read from the pages of the scriptural library together, and then discuss freely the beautiful stories and thoughts according to the understanding of all. Often youth and little ones have amazing insight into and appreciation for the basic literature of religion.

We should not be haphazard in our reading but rather develop a systematic plan for study. There are some who read to a schedule of a number of pages or a set number of chapters each day or week. This may be perfectly justifiable and may be enjoyable if one is reading for pleasure, but it does not constitute meaningful study. It is better to have a set amount of time to give scriptural study each day than to have a set amount of chapters to read. Sometimes we find that the study of a single verse will occupy the whole time.[10]

4

Contemplating the brief scriptural account of Jairus brings a great depth of understanding and meaning.

The life, acts, and teachings of Jesus can be read rapidly. The stories are simple in most instances and the stories are simply told. The Master used few words in his teachings, but each one is so concise in meaning that together they portray a clear image to the reader. Sometimes, however, many hours might be spent in contemplation of profound thoughts expressed in a few simple words.

There was an incident in the life of the Savior that was mentioned by Matthew, Mark, and Luke. A significant part of the story is told by Mark in only two short verses and five words of the following verse. . . .

"And, behold, there cometh one of the rulers of the synagogue, Jairus by name; and when he saw him [that is, when he saw Jesus], he fell at his feet,

"And besought him greatly, saying, My little daughter lieth at the point of death: I pray thee, come and lay thy hands on her, that she may be healed; and she shall live.

"And Jesus went with him" (Mark 5:22–24).

The reading time of that portion of the story is about thirty seconds. It is short and uncomplicated. The visual picture is clear and even a child could repeat it without difficulty. But as we spend time in thought and contemplation, a great depth of understanding and meaning comes to us. . . .

. . . Jesus and those who were with him had just recrossed the Sea of Galilee, and a multitude of people who had been waiting met him on the shore near Capernaum. "And, behold, there cometh one of the rulers of the synagogue." The larger synagogues of that day were presided over by a college of elders under the direction of a chief or a ruler. This was a man of rank and prestige whom the Jews looked upon with great respect.

Matthew doesn't give the name of this chief elder, but Mark identifies him by adding to his title the words, "Jairus by name." Nowhere else in the scriptures does this man or his name appear except on this occasion, yet his memory lives in history because of a brief contact with Jesus. Many, many lives have become memorable that otherwise would have been lost in obscurity had it not been for the touch of the Master's hand that made a significant change of thought and action and a new and better life.

"And when he saw him [that is, when Jairus saw Jesus], he fell at his feet."

This was an unusual circumstance for a man of rank and prestige, a ruler of the synagogue, to kneel at Jesus' feet—at the feet of one considered to be an itinerant teacher with the gift of healing. Many others of learning and prestige saw Jesus also but ignored him. Their minds were closed. Today is no different; obstacles stand in the way of many to accept him.

"And [Jairus] besought him greatly, saying, My little daughter lieth at the point of death." This is typical of what happens frequently when a man comes to Christ, not so much for his own need, but because of the desperate need of a loved one. The tremor we hear in Jairus's voice as he speaks of "My little daughter" stirs our souls with sympathy as we think of this man of high position in the synagogue on his knees before the Savior.

Then comes a great acknowledgement of faith: "I pray thee, come and lay thy hands on her, that she may be healed; and she shall live." These are not only the words of faith of a father torn with grief but are also a reminder to us that whatever Jesus lays his hands upon lives. If Jesus lays his hands upon a marriage, it lives. If he is allowed to lay his hands on the family, it lives.

The words, "and Jesus went with him" follow. We would not suppose that this event had been within the plans for the day. The Master had come back across the sea where the multitude was waiting on the shore for him to teach them. . . . He was interrupted by the plea of a father. He could have ignored the request because many others were waiting. He could have said to Jairus that he would come to see his daughter tomorrow, but "Jesus went with him." If we follow in the footsteps of the Master, would we ever be too busy to ignore the needs of our fellowmen?

It is not necessary to read the remainder of the story. When they got to the home of the ruler of the synagogue, Jesus took the little girl by the hand and raised her from the dead. In like manner, he will lift and raise every man to a new and better life who will permit the Savior to take him by the hand.[11]

5

The Book of Mormon and Doctrine and Covenants will bring us closer to Christ.

The Book of Mormon

One of the most significant resources the Lord has provided to assist us in accomplishing this divine work is the Book of Mormon, subtitled "Another Testament of Jesus Christ." [President Ezra Taft Benson] forthrightly admonished us not to neglect reading and abiding by the precepts of this sacred volume of scripture. "Its great mission," he taught us, "is to bring men to Christ [and thus to the Father], and all other things are secondary." (*Ensign,* May 1986, p. 105.) We hope you brothers and sisters are feeding your spirits by regularly reading the Book of Mormon and the other scriptures and using them in your ministries.[12]

The Book of Mormon is the word of God. We invite you to read this wonderful record. It is the most remarkable volume in existence today. Read it carefully and prayerfully, and as you do, God will give you a testimony of its truthfulness as promised by Moroni (see Moroni 10:4).[13]

It is through reading and studying the Book of Mormon, and prayerfully seeking confirmation of its contents, that we receive a testimony that Joseph Smith was a prophet of God and that the Church of Jesus Christ has been restored to the earth.[14]

Reading [the Book of Mormon] will have a profound effect on your life. It will expand your knowledge of the way God deals with man and will give you a greater desire to live in harmony with his gospel teachings. It will also provide for you a powerful testimony of Jesus.[15]

The Doctrine and Covenants

The Doctrine and Covenants is a unique book. It is the only book on the face of the entire earth with a preface composed by the Creator himself. Furthermore, this book of scripture contains more direct quotations from the Lord than any other existing book of scripture.

It is not a translation of an ancient document, but is of modern origin. It is a book of revelation for our day. It is a unique and divinely inspired selection of revelations that came through prophets of God in our day in answer to questions, concerns, and challenges they and others faced. It contains divine answers to real-life problems involving real people. . . .

Did you realize that by reading the Doctrine and Covenants you can hear the voice of the Lord through scripture? [see D&C 18:33–36]. . . . That voice of enlightenment will usually come into your mind as "thoughts" and into your heart as "feelings" (see D&C 8:1–3). The promise of that witness is . . . available to every worthy man, woman, and child who prayerfully seeks for such a witness. Should not each of us resolve to read, study, ponder, and pray over these sacred revelations?[16]

Suggestions for Study and Teaching

Questions
- What experiences have helped you learn that studying the scriptures "is the most profitable of all study"? (See section 1.) How can we strengthen our commitment to be "women and men who know the scriptures thoroughly"?

- How does studying the scriptures help us be more obedient? (See section 2.) How have you seen that "the words of Christ will tell you all things what ye should do"? (2 Nephi 32:3).

- What aspects of President Hunter's counsel about how to study the scriptures could help you? (See section 3.) How has consistent, prayerful study of the scriptures blessed you?

- What insights can we gain from President Hunter's account of the Savior healing the daughter of Jairus? (See section 4.) How can pondering just a few verses like this enrich your scripture study?

- How have the Book of Mormon and the Doctrine and Covenants helped you draw closer to the Savior? (See section 5.) What are some other ways these sacred volumes have influenced you? Consider sharing your testimony of these scriptures with family members and others.

Related Scriptures

Joshua 1:8; Proverbs 30:5; 1 Nephi 15:23–24; 2 Nephi 3:12; Alma 31:5; 37:44; Helaman 3:29–30; D&C 98:11

Study Help

"Reading, studying, and pondering are not the same. We read words and we may get ideas. We study and we may discover patterns and connections in scripture. But when we ponder, we invite revelation by the Spirit. Pondering, to me, is the thinking and the praying I do after reading and studying in the scriptures carefully" (Henry B. Eyring, "Serve with the Spirit," *Ensign* or *Liahona,* Nov. 2010, 60).

Notes

1. "Reading the Scriptures," *Ensign,* Nov. 1979, 65.
2. *The Teachings of Howard W. Hunter,* ed. Clyde J. Williams (1997), 50.
3. "Reading the Scriptures," 64.
4. *The Teachings of Howard W. Hunter,* 53–54.
5. *The Teachings of Howard W. Hunter,* 51.

6. "Obedience" (address given at the Hawaii Area Conference, June 18, 1978), 3–5, Church History Library, Salt Lake City; the last paragraph is also in *The Teachings of Howard W. Hunter,* 52.
7. "Eternal Investments" (address to CES religious educators, Feb. 10, 1989), 3; si.lds.org.

8. "Fear Not, Little Flock" (address given at Brigham Young University, Mar. 14, 1989), 2; speeches.byu.edu.

9. *The Teachings of Howard W. Hunter,* 51–52.

10. "Reading the Scriptures," 64.

11. "Reading the Scriptures," 64–65.

12. "The Mission of the Church" (address given at the regional representatives' seminar, Mar. 30, 1990), 2.

13. *The Teachings of Howard W. Hunter,* 54.

14. "The Pillars of Our Faith," *Ensign,* Sept. 1994, 54.

15. "Evidences of the Resurrection," *Ensign,* May 1983, 16.

16. *The Teachings of Howard W. Hunter,* 55–56.

True Greatness

"Giving consistent effort in the little things in day-to-day life leads to true greatness."

From the Life of Howard W. Hunter

President Howard W. Hunter taught that true greatness comes not from worldly success but from "thousands of little deeds . . . of service and sacrifice that constitute the giving, or losing, of one's life for others and for the Lord."[1] President Hunter lived his life according to this teaching. Rather than seeking the spotlight or the acclaim of others, he performed daily deeds of service and sacrifice that were often unnoticed.

One example of President Hunter's relatively unnoticed service was the care he gave to his wife as she struggled with declining health for more than a decade. In the early 1970s, Claire Hunter began experiencing headaches and memory loss. She later suffered several small strokes, which made it difficult for her to talk or use her hands. When she began to need constant care, President Hunter provided as much as he could while also fulfilling his responsibilities as an Apostle. He arranged for someone to stay with Claire during the day, but he cared for her at night.

A cerebral hemorrhage in 1981 left Claire unable to walk or speak. Nevertheless, President Hunter sometimes helped her out of her wheelchair and held her tightly so they could dance as they had done years earlier.

After Claire experienced a second cerebral hemorrhage, doctors insisted that she be placed in a care center, and she remained there for the last 18 months of her life. During that time, President Hunter went to see her each day except when traveling on Church assignments. When he returned home, he went directly from the airport

Howard and Claire Hunter

to be with her. Most of the time she was either in a deep sleep or did not recognize him, but he continued to tell her of his love and to make sure that she was comfortable.

Elder James E. Faust of the Quorum of the Twelve later said that President Hunter's "tender loving care of his wife Claire for more than ten years while she was not well was the most noble devotion of a man to a woman that many of us have seen in our lives."[2]

After President Hunter died, a biography in the *Ensign* quoted his teachings about true greatness and summarized how they had guided his life:

"Though deep-seated modesty would prevent him from ever making the comparison, President Hunter met his own definition of greatness. His greatness emerged in periods of his life far from the spotlight as he made pivotal choices to work hard, to try again after failing, and to help his fellowman. Those attributes were reflected in his remarkable ability to succeed in endeavors as diverse as music, law, business, international relations, carpentry, and, above all, being a 'good and faithful servant' of the Lord [Matthew 25:21]. . . .

"For the fourteenth President of the Church, fulfilling the Lord's purposes came as selflessly and naturally as had his labors as a schoolboy, a young father, a devoted bishop, and a tireless Apostle. The Lord's vineyard, as Howard W. Hunter saw it, requires constant upkeep, and all that his Master required of him was to be a 'good and faithful servant.' This President Hunter fulfilled with true greatness, with constant attention to the example of the Savior, whom he served until the end."[3]

Teachings of Howard W. Hunter

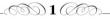 1

The world's definition of greatness is often misleading and can prompt damaging comparisons.

Many Latter-day Saints are happy and enjoying the opportunities life offers. Yet I am concerned that some among us are unhappy. Some of us feel that we are falling short of our expected ideals. I have particular concern for those who have lived righteously but think—because they haven't achieved in the world or in the Church what others have achieved—that they have failed. Each of us desires to achieve a measure of greatness in this life. And why shouldn't we? As someone once noted, there is within each of us a giant struggling with celestial homesickness. (See Heb. 11:13–16; D&C 45:11–14.)

Realizing who we are and what we may become assures us that with God nothing is really impossible. From the time we learn that Jesus wants us for a Sunbeam through the time we learn more fully the basic principles of the gospel, we are taught to strive for perfection. It is not new to us, then, to talk of the importance of achievement. The difficulty arises when inflated expectations of the world alter the definition of greatness.

What is true greatness? What is it that makes a person great?

We live in a world that seems to worship its own kind of greatness and to produce its own kind of heroes. A recent survey of young people ages eighteen through twenty-four revealed that today's youth prefer the "strong, go-it-alone, conquer-against-all-odds" individuals and that they clearly seek to pattern their lives after the glamorous and "boundlessly rich." During the 1950s, heroes included Winston Churchill, Albert Schweitzer, President Harry Truman, Queen Elizabeth, and Helen Keller—the blind and deaf writer-lecturer. These were figures who either helped shape history or were noted for their inspiring lives. Today, many of the top ten heroes are movie stars and other entertainers, which suggests something of a shift in our attitudes. (See *U.S. News & World Report,* 22 Apr. 1985, pp. 44–48.)

It's true that the world's heroes don't last very long in the public mind; but, nevertheless, there is never a lack of champions and great achievers. We hear almost daily of athletes breaking records; scientists inventing marvelous new devices, machines, and processes; and doctors saving lives in new ways. We are constantly being exposed to exceptionally gifted musicians and entertainers and to unusually talented artists, architects, and builders. Magazines, billboards, and television commercials bombard us with pictures of individuals with perfect teeth and flawless features, wearing stylish clothes and doing whatever it is that "successful" people do.

*"True greatness [comes from] the thousands of little deeds
and tasks of service and sacrifice that constitute the giving,
or losing, of one's life for others and for the Lord."*

Because we are being constantly exposed to the world's definition of *greatness,* it is understandable that we make comparisons between what we are and what others are—or seem to be—and also between what we have and what others have. Although it is true that making comparisons can be beneficial and may motivate us to accomplish much good and to improve our lives, we often allow unfair and improper comparisons to destroy our happiness when they cause us to feel unfulfilled or inadequate or unsuccessful. Sometimes, because of these feelings, we are led into error and dwell on our failures while ignoring aspects of our lives that may contain elements of true greatness.[4]

 **2**

Giving consistent effort in the little things in day-to-day life leads to true greatness.

In 1905, President Joseph F. Smith made this most profound statement about true greatness:

"Those things which we call extraordinary, remarkable, or unusual may make history, but they do not make real life.

"After all, to do well those things which God ordained to be the common lot of all mankind, is the truest greatness. To be a successful father or a successful mother is greater than to be a successful general or a successful statesman." (*Juvenile Instructor,* 15 Dec. 1905, p. 752.)

This statement raises a query: What are the things God has ordained to be "the common lot of all mankind"? Surely they include the things that must be done in order to be a good father or a good mother, a good son or a good daughter, a good student or a good roommate or a good neighbor.

. . . Giving consistent effort in the little things in day-to-day life leads to true greatness. Specifically, it is the thousands of little deeds and tasks of service and sacrifice that constitute the giving, or losing, of one's life for others and for the Lord. They include gaining a knowledge of our Father in Heaven and the gospel. They also include bringing others into the faith and fellowship of his kingdom. These things do not usually receive the attention or the adulation of the world.[5]

 **3**

The Prophet Joseph was concerned with the daily tasks of service and caring for others.

Joseph Smith is not generally remembered as a general, mayor, architect, editor, or presidential candidate. We remember him as the prophet of the Restoration, a man committed to the love of God and the furthering of His work. The Prophet Joseph was an everyday Christian. He was concerned about the small things, the daily tasks of service and caring for others. As a thirteen-year-old boy, Lyman O. Littlefield accompanied the camp of Zion, which went up to Missouri. He later narrated this incident of a small yet personally significant act of service in the life of the Prophet:

"The journey was extremely toilsome for all, and the physical suffering, coupled with the knowledge of the persecutions endured by our brethren whom we were traveling to succor, caused me to lapse one day into a state of melancholy. As the camp was making ready

"The Prophet Joseph was an everyday Christian. He was concerned about the small things, the daily tasks of service and caring for others."

to depart I sat tired and brooding by the roadside. The Prophet was the busiest man of the camp; and yet when he saw me, he turned from the great press of other duties to say a word of comfort to a child. Placing his hand upon my head, he said, 'Is there no place for you, my boy? If not, we must make one.' This circumstance made an impression upon my mind which long lapse of time and cares of riper years have not effaced." (In George Q. Cannon, *Life of Joseph Smith the Prophet,* Salt Lake City: Deseret Book Co., 1986, p. 344.)

On another occasion, when Governor Carlin of Illinois sent Sheriff Thomas King of Adams County and several others as a posse to apprehend the Prophet and deliver him to the emissaries of Governor

Boggs of Missouri, Sheriff King became deathly ill. At Nauvoo the Prophet took the sheriff to his home and nursed him like a brother for four days. (Ibid., p. 372.) Small, kind, and yet significant acts of service were not occasional for the Prophet.

Writing about the opening of the [Prophet Joseph Smith's] store in Nauvoo, Elder George Q. Cannon recorded:

"The Prophet himself did not hesitate to engage in mercantile and industrial pursuits; the gospel which he preached was one of temporal salvation as well as spiritual exaltation; and he was willing to perform his share of the practical labor. This he did with no thought of personal gain." (Ibid., p. 385.)

And in a letter, the Prophet wrote:

"The [Red Brick Store in Nauvoo] has been filled to overflowing and I have stood behind the counter all day, distributing goods as steadily as any clerk you ever saw, to oblige those who were compelled to go without their Christmas and New Year's dinners for the want of a little sugar, molasses, raisins, etc.; and to please myself also, for I love to wait upon the Saints and to be a servant to all, hoping that I may be exalted in the due time of the Lord." (Ibid., p. 386.)

About this scene, George Q. Cannon commented:

"What a picture is presented here! A man chosen by the Lord to lay the foundation of His Church and to be its Prophet and President, takes joy and pride in waiting upon his brethren and sisters like a servant. . . . Joseph never saw the day when he did not feel that he was serving God and obtaining favor in the sight of Jesus Christ by showing kindness and attention 'even unto the least of these.'" (Ibid., p. 386.)[6]

True greatness comes from persevering in the difficulties of life and from serving in ways that are often unnoticed.

To be a successful elders quorum secretary or Relief Society teacher or loving neighbor or listening friend is much of what true greatness is all about. To do one's best in the face of the commonplace struggles of life—and possibly in the face of failure—and to continue to endure and to persevere in the ongoing difficulties of life when those struggles and tasks contribute to others' progress and happiness and one's own eternal salvation—this is true greatness.

We all want to achieve a measure of greatness in this life. Many have already achieved great things; others are striving to achieve greatness. Let me encourage you to achieve and, at the same time, to remember who you are. Don't let the illusion of fleeting worldly greatness overcome you. Many people are losing their souls to such temptations. Your good name is not worth selling—for any price. True greatness is to remain true—"True to the faith that our parents have cherished, True to the truth for which martyrs have perished." (*Hymns,* 1985, no. 254.)

I am confident that there are many great, unnoticed, and forgotten heroes among us. I am speaking of those of you who quietly and consistently do the things you ought to do. I am talking about those who are always there and always willing. I am referring to the uncommon valor of the mother who, hour after hour, day and night, stays with and cares for a sick child while her husband is at work or in school. I am including those who volunteer to give blood or to work with the elderly. I am thinking about those of you who faithfully fulfill your priesthood and church responsibilities and of the students who write home regularly to thank their parents for their love and support.

I am also talking about those who instill in others faith and a desire to live the gospel—those who actively work to build and mold the lives of others physically, socially, and spiritually. I am referring to those who are honest and kind and hardworking in their daily tasks, but who are also servants of the Master and shepherds of his sheep.

Now, I do not mean to discount the great accomplishments of the world that have given us so many opportunities and that provide culture and order and excitement in our lives. I am merely suggesting that we try to focus more clearly on the things in life that will be of greatest worth. You will remember that it was the Savior who said, "He that is greatest among you shall be your servant." (Matt. 23:11.)[7]

5

True greatness requires consistent, small, and sometimes ordinary steps over a long period of time.

Each of us has seen individuals become wealthy or successful almost instantaneously—almost overnight. But I believe that even though this kind of success may come to some without prolonged struggle, there is no such thing as instant greatness. The achievement of true greatness is a long-term process. It may involve occasional setbacks. The end result may not always be clearly visible, but it seems that it always requires regular, consistent, small, and sometimes ordinary and mundane steps over a long period of time. We should remember that it was the Lord who said, "Out of small things proceedeth that which is great." (D&C 64:33.)

True greatness is never a result of a chance occurrence or a one-time effort or achievement. Greatness requires the development of character. It requires a multitude of correct decisions in the everyday choices between good and evil that Elder Boyd K. Packer spoke about when he said, "Over the years these little choices will be bundled together and show clearly what we value." (*Ensign,* Nov. 1980, p. 21.) Those choices will also show clearly what we are.[8]

6

Commonplace tasks often have the greatest positive effect on others.

As we evaluate our lives, it is important that we look, not only at our accomplishments but also at the conditions under which we have labored. We are each different and unique; we have each had different starting points in the race of life; we each have a unique mixture of talents and skills; we each have our own set of challenges and constraints with which to contend. Therefore, our judgment of ourselves and our achievements should not merely include the size or magnitude and number of our accomplishments; it should also include the conditions that have existed and the effect that our efforts have had on others.

It is this last aspect of our self-evaluation—the effect of our lives on the lives of others—that will help us understand why some of the common, ordinary work of life should be valued so highly. Frequently it is the commonplace tasks we perform that have the greatest positive effect on the lives of others, as compared with the things that the world so often relates to greatness.[9]

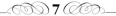

Doing the things that God has ordained to be important will lead to true greatness.

It appears to me that the kind of greatness that our Father in Heaven would have us pursue is within the grasp of all who are within the gospel net. We have an unlimited number of opportunities to do the many simple and minor things that will ultimately make us great. To those who have devoted their lives to service and sacrifice for their families, for others, and for the Lord, the best counsel is simply to do more of the same.

To those who are furthering the work of the Lord in so many quiet but significant ways, to those who are the salt of the earth and the strength of the world and the backbone of each nation—to you we would simply express our admiration. If you endure to the end, and if you are valiant in the testimony of Jesus, you will achieve true greatness and will one day live in the presence of our Father in Heaven.

As President Joseph F. Smith has said, "Let us not be trying to substitute an artificial life for the true one." (*Juvenile Instructor,* 15 Dec. 1905, p. 753.) Let us remember that doing the things that have been ordained by God to be important and needful and necessary, even though the world may view them as unimportant and insignificant, will eventually lead to true greatness.

We should strive to remember the words of the Apostle Paul, especially if we are unhappy with our lives and feeling that we have not achieved some form of greatness. He wrote:

"For our light affliction, which is but for a moment, worketh for us a far more exceeding and eternal weight of glory;

"While we look not at the things which are seen, but at the things which are not seen: for the things which are seen are temporal; but the things which are not seen are eternal." (2 Cor. 4:17–18.)

The small things are significant. We remember not the amount offered by the Pharisee but the widow's mite, not the power and strength of the Philistine army but the courage and conviction of David.

May we never be discouraged in doing those daily tasks which God has ordained to be "the common lot of man." [10]

Suggestions for Study and Teaching

Questions

- Why are we sometimes confused about what true greatness is? (See section 1.) Why does the world's definition of greatness lead some people to feel unfulfilled and unhappy?

- How does President Hunter's definition of true greatness differ from the world's definition? (See section 2.) How can this definition of true greatness help you in your life? Contemplate some specific "little things" that would be good to give more time and attention to.

- What impresses you about Joseph Smith's small acts of service, as outlined in section 3? What are some small acts of service that have blessed you?

- Review the examples in section 4 of what constitutes true greatness. How have you seen people manifest true greatness in these ways?

- What can we learn from the teachings in section 5 about how to achieve true greatness?

- What are some examples you have seen of "commonplace tasks we perform [having] the greatest positive effect on the lives of others"? (See section 6.)

- Ponder President Hunter's teachings in section 7. How do service and sacrifice lead to true greatness? How does being "valiant in the testimony of Jesus" help us achieve true greatness?

Related Scriptures

1 Samuel 16:7; 1 Timothy 4:12; Mosiah 2:17; Alma 17:24–25; 37:6; Moroni 10:32; D&C 12:8; 59:23; 76:5–6; 88:125

Teaching Help

"As you prayerfully prepare to teach you may be led to emphasize certain principles. You may gain an understanding of how best to present certain ideas. You may discover examples, object lessons, and inspiring stories in the simple activities of life. You may feel impressed to invite a particular person to assist with the lesson. You may be reminded of a personal experience that you can share" (*Teaching, No Greater Call* [1999], 48).

Notes

1. "What Is True Greatness?" *Ensign,* Sept. 1987, 71.
2. James E. Faust, "Howard W. Hunter: Man of God," *Ensign,* Apr. 1995, 28.
3. "President Howard W. Hunter: The Lord's 'Good and Faithful Servant,'" *Ensign,* Apr. 1995, 9, 16.
4. "What Is True Greatness?" 70.
5. "What Is True Greatness?" 70–71.
6. "What Is True Greatness?" 71.
7. "What Is True Greatness?" 71–72.
8. "What Is True Greatness?" 72.
9. "What Is True Greatness?" 72.
10. "What Is True Greatness?" 72.

"Each of us should read and reread the parable of the lost sheep. . . . I hope the message of that parable will be impressed on the hearts of each of us."

Come Back and Feast at the Table of the Lord

"Reach out to the less active and realize the joy that will come to you and those you help."

From the Life of Howard W. Hunter

The day after Howard W. Hunter became President of the Church, he extended this loving invitation to Church members who were not actively participating:

"To those who have transgressed or been offended, we say, come back. To those who are hurt and struggling and afraid, we say, let us stand with you and dry your tears. To those who are confused and assailed by error on every side, we say, come to the God of all truth and the Church of continuing revelation. Come back. Stand with us. Carry on. Be believing. All is well, and all will be well. Feast at the table laid before you in The Church of Jesus Christ of Latter-day Saints and strive to follow the Good Shepherd who has provided it. Have hope, exert faith, receive—and give—charity, the pure love of Christ."[1]

In his first general conference address as President of the Church a few months later, President Hunter said he felt impressed to continue this emphasis. "Come back," he repeated. "Take literally [the Savior's] invitation to 'come, follow me.' . . . He is the only sure way; he is the light of the world."[2]

Throughout his life, President Hunter helped many Church members return to activity. Relating such an experience from early adulthood, he said:

"My ward bishop assigned me as a ward teacher to a brother who boasted he was the oldest deacon in the Church. Home teaching was ward teaching in those days. His problem was that he loved to play golf on Sunday. It was discouraging to meet month after month with him and his wife and see no apparent progress. But finally, the right word was said to him and it struck a responsive chord. The word was *covenant*. We asked him, 'What does the covenant of baptism mean to you?' His expression changed, and for the first time we saw a serious side to him. Eventually he came to our classes, gave up golf, and took his wife to the temple."[3]

Teachings of Howard W. Hunter

 **1**

The parable of the lost sheep teaches us to seek after those who are lost.

The First Presidency [extended] to the membership of the Church a significant invitation . . . :

"To those who have ceased activity and to those who have become critical, we say, 'Come back. Come back and feast at the table of the Lord, and taste again the sweet and satisfying fruits of fellowship with the Saints.'

"We are confident that many have longed to return, but have felt awkward about doing so. We assure you that you will find open arms to receive you and willing hands to assist you." (*Ensign,* March 1986, p. 88.)

I think all of us were impressed by this magnanimous appeal akin to what the prophet Alma stated in the Book of Mormon regarding an invitation that was extended by the Lord. He said:

"Behold, he sendeth an invitation unto all men, for the arms of mercy are extended towards them, and he saith: Repent, and I will receive you.

"Yea, he saith: Come unto me and ye shall partake of the fruit of the tree of life; yea, ye shall eat and drink of the bread and the waters of life freely;

"Yea, come unto me and bring forth works of righteousness." (Alma 5:33–35.)

Each of us should read and reread the parable of the lost sheep found in the fifteenth chapter of Luke, commencing with the fourth verse:

"What man of you, having an hundred sheep, if he lose one of them, doth not leave the ninety and nine in the wilderness, and go after that which is lost, until he find it?

"And when he hath found it, he layeth it on his shoulders, rejoicing.

"And when he cometh home, he calleth together his friends and neighbours, saying unto them, Rejoice with me; for I have found my sheep which was lost" [Luke 15:4–6]. . . .

The Prophet Joseph Smith significantly altered one verse in the Joseph Smith Translation. It reads: "What man of you, having an hundred sheep, if he lose one of them, doth not leave the ninety and nine *and go into the wilderness after that which is lost,* until he find it?" (JST, Luke 15:4; italics added.)

That translation suggests that the shepherd leave his secure flock and go out into the wilderness—that is, go out into the world after him who is lost. Lost from what? Lost from the flock where there is protection and security. I hope the message of that parable will be impressed on the hearts of each of us.[4]

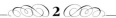

The Lord expects us to be His undershepherds and recover those who are struggling or lost.

What should we do to help those who have lost their way in the wilderness?

Because of what the Master has said about leaving the ninety-nine and going into the wilderness to seek the one that is lost, and because of the invitation of the First Presidency to those who have ceased activity or have been critical to "come back," we invite you to become involved in saving souls. Reach out to the less active and realize the joy that will come to you and those you help if you and they will take part in extending invitations to come back and feast at the table of the Lord.

The Lord, our Good Shepherd, expects us to be his undershepherds and recover those who are struggling or are lost. We can't tell you how to do it, but as you become involved and seek inspiration, success will result from efforts in your areas, . . . stakes, and wards. Some stakes have responded to previous pleadings and have had remarkable success.

The words of a familiar hymn contain the Savior's appeal to us:

Hark! he is earnestly calling,
Tenderly pleading today:
"Will you not seek for my lost ones,
Off from my shelter astray?"

And that hymn, sung often, indicates what our response should be:

"Make us thy true undershepherds;
Give us a love that is deep.
Send us out into the desert,
Seeking thy wandering sheep."
(*Hymns,* 1985, no. 221.)

If we do this, eternal blessings will come to us.[5]

Seeking after the lost, the wayward, and the straying is the Lord's business. . . . The prayerful plea of Alma is a good reminder of the sacredness of our task:

"O Lord, wilt thou grant unto us that we may have success in bringing [souls] again unto thee in Christ.

"Behold, O Lord, their souls are precious." (Alma 31:34–35.)[6]

Our grand objective is to help people return to God's presence.

Over the years the Church has made some monumental efforts to recover those who are less active. . . . And all to what end? It is to save the souls of our brothers and sisters and see that they have the ordinances of exaltation.

While I was serving as a stake president in the Los Angeles area, my counselors and I asked our bishops to carefully select four or

*"O Lord, wilt thou grant unto us that we may have success
in bringing [souls] again unto thee in Christ. Behold,
O Lord, their souls are precious" (Alma 31:34–35).*

five couples who wanted to further their progress in the Church. Some were less active, others new converts—but they were motivated to spiritually progress. We got them together in a stake class and taught them the gospel. Rather than emphasizing the temple, we stressed a better relationship with our Heavenly Father and his Son, Jesus Christ. Our careful selection process assured success, and the majority of these couples did become active and go to the temple.

Let me share [another] experience. . . . We had a brother in one of the wards who didn't attend any meetings. His wife was not a member. She was somewhat hostile, so we could not send home teachers to the home. The bishop approached this brother by telling him that the brother had a relationship with the Savior he needed to expand and enlarge. The brother explained to the bishop the problem with his nonmember wife, so the bishop talked to her, emphasizing the same approach—a relationship with the Lord that needed to be expanded. She still was not receptive but was happy to learn that Latter-day Saints believed in Christ, and consequently dropped some of her defenses.

Success did not come immediately, but those who visited the home kept stressing the couple's relationship with the Lord. In time she became friendly, and finally consented to come with her husband to the stake class taught by members of the high council. We stressed the covenant one makes at baptism and other covenants. Eventually she became a member of the Church and he became a productive priesthood leader. . . .

I am impressed by a statement on the title page of the Book of Mormon that describes one of the purposes of that sacred book: "That they [the House of Israel in the latter days] may know *the covenants of the Lord*." (Italics added.) That was the emphasis we as a stake presidency felt impressed to make to those less active. We tried to appeal to them on the basis of the importance of the covenants they had made with the Lord; then we taught them the importance of the covenant of baptism and additional covenants that they could make which would unite them as an eternal family.[7]

The whole purpose of the Church operating smoothly at the local level is to qualify individuals to return to the presence of God. That can only be done by their receiving the ordinances and making covenants in the temple.[8]

Our efforts focus on making the saving covenants and ordinances of the gospel available to all mankind: to the nonmember through our missionary work; to the less-active through fellowshipping and activation efforts; to active members through participation and service in the Church, and to those who have passed beyond the veil through the work of redemption for the dead.[9]

We are leading toward one objective for each individual member of the Church. That is for all to receive the ordinances of the gospel and make covenants with our Heavenly Father so they may return to his presence. That is our grand objective. The ordinances and covenants are the means to achieving that divine nature that will return us into his presence again. . . .

Keep in mind the purpose: to invite all to come unto Christ. . . .

I testify, my brethren and sisters, to his divinity and power to save those who will come to him with broken hearts and contrite spirits. Through the ordinances and his Holy Spirit, each individual may become clean.[10]

Suggestions for Study and Teaching

Questions

- President Hunter encourages every Church member to read and reread the parable of the lost sheep (see section 1; Luke 15:4–7). What messages do you receive from that parable and the other teachings in the first section? Consider how those teachings can guide you as you serve in the Church.

- What is our responsibility as the Lord's undershepherds? (See section 2.) How can we help people return to Church activity? How have you (or someone you know) been blessed by a person who reached out to you when you were "struggling or lost"?

- What can we learn from the experiences that President Hunter relates in section 3? How can an emphasis on covenants help Church members return to activity?

Related Scriptures

Ezekiel 34:1–16; Luke 15:11–32; John 10:1–16, 26–28; 13:35; 1 John 1:7; Mosiah 18:8–10; Helaman 6:3; 3 Nephi 18:32; Moroni 6:4–6; D&C 38:24

Study Help

A principle is a truth that guides decisions and actions. "As you read, ask yourself, 'What gospel principle is taught in this passage? How can I apply this in my life?'" (*Teaching, No Greater Call* [1999], 17).

Notes

1. In Jay M. Todd, "President Howard W. Hunter: Fourteenth President of the Church," *Ensign,* July 1994, 5.
2. "Exceeding Great and Precious Promises," *Ensign,* Nov. 1994, 8.
3. "Make Us Thy True Undershepherds," *Ensign,* Sept. 1986, 9.
4. "Make Us Thy True Undershepherds," 7–8.
5. "Make Us Thy True Undershepherds," 9.
6. "The Mission of the Church" (address given at the regional representatives' seminar, Mar. 30, 1990), 4.
7. "Make Us Thy True Undershepherds," 8–9.
8. *The Teachings of Howard W. Hunter,* ed. Clyde J. Williams (1997), 218.
9. *The Teachings of Howard W. Hunter,* 245–46.
10. *The Teachings of Howard W. Hunter,* 218.

The Mesa Arizona Temple, where President Howard W. Hunter was sealed to his parents in 1953

The Temple—The Great Symbol of Our Membership

"It is the deepest desire of my heart to have every member of the Church worthy to enter the temple."

From the Life of Howard W. Hunter

Howard W. Hunter's mother was a faithful member of the Church throughout her life, but his father was not baptized until Howard was 19. Years later, when Howard was a stake president in California, stake members traveled to the Mesa Arizona Temple to do temple work. Before a session began, the temple president asked him to address those who were assembled in the chapel. It was President Hunter's 46th birthday. He later wrote of that experience:

"While I was speaking to the congregation, . . . my father and mother came into the chapel dressed in white. I had no idea my father was prepared for his temple blessings, although Mother had been anxious about it for some time. I was so overcome with emotion that I was unable to continue to speak. President Pierce [the temple president] came to my side and explained the reason for the interruption. When my father and mother came to the temple that morning they asked the president not to mention to me that they were there because they wanted it to be a birthday surprise. This was a birthday I have never forgotten because on that day they were endowed and I had the privilege of witnessing their sealing, following which I was sealed to them."[1]

A little more than 40 years later, when Howard W. Hunter made his first public statement as President of the Church, one of his primary messages was for members to seek the blessings of the temple with greater devotion.[2] He continued to emphasize that message throughout his service as President. Speaking at the site of the Nauvoo Temple in June 1994, he said:

"Earlier this month I began my ministry by expressing a deep desire to have more and more Church members become temple worthy. As in [Joseph Smith's] day, having worthy and endowed members is the key to building the kingdom in all the world. Temple worthiness ensures that our lives are in harmony with the will of the Lord, and we are attuned to receive His guidance in our lives."[3]

Several months later, in January 1995, President Hunter's last public activity was the dedication of the Bountiful Utah Temple. In the dedicatory prayer, he asked that the blessings of the temple would enrich the lives of all who entered:

"We humbly pray that thou wilt accept this edifice and let thy blessings be upon it. Let thy spirit attend and guide all who officiate herein, that holiness will prevail in every room. May all who enter have clean hands and pure hearts. May they be built up in their faith and depart with a feeling of peace, praising thy holy name. . . .

"May this House provide a spirit of peace to all who observe its majesty, and especially to those who enter for their own sacred ordinances and to perform the work for their loved ones beyond the veil. Let them feel of thy divine love and mercy. May they be privileged to say, as did the Psalmist of old, 'We took sweet counsel together, and walked unto the house of God in company.'

"As we dedicate this sacred edifice, we rededicate our very lives to thee and to thy work."[4]

Teachings of Howard W. Hunter

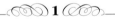 1

We are encouraged to establish the temple as the great symbol of our membership.

At the time of my call to this sacred office [President of the Church], an invitation was given for all members of the Church to establish the temple of the Lord as the great symbol of their membership and the supernal setting for their most sacred covenants.

When I contemplate the temple, I think of these words:

"The temple is a place of instruction where profound truths pertaining to the Kingdom of God are unfolded. It is a place of peace where minds can be centered upon things of the spirit and the worries of the world can be laid aside. In the temple we make covenants to obey the laws of God, and promises are made to us, conditioned always on our faithfulness, which extend into eternity" (*The Priesthood and You,* Melchizedek Priesthood Lessons—1966, Salt Lake City: The Church of Jesus Christ of Latter-day Saints, 1966, p. 293).

It is the Lord Himself who, in His revelations to us, has made the temple the great symbol for members of the Church. Think of the attitudes and righteous behaviors that the Lord pointed us toward in the counsel He gave to the Kirtland Saints through the Prophet Joseph Smith as they were preparing to build a temple. This counsel is still applicable:

"Organize yourselves; prepare every needful thing; and establish a house, even a house of prayer, a house of fasting, a house of faith, a house of learning, a house of glory, a house of order, a house of God" (D&C 88:119). Are these attitudes and behaviors indeed reflective of what each of us desires and seeks to be? . . .

. . . To have the temple indeed be a symbol unto us, we must desire it to be so. We must live worthy to enter the temple. We must keep the commandments of our Lord. If we can pattern our life after the Master, and take His teaching and example as the supreme pattern for our own, we will not find it difficult to be temple worthy, to be consistent and loyal in every walk of life, for we will be committed to a single, sacred standard of conduct and belief. Whether at home or in the marketplace, whether at school or long after school is behind us, whether we are acting totally alone or in concert with a host of other people, our course will be clear and our standards will be obvious.

The ability to stand by one's principles, to live with integrity and faith according to one's belief—that is what matters. That devotion to true principle—in our individual lives, in our homes and families, and in all places that we meet and influence other people—that devotion is what God is ultimately requesting of us. It requires commitment—whole-souled, deeply held, eternally cherished commitment to the principles we know to be true in the commandments God has given. If we will be true and faithful to the Lord's principles, then we will always be temple worthy, and the Lord and His holy temples will be the great symbols of our discipleship with Him.[5]

Each of us should strive to be worthy to receive a temple recommend.

It is the deepest desire of my heart to have every member of the Church worthy to enter the temple. It would please the Lord if every adult member would be worthy of—and carry—a current temple recommend. The things that we must do and not do to be worthy of a temple recommend are the very things that ensure we will be happy as individuals and as families.[6]

Our Heavenly Father has clearly outlined that those who enter the temple must be clean and free from the sins of the world. He said, "And inasmuch as my people build a house unto me in the name of the Lord, and do not suffer any unclean thing to come into it, that it be not defiled, my glory shall rest upon it; . . . But if it be defiled I will not come into it, and my glory shall not be there; for I will not come into unholy temples" (D&C 97:15, 17).

It might be interesting for you to know that the President of the Church used to sign each temple recommend. That's how strongly the early presidents felt about worthiness to enter the temple. In 1891 the responsibility was placed on bishops and stake presidents, who ask you several questions concerning your worthiness to qualify for a temple recommend. You should know what is expected of you in order to qualify for a temple recommend.

You must believe in God the Eternal Father, in his Son Jesus Christ, and in the Holy Ghost. You must believe that this is their sacred and divine work. We encourage you to work daily on building your testimony of our Heavenly Father and the Lord Jesus Christ. The Spirit that you feel is the Holy Ghost testifying to you of their reality. Later, in the temple, you will learn more about the Godhead through the revealed instruction and ordinances.

*"Bishops and stake presidents . . . ask you several questions
concerning your worthiness to qualify for a temple recommend."*

*You must sustain the General Authorities and local authorities
of the Church.* When you raise your arm to the square when these
leaders' names are presented, you signify that you will sustain them
in their responsibilities and in the counsel they give you.

This is not an exercise in paying homage to those whom the Lord
has called to preside. Rather, it is a recognition of the fact that God
has called prophets, seers, and revelators, and others as General
Authorities. It is a commitment that you will follow the instructions
that come from the presiding officers of the Church. Likewise you
should feel loyalty toward the bishop and stake president and other
Church leaders. Failure to sustain those in authority is incompatible
with service in the temple.

You must be morally clean to enter into the holy temple. The law
of chastity requires that you not have sexual relations with anyone other than your husband or wife. We especially encourage
you to guard against the enticements of Satan to sully your moral
cleanliness.

*You must ensure that there is nothing in your relationship with
family members that is out of harmony with the teachings of the*

Church. We especially encourage [youth] to obey [their] parents in righteousness. Parents must be vigilant to ensure that their relationships with family members are in harmony with the teachings of the gospel and never involve abuse or neglect.

To enter the temple you must be honest in all of your dealings with others. As Latter-day Saints we have a sacred obligation to never be deceitful or dishonest. Our basic integrity is at stake when we violate this covenant.

To qualify for a temple recommend, you should strive to do your duty in the Church, attending your sacrament, priesthood, and other meetings. You must also strive to obey the rules, laws, and commandments of the gospel. Learn . . . to accept callings and other responsibilities that come to you. Be active participants in your wards and branches, and be one your leaders can depend on.

To enter the temple you must be a full-tithe payer and live the Word of Wisdom. These two commandments, simple in their instruction but enormously important in our spiritual growth, are essential in certifying our personal worthiness. Observation over many years has shown that those who faithfully pay their tithing and observe the Word of Wisdom are usually faithful in all other matters that relate to entering the holy temple.

These are not matters to be taken lightly. Once having been found worthy to enter the temple, we perform ordinances that are the most sacred administered anywhere on the earth. These ordinances are concerned with the things of eternity.[7]

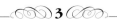 **3**

Doing temple work brings great blessings to individuals and families.

What a glorious thing it is for us to have the privilege of going to the temple for our own blessings. Then after going to the temple for our own blessings, what a glorious privilege to do the work for those who have gone on before us. This aspect of temple work is an unselfish work. Yet whenever we do temple work for other people, there is a blessing that comes back to us. Thus it should be no surprise to us that the Lord does desire that his people be a temple-motivated people. . . .

. . . We should go not only for our kindred dead but also for the personal blessing of temple worship, for the sanctity and safety that are within those hallowed and consecrated walls. As we attend the temple, we learn more richly and deeply the purpose of life and the significance of the atoning sacrifice of the Lord Jesus Christ. Let us make the temple, with temple worship and temple covenants and temple marriage, our ultimate earthly goal and the supreme mortal experience.[8]

Several things are accomplished by our attendance at the temple—we comply with the instructions of the Lord to accomplish our own ordinance work, we bless our families by the sealing ordinances, and we share our blessings with others by doing for them what they cannot do for themselves. In addition to these, we lift our own thoughts, grow closer to the Lord, honor [the] priesthood, and spiritualize our lives.[9]

We receive personal blessings as we attend the temple. Commenting on how our lives are blessed by temple attendance Elder John A. Widtsoe stated:

"Temple work . . . gives a wonderful opportunity for keeping alive our spiritual knowledge and strength. . . . The mighty perspective of eternity is unraveled before us in the holy temples; we see time from its infinite beginning to its endless end; and the drama of eternal life is unfolded before us. Then I see more clearly my place amidst the things of the universe, my place among the purposes of God; I am better able to place myself where I belong, and I am better able to value and to weigh, to separate and to organize the common, ordinary duties of my life so that the little things shall not oppress me or take away my vision of the greater things that God has given us" (in Conference Report, Apr. 1922, pp. 97–98).[10]

Consider the majestic teachings in the great dedicatory prayer of the Kirtland Temple, a prayer the Prophet Joseph Smith said was given to him by revelation. It is a prayer that continues to be answered upon us individually, upon us as families, and upon us as a people because of the priesthood power the Lord has given us to use in His holy temples.

"And now, Holy Father," pleaded the Prophet Joseph Smith, "we ask thee to assist us, thy people, with thy grace . . . that we may be found worthy, in thy sight, to secure a fulfilment of the promises which thou hast made unto us, thy people, in the revelations given unto us;

"That thy glory may rest down upon thy people. . . .

"And we ask thee, Holy Father, that thy servants may go forth from this house armed with thy power, and that thy name may be upon them, and thy glory be round about them, and thine angels have charge over them" [D&C 109:10–12, 22].[11]

Temple attendance creates spirituality. It is one of the finest programs we have in the Church to develop spirituality. This turns the hearts of the children to their fathers and the hearts of the fathers to their children (Malachi 4:6). This promotes family solidarity and unity.[12]

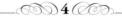

4

Let us hasten to the temple.

Let us share with our children the spiritual feelings we have in the temple. And let us teach them more earnestly and more comfortably the things we can appropriately say about the purposes of the house of the Lord. Keep a picture of a temple in your home that your children may see it. Teach them about the purposes of the house of the Lord. Have them plan from their earliest years to go there and to remain worthy of that blessing. Let us prepare every missionary to go to the temple worthily and to make that experience an even greater highlight than receiving the mission call. Let us plan for and teach and plead with our children to marry in the house of the Lord. Let us reaffirm more vigorously than we ever have in the past that it does matter where you marry and by what authority you are pronounced man and wife.[13]

It is pleasing to the Lord for our youth to worthily go to the temple and perform vicarious baptism for those who did not have the opportunity to be baptized in life. It is pleasing to the Lord when we worthily go to the temple to personally make our own covenants with Him and to be sealed as couples and as families. And it is pleasing to the Lord when we worthily go to the temple to perform these same saving ordinances for those who have died, many of whom eagerly await the completion of these ordinances in their behalf.[14]

To those who have not received their temple blessings, or who do not hold a current temple recommend, may I encourage you in humility and love to work towards the day that you can enter into the house of the Lord. He has promised those who are faithful to their covenants, "If my people will hearken unto my voice, and unto the voice of my servants whom I have appointed to lead my people, behold, verily I say unto you, they shall not be moved out of their place" (D&C 124:45). . . . I promise you that your personal spirituality, relationship with your husband or wife, and family relationships will be blessed and strengthened as you regularly attend the temple.[15]

Let us be a temple-attending and a temple-loving people. Let us hasten to the temple as frequently as time and means and personal circumstances allow. Let us go not only for our kindred dead, but let us also go for the personal blessing of temple worship, for the sanctity and safety which is provided within those hallowed and consecrated walls. The temple is a place of beauty, it is a place of revelation, it is a place of peace. It is the house of the Lord. It is holy unto the Lord. It should be holy unto us.[16]

Suggestions for Study and Teaching

Questions
- Ponder President Hunter's teachings in section 1. How can we "establish the temple of the Lord as the great symbol of [our] membership"?

- Review the requirements for a temple recommend as outlined in section 2. How has living by these requirements blessed you and your family? Why are we required to strive to be "clean and free from the sins of the world" as we enter the temple?

- Review President Hunter's teachings about the blessings of doing temple work (see section 3). How has participating in temple ordinances blessed you and your family? How can you more fully benefit from the blessings of the temple? Can you share a time when you felt spiritual strength or direction in the temple? If you have not yet been to the temple, ponder how you can prepare to receive that blessing.

- What are some ways we can help children and youth learn about temples and develop a love for them? (See section 4.) How can we help children and youth desire to marry in the house of the Lord? Why is it important that we go to the temple "as frequently as time and means and personal circumstances allow"?

Related Scriptures

Psalm 55:14; Isaiah 2:2–3; D&C 97:12–17; 110:6–10; 124:39–41; 138:53–54; Bible Dictionary, "Temple"

Teaching Help

"Often a lesson will contain more material than you are able to teach in the time you are given. In such cases, you should select the material that will be most helpful for those you teach" (*Teaching, No Greater Call* [1999], 98).

Notes

1. In Eleanor Knowles, *Howard W. Hunter* (1994), 135.
2. See Jay M. Todd, "President Howard W. Hunter: Fourteenth President of the Church," *Ensign,* July 1994, 4–5.
3. "The Temple of Nauvoo," *Ensign,* Sept. 1994, 62–63.
4. Text of the Bountiful Utah Temple dedicatory prayer, in "'Magnificent Edifice' Consecrated to [the] Lord," *Church News,* Jan. 14, 1995, 4.
5. "The Great Symbol of Our Membership," *Ensign,* Oct. 1994, 2, 5.
6. "Exceeding Great and Precious Promises," *Ensign,* Nov. 1994, 8.
7. "Your Temple Recommend," *New Era,* Apr. 1995, 6–9.
8. "A Temple-Motivated People," *Ensign,* Feb. 1995, 5.
9. *The Teachings of Howard W. Hunter,* ed. Clyde J. Williams (1997), 240.
10. "We Have a Work to Do," *Ensign,* Mar. 1995, 65.
11. "The Great Symbol of Our Membership," 4.
12. *The Teachings of Howard W. Hunter,* 239–40.
13. "A Temple-Motivated People," 5.
14. "The Great Symbol of Our Membership," 5.
15. *The Teachings of Howard W. Hunter,* 240–41.
16. "The Great Symbol of Our Membership," 5.

Hastening Family History and Temple Work

"Surely the Lord will support us if we use our best efforts in carrying out the commandment to do family history research and temple work."

From the Life of Howard W. Hunter

Family history was always close to President Howard W. Hunter's heart. From the time he was a boy, he listened to stories about his ancestors with great interest. As he grew older, he devoted substantial time to researching his family history.[1] In 1972, while he was in Europe on a Church assignment, he and his wife, Claire, visited places in Denmark where his ancestors had lived. In one of the villages, they found the church where President Hunter's great-grandfather Rasmussen had been christened and where the family had worshipped. This experience deepened President Hunter's appreciation for his maternal ancestors. He made similar visits to areas of Norway and Scotland where other ancestors had lived.[2]

President Hunter's son Richard recalled his father's love for family history:

"He was an avid researcher all of his life. He would often take time from his law practice to go to the Los Angeles public library to do research in its extensive genealogy section. He kept his research, family group sheets, pedigree charts, and the narrative histories he personally wrote in ledger books.

"Occasionally I would travel with him to various conference assignments. He would put a few of the ledgers in the car trunk, and after the stake conference he would say, 'Let's go to [this] cousin's home for a few minutes. There are some dates I want to verify.' We would go to [the] cousin's home. He would get the ledgers from

*Howard W. Hunter's parents, John William (Will) Hunter
and Nellie Marie Rasmussen Hunter*

the trunk, and soon the dining room table would be covered with family group sheets.

"If one of the family members wanted to make sure they had the right information for their own research, they would call or write Dad to verify the facts because they knew he would have it right. The work he did was prodigious."[3]

One time while President Hunter was serving in the Quorum of the Twelve, his home teachers visited and said, "We wanted to show you our family group sheets that we have prepared. . . . We don't have time to see yours tonight, but next time we come we'd like to take a look at them."

"Now this was quite interesting to me," President Hunter said. "I worked a month getting prepared for the next home teachers' visit."[4]

From 1964 to 1972, Howard W. Hunter presided over the Genealogical Society of Utah (see page 19). In 1994, at a meeting honoring President Hunter and commemorating the 100th anniversary of the Genealogical Society, he said:

"On the eve of my eighty-seventh birthday, I look back in wonder at the tapestry woven by the Lord in the furthering of temple and family history work. When I was president of the Genealogical Society of Utah, we had visions of how it would move forward mightily. Now we are observing something glorious occurring throughout the world. The gospel is moving forward to encompass every nation, kindred, tongue, and people. Temples are located throughout the earth, and the spirit of Elijah is touching the hearts of many members, who are doing family history and temple ordinance work at an unprecedented pace."[5]

Teachings of Howard W. Hunter

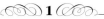

1

Temples are built for performing ordinances that are essential for the salvation and exaltation of God's children.

Temples are sacred for the closest communion between the Lord and those receiving the highest and most sacred ordinances of the holy priesthood. It is in the temple that things of the earth are joined with the things of heaven. . . . The great family of God will be united through the saving ordinances of the gospel. Vicarious work for the dead and ordinances for the living are the purposes of temples.[6]

The gospel proclaimed to the world by the Latter-day Saints is the gospel of Jesus Christ as restored to the earth in this dispensation and is for the redemption of all mankind. The Lord himself has revealed what is essential for the salvation and exaltation of his children. One of these essentials is that temples are to be erected for the performance of ordinances that cannot be performed in any other place.

When this is explained to people from all over the world who come and look at our temples, the question these people most frequently ask is, what are the ordinances that are performed in temples?

Baptism for the dead

In response, we often first explain the ordinance known as baptism for the dead. We note that many Christians believe that at the time of death, our status before the Lord is determined for all eternity, for did not Christ say to Nicodemus, "Verily, verily, I say unto thee, Except a man be born of water and of the Spirit, he cannot enter into the kingdom of God" (John 3:5)? Yet we know that many people have died without the ordinance of baptism, and thus, according to Christ's statement to Nicodemus, they would be eliminated from entering into the kingdom of God. This raises the question, is God just?

The answer is, of course God is just. It is evident that the Savior's statement to Nicodemus presupposes that baptisms may be done for those who have died who have not been baptized. Latter-day prophets have told us that baptism is an earthly ordinance that can be performed only by the living. How then can those who are dead be baptized if only the living can perform the ordinance? That was the theme of the Apostle Paul's writing to the Corinthians when he asked this question:

"Else what shall they do which are baptized for the dead, if the dead rise not at all? why are they then baptized for the dead?" (1 Cor. 15:29.)[7]

Does it seem reasonable that persons who have lived upon the earth and died without the opportunity of baptism should be deprived throughout eternity? Is there anything unreasonable about the living performing the baptisms for the dead? Perhaps the greatest example of vicarious work for the dead is the Master himself. He gave his life as a vicarious atonement, that all who die shall live again and have life everlasting. He did for us what we could not do for ourselves. In a similar way we can perform ordinances for those who did not have the opportunity to do them in [their] lifetime.[8]

The endowment

The endowment is another ordinance performed in our temples. It consists of two parts: first, a series of instructions, and second, promises or covenants that the person receiving the endowment makes—promises to live righteously and comply with the requirements of the gospel of Jesus Christ. The endowment is an ordinance for the great blessing of the Saints—both living and dead. Thus it is also an ordinance performed by the living in behalf of deceased individuals; it is performed for those for whom baptismal work has already been performed.

Celestial marriage

Another temple ordinance is that of celestial marriage, where wife is sealed to husband and husband sealed to wife for eternity. We know, of course, that civil marriages end at death; but eternal marriages performed in the temple may exist forever. Children born to a husband and wife after an eternal marriage are automatically sealed to their parents for eternity. If children are born before the wife is sealed to her husband, there is a temple sealing ordinance that can seal these children to their parents for eternity, and so it is that children can be sealed vicariously to parents who have passed away. . . .

All of these priesthood ordinances are essential for the salvation and exaltation of our Father in Heaven's children.[9]

"Truly there is no work equal to that done in the temple."

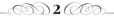

The objective of family history work is to make the blessings of the temple available to all people.

Surely we on this side of the veil have a great work to do. . . .
The building of temples has deep significance for ourselves and
mankind, and our responsibilities become clear. We must accomplish the priesthood temple ordinance work necessary for our own
exaltation; then we must do the necessary work for those who did
not have the opportunity to accept the gospel in life. Doing work
for others is accomplished in two steps: first, by family history research to ascertain our progenitors; and second, by performing the
temple ordinances to give them the same opportunities afforded
to the living.

Yet there are many members of the Church who have only limited access to the temples. They do the best they can. They pursue
family history research and have the temple ordinance work done
by others. Conversely, there are some members who engage in
temple work but fail to do family history research on their own
family lines. Although they perform a divine service in assisting

others, they lose a blessing by not seeking their own kindred dead as divinely directed by latter-day prophets.

I recall an experience of a few years ago that is analogous to this condition. At the close of a fast and testimony meeting, the bishop remarked, "We have had a spiritual experience today listening to the testimonies borne by each other. This is because we have come fasting according to the law of the Lord. But let us never forget that the law consists of two parts: that we fast by abstaining from food and drink and that we contribute what we have thereby saved to the bishop's storehouse for the benefit of those who are less fortunate." Then he added: "I hope no one of us will leave today with only half a blessing."

I have learned that those who engage in family history research and then perform the temple ordinance work for those whose names they have found will know the additional joy of receiving both halves of the blessing.

Furthermore, the dead are anxiously waiting for the Latter-day Saints to search out their names and then go into the temples to officiate in their behalf, that they may be liberated from their prison house in the spirit world. All of us should find joy in this magnificent labor of love.[10]

The objective of family history work is to make the blessings of the temple available to all people, both living and dead. As we attend the temple and perform work for the dead, we accomplish a deep sense of alliance with God and a better understanding of his plan for the salvation of the human race. We learn to love our neighbors as ourselves. Truly there is no work equal to that done in the temple.[11]

 **3**

May we be valiant in hastening our family history and temple work.

As we do the work in [the] temple for those who have gone beyond, we are reminded of the inspired counsel of President Joseph F. Smith who declared: "Through our efforts in their behalf, their chains of bondage will fall from them, and the darkness surrounding them will clear away, that light may shine upon them; and they shall hear in the spirit world of the work that has been done for them by their children here, and will rejoice" [in Conference Report, Oct. 1916, 6].[12]

This sacred work [family history and temple work] has a prominent place in the hearts and minds of the First Presidency and Quorum of the Twelve. I speak for all of the Brethren when I thank those who have given valuable contributions in providing the saving ordinances for those beyond the veil. . . . We are grateful to the army of volunteers who move this mighty work forward throughout the world. Thank you all for what you are doing so well.

The Prophet Joseph Smith stated, "The greatest responsibility in this world that God has laid upon us is to seek after our dead" [*Teachings of Presidents of the Church: Joseph Smith* (2007), 475]. He also stated: . . . "Those Saints who neglect it in behalf of their deceased relatives, do it at the peril of their own salvation" [*Teachings of Presidents of the Church: Joseph Smith,* 471–72].

Catching the same vision of this important revelation, President Brigham Young said: "We have a work to do just as important in its sphere as the Savior's work was in its sphere. Our fathers cannot be made perfect without us; we cannot be made perfect without them. They have done their work and now sleep. We are now called upon to do ours; which is to be the greatest work man ever performed on the earth" (*Discourses of Brigham Young,* sel. John A. Widtsoe, Salt Lake City: Deseret Book Co., 1941, p. 406).

Every prophet who has led this church from the days of Joseph Smith until the present has repeated this same sublime truth. Guided by these truths, the Church has been from the beginning of this dispensation engaged in the work of salvation and exaltation for all the sons and daughters of God, regardless of when they lived on the earth.

We who live in this day are those whom God appointed before birth to be his representatives on earth in this dispensation. We are of the house of Israel. In our hands lie the sacred powers of being saviors on Mount Zion in the latter days [see Obadiah 1:21].

With regard to temple and family history work, I have one overriding message: This work must hasten. The work waiting to be done is staggering and escapes human comprehension. Last year [1993] we performed proxy temple endowments for about five and a half million persons, but during that year about fifty million persons died. This might suggest futility in the work that lies before us, but we cannot think of futility. Surely the Lord will support us if we use our best efforts in carrying out the commandment to do family history research and temple work. The great work of the temples and all that supports it must expand. It is imperative! . . .

My beloved brothers and sisters, may we be valiant in hastening our family history and temple work. The Lord said, "Let the work of my temple, and all the works which I have appointed unto you, be continued on and not cease; and let your diligence, and your perseverance, and patience, and your works be redoubled, and you shall in nowise lose your reward, saith the Lord of Hosts" (D&C 127:4).

I encourage you in your efforts with these words of the Prophet Joseph Smith: "Brethren, shall we not go on in so great a cause? Go forward and not backward. Courage, brethren; and on, on to the victory! Let your hearts rejoice, and be exceedingly glad. Let the earth break forth into singing. Let the dead speak forth anthems of eternal praise to the King Immanuel, who hath ordained, before the world was, that which would enable us to redeem them out of their prison; for the prisoners shall go free" (D&C 128:22).

I love this work. I know the Lord will provide all that will be required to accomplish it as we devotedly do our part. May the Lord bless each of us as we make our contribution to this great work, which we must accomplish in our day.[13]

Suggestions for Study and Teaching

Questions
- Ponder the opening sentence in section 1. How has performing ordinances in the temple helped you draw closer to God? What information in this section could help you explain the purposes of temples to someone who does not understand them?

- How have you experienced "both halves of the blessing" of family history research and temple work? (See section 2.) How can we include children and other family members in this important work?

• As you review President Hunter's teachings in section 3, consider the importance the Lord places on family history and temple work. How are family history and temple work hastening today? How can we increase our participation in this work?

Related Scriptures

Isaiah 42:6–7; Malachi 4:5–6; 1 Peter 3:18–20; 4:6; D&C 2; 110:12–15; 124:28–30; 128:15–18; 138:57–59

Study Help

To liken the words of a prophet to yourself, think about how his teachings relate to you (see *Teaching, No Greater Call* [1999], 170). During your study, consider asking yourself how those teachings can help you with concerns, questions, and challenges in your life.

Notes

1. See Eleanor Knowles, *Howard W. Hunter* (1994), 186.

2. See Francis M. Gibbons, *Howard W. Hunter: Man of Thought and Independence, Prophet of God* (2011), 16–18.

3. Unpublished manuscript by Richard A. Hunter.

4. In Knowles, *Howard W. Hunter,* 192.

5. "We Have a Work to Do," *Ensign,* Mar. 1995, 64.

6. "The Great Symbol of Our Membership," *Ensign,* Oct. 1994, 2.

7. "A Temple-Motivated People," *Ensign,* Feb. 1995, 2.

8. "Elijah the Prophet," *Ensign,* Dec. 1971, 71.

9. "A Temple-Motivated People," 2, 4.

10. "A Temple-Motivated People," 4–5.

11. "We Have a Work to Do," 65.

12. Text of the Bountiful Utah Temple dedicatory prayer, in "'Magnificent Edifice' Consecrated to [the] Lord," *Church News,* Jan. 14, 1995, 4.

13. "We Have a Work to Do," 64–65.

The Sacrament of the Lord's Supper

"As [Jesus] took the bread and broke it, and took the cup and blessed it, he was presenting himself as the Lamb of God who would provide spiritual nourishment and eternal salvation."

From the Life of Howard W. Hunter

Howard W. Hunter was raised by an active Latter-day Saint mother and a good father who was not then affiliated with any church. His father did not object to the family's participation in the Church—he even attended sacrament meetings with them occasionally—but he did not want his children to be baptized when they were 8 years old. He felt that they should not make that decision until they were older. When Howard turned 12, he could not receive the Aaronic Priesthood and be ordained a deacon because he had not been baptized. Even though he was able to participate with the young men in other activities, Howard was deeply disappointed that he could not pass the sacrament with them.

"I sat in sacrament meetings with the other boys," he recalled. "When it was time for them to pass the sacrament, I would slump down in my seat. I felt so left out. I wanted to pass the sacrament, but couldn't because I had not been baptized."[1]

Nearly five months after his 12th birthday, Howard persuaded his father to let him be baptized. Soon afterward, he was ordained a deacon. "I remember the first time I passed the sacrament," he said. "I was frightened, but thrilled to have the privilege. After the meeting the bishop complimented me on the way I had conducted myself."[2]

"This do in remembrance of me" (Luke 22:19).

When Howard W. Hunter was called as an Apostle, he regularly participated in the ordinance of the sacrament with other General Authorities in the Salt Lake Temple. Elder David B. Haight, who served with Elder Hunter in the Quorum of the Twelve, described the experience of hearing him bless the sacrament:

"I wish the Aaronic Priesthood boys throughout the Church could have the same opportunity of hearing Elder Howard W. Hunter bless the sacrament as we have had in the temple. He is a special witness of Christ. As I have listened to him ask our Heavenly Father to bless the sacrament, I have felt of the deep spirituality in his soul. Every word was clear and meaningful. He was not in a hurry, not rushed. He was the spokesman for all of the Apostles in addressing our Heavenly Father."[3]

These accounts illustrate President Hunter's lifelong reverence for the sacred emblems of Christ's atoning sacrifice.

As the teachings in this chapter show, one way President Hunter sought to help Church members understand the significance of the sacrament was to explain its connection to the ancient celebration of the Passover and to review the Savior's introduction of this ordinance during a Passover meal with His disciples.

Teachings of Howard W. Hunter

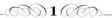

1

The Passover declares that death has no permanent power on us.

[The Passover] is the oldest of the Jewish festivals, celebrating an event in advance of receiving the traditional Mosaic Law. It reminds every generation of the return of the children of Israel to the promised land and of the great travail in Egypt which preceded it. It commemorates the passage of a people from subjection and bondage to freedom and deliverance. It is the Old Testament festival of springtime when the world of nature awakens to life, growth, and fruition.

Passover is linked with the Christian observance of Easter. . . . The Passover [and Easter] testify of the great gift God has given and of the sacrifice that was involved in its bestowal. Both of these great religious commemorations declare that death would "pass over" us and could have no permanent power upon us, and that the grave would have no victory.

In delivering the children of Israel out of Egypt, Jehovah himself spoke to Moses out of the burning bush at Sinai saying:

"I have surely seen the affliction of my people which are in Egypt, and have heard their cry by reason of their taskmasters; for I know their sorrows. . . .

"Come now therefore, and I will send thee unto Pharaoh, that thou mayest bring forth my people the children of Israel out of Egypt." (Ex. 3:7, 10.)

Because Pharaoh was unyielding, many plagues were brought upon Egypt, but still "the heart of Pharaoh was hardened, neither would he let the children of Israel go." (Ex. 9:35.)

In response to that refusal by Pharaoh, the Lord said, "And all the firstborn in the land of Egypt shall die, from the firstborn of Pharaoh that sitteth upon his throne, even unto the firstborn of the maidservant that is behind the mill; and all the firstborn of beasts." (Ex. 11:5.)

As a protection against this last and most terrible punishment inflicted upon the Egyptians, the Lord instructed Moses to have the children of Israel take to them every man a lamb without blemish.

"And they shall take of the blood, and strike it on the two side posts and on the upper door post of the houses, wherein they shall eat it.

"And they shall eat the flesh in that night, roast with fire, and unleavened bread; and with bitter herbs they shall eat it. . . .

"And thus shall ye eat it; with your loins girded, your shoes on your feet, and your staff in your hand; and ye shall eat it in haste: it is the Lord's passover. . . .

"And it shall come to pass, when your children shall say unto you, What mean ye by this service?

"That ye shall say, It is the sacrifice of the Lord's passover, who passed over the houses of the children of Israel in Egypt." (Ex. 12:7–8, 11, 26–27.)

After the Israelites had escaped from Pharaoh's grasp and death came to the firstborn of the Egyptians, the Israelites eventually crossed over Jordan. It is recorded that "the children of Israel encamped in Gilgal, and kept the passover on the fourteenth day of the month at even in the plains of Jericho." (Josh. 5:10.) And so it was with Jewish families year after year thereafter, including the family of Joseph and Mary and the young boy, Jesus.[4]

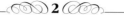

2

During a feast commemorating the Passover, the Savior instituted the ordinance of the sacrament.

As the Gospel of John makes clear, the feast of the Passover marked significant milestones during the mortal ministry of Christ. At the first Passover in his ministry, Jesus made his mission known by purifying the temple when he drove from its portals the money changers and those who sold animals. In the second Passover Jesus manifested his power by the miracle of the loaves and fishes. Christ here introduced the symbols that would later have even greater meaning in the Upper Room. "I am the bread of life," he said. "He that cometh to me shall never hunger; and he that believeth on me shall never thirst." (John 6:35.)

Of course, it would be the feast of his last Passover that would give full expression to this ancient celebration. By that final week of his mortal ministry, Jesus knew clearly what this particular Passover would mean to him. Trouble was already in the air. Matthew records:

"When Jesus had finished all these sayings, he said unto his disciples,

"Ye know that after two days is the feast of the passover, and the Son of man is betrayed to be crucified." (Matt. 26:1–2.)

Knowing full well what awaited him, Jesus asked Peter and John to make arrangements for the paschal meal. He told them to ask of the master of a local house, "Where is the guestchamber, where I shall eat the passover with my disciples?" (Luke 22:11.)

The loneliness of his birth was to be, in a sense, duplicated in the loneliness of his death. Foxes had holes and birds had nests, but

"As he took the bread and broke it, and took the cup and blessed it, he was presenting himself as the Lamb of God."

the Son of Man had nowhere to lay his head either in his nativity or in his last hours of mortality [see Matthew 8:20].

Finally, preparations for the Passover meal were complete, in keeping with nearly fifteen hundred years of tradition. Jesus sat down with his disciples and, after the eating of the sacrificial lamb and of the bread and wine of this ancient feast, he taught them a newer and holier meaning of that ancient blessing from God.

He took one of the flat, round loaves of unleavened bread, said the blessing over it, and broke it into pieces that he distributed to the Apostles, saying: "This is my body which is given for you: this do in remembrance of me." (Luke 22:19.)

As the cup was being poured, he took it and, giving thanks, invited them to drink of it, saying, "This cup is the new testament in my blood, which is shed for you." (Luke 22:20.) Paul said of it: "For as often as ye eat this bread, and drink this cup, ye do shew the Lord's death till he come." (1 Cor. 11:26.)

The bread and wine, rather than the animals and herbs, would become emblems of the great Lamb's body and blood, emblems to be eaten and drunk reverently and in remembrance of him forever.

In this simple but impressive manner the Savior instituted the ordinance now known as the sacrament of the Lord's Supper. With the suffering of Gethsemane, the sacrifice of Calvary, and the resurrection from a garden tomb, Jesus fulfilled the ancient law and ushered in a new dispensation based on a higher, holier understanding of the law of sacrifice. No more would men be required to offer the firstborn lamb from their flock, because the Firstborn of God had come to offer himself as an "infinite and eternal sacrifice."

This is the majesty of the Atonement and Resurrection, not just a passover from death, but a gift of eternal life by an infinite sacrifice.[5]

How fitting it was during the observance of this ancient covenant of protection [the Passover meal] that Jesus should institute the emblems of the new covenant of safety—the emblems of his own body and blood. As he took the bread and broke it, and took the cup and blessed it, he was presenting himself as *the* Lamb of God who would provide spiritual nourishment and eternal salvation.[6]

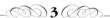 3

Our participation in the sacrament is an opportunity to review our lives and renew our covenants.

Not long ago I . . . [had] the privilege of attending the sacrament service in our own home ward. . . . While the priests were preparing the sacrament, we were led in singing:

God, our Father, hear us pray;
Send thy grace this holy day.
As we take of emblems blest,
On our Savior's love we rest.
[*Hymns,* no. 170]

"O Lord, I do remember Thee!"

A priest kneeled over the broken bread and prayed: "That they may eat in remembrance of the body of thy Son, and witness unto thee, O God, the Eternal Father, that they are willing to take upon them the name of thy Son, and always remember him and keep his commandments." (D&C 20:77.) The deacons dispersed throughout the chapel to serve the broken bread. One of them came to our row and held the silver tray while I partook. Then I held the tray so Sister Hunter could partake, and she held it for the person next to her. Thus the tray went down the row, each serving and being served.

I thought of the events that took place on the evening nearly two thousand years ago when Jesus was betrayed. . . . The sacrament of the Lord's Supper [was] introduced to replace [animal] sacrifice and be a reminder to all those who partake that He truly made a sacrifice for them; and to be an additional reminder of the covenants they have made to follow Him, keep His commandments, and be faithful to the end.

While [I was] thinking about this, the admonition of Paul in his letter to the church in Corinth came to my mind. He said: "Wherefore whosoever shall eat this bread, and drink this cup of the Lord, unworthily, shall be guilty of the body and blood of the Lord.

"But let a man examine himself, and so let him eat of that bread, and drink of that cup.

"For he that eateth and drinketh unworthily, eateth and drinketh damnation to himself, not discerning the Lord's body." (1 Cor. 11:27–29.)

I was troubled. I asked myself this question: "Do I place God above all other things and keep all of His commandments?" Then came reflection and resolution. To make a covenant with the Lord to always keep His commandments is a serious obligation, and to renew that covenant by partaking of the sacrament is equally serious. The solemn moments of thought while the sacrament is being served have great significance. They are moments of self-examination, introspection, self-discernment—a time to reflect and to resolve.

By this time the other priest was kneeling at the table, praying that all who should drink "may do it in remembrance of the blood of thy Son, which was shed for them; . . . that they do always remember him, that they may have his Spirit to be with them." (D&C 20:79.)

There was quiet meditation, the silence broken only by the voice of a tiny babe whose mother quickly held him close. Anything that breaks the silence during this sacred ordinance seems out of place; but surely the sound of a little one would not displease the Lord. He, too, had been cradled by a loving mother at the beginning of a mortal life that commenced in Bethlehem and ended on the cross of Calvary.

The young men concluded serving the sacrament. Then followed words of encouragement and instruction, a closing hymn and prayer; and the sacred moments "unmarred by earthly care" had come to a close [see "Secret Prayer," *Hymns,* no. 144]. On the way home . . . this thought came to my mind: What a wonderful thing it would be if all persons had an understanding of the purpose of baptism and the willingness to accept it; the desire to keep the covenants made in that ordinance to serve the Lord and live His commandments; and, in addition, the desire to partake of the sacrament on the Sabbath day to renew those covenants to serve Him and be faithful to the end. . . .

Having attended sacrament meeting and partaken of the sacrament made the day more meaningful, and I felt that I better understood the reason why the Lord said, "And that thou mayest more fully keep thyself unspotted from the world, thou shalt go to the house of prayer and offer up thy sacraments upon my holy day;

"For verily this is a day appointed unto you to rest from your labors, and to pay thy devotions unto the Most High." (D&C 59:9–10.)[7]

Suggestions for Study and Teaching

Questions
- Review President Hunter's teachings about the Passover in ancient Israel (see section 1). What can we learn from the Passover? How is the Passover linked with the observance of Easter?

- Review President Hunter's account of the Savior instituting the sacrament (see section 2). Why is this event significant to you? In what ways is the sacrament a "covenant of safety" for us?

- What impresses you about President Hunter's account of partaking of the sacrament in section 3? What can we learn from this account to make the sacrament more meaningful? How is partaking of the sacrament a blessing to you?

Related Scriptures

1 Corinthians 5:7–8; 11:23–29; 3 Nephi 18:3–14; 20:8–9; Moroni 6:5–6; D&C 20:75–79; 27:1–2

Teaching Help

"As we teach the gospel, we should humbly recognize that the Holy Ghost is the true teacher. Our privilege is to serve as instruments through whom the Holy Ghost can teach, testify, comfort, and inspire" (*Teaching, No Greater Call* [1999], 41).

Notes

1. In Gerry Avant, "Elder Hunter—Packed Away Musician's Career for Marriage," *Church News,* May 19, 1985, 4.

2. In J M. Heslop, "He Found Pleasure in Work," *Church News,* Nov. 16, 1974, 4.

3. David B. Haight, "The Sacrament," *Ensign,* May 1983, 13.

4. "Christ, Our Passover," *Ensign,* May 1985, 17–18.

5. "Christ, Our Passover," 18–19.

6. "His Final Hours," *Ensign,* May 1974, 18.

7. "Thoughts on the Sacrament," *Ensign,* May 1977, 24–25.

Marriage—An Eternal Partnership

"Life's greatest partnership is in marriage—that relationship which has lasting and eternal significance."

From the Life of Howard W. Hunter

When Howard W. Hunter was 20 years old, he met Claire Jeffs at a Church dance in Los Angeles, California, while she was on a date with one of his friends. After the dance, a few of the young adults went wading in the ocean surf. Howard lost his tie, and Claire volunteered to walk along the beach with him to help find it. Howard later said, "The next time we went out, I took Claire, and [my friend] went with someone else."[1]

The following year they began dating seriously, and on a spring evening nearly three years after they met, Howard took Claire to a beautiful overlook above the ocean. "We [watched] the waves roll in from the Pacific and break over the rocks in the light of a full moon," he wrote. That night Howard proposed marriage, and Claire accepted. "We talked about our plans," he said, "[and] made many decisions that night and some strong resolutions regarding our lives."[2]

Howard and Claire were married in the Salt Lake Temple on June 10, 1931. During the next 52 years, their love deepened as they raised their sons, served in the Church, and faced their challenges with faith.

Their happiness as a couple was evident to their family. Robert Hunter, their oldest grandson, said: "When I think of Grandpa Hunter, I think more than anything of an example of a loving husband. . . . You could really sense a loving bond between the two of them."[3]

"In the temple we receive the highest ordinance available to men and women, the sealing of husbands and wives together for eternity."

President Hunter's love for his wife was especially apparent as he cared for her during the last decade of her life, when she struggled with serious health problems. When Claire passed away on October 9, 1983, it was "a crushing blow" to President Hunter.[4] He wrote that when he arrived home on the day she died, "the house seemed cold, and as I walked about, everything reminded me of her."[5]

After nearly seven years alone, President Hunter married Inis Stanton in April 1990. President Gordon B. Hinckley performed the ceremony in the Salt Lake Temple. Inis was a source of great comfort and strength to President Hunter during his service as President of the Quorum of the Twelve and President of the Church. She accompanied him on many of his travels to meet with the Saints all over the world.

Elder James E. Faust of the Quorum of the Twelve spoke of the blessing Inis was to President Hunter: "After [Claire's] passing, it was a lonely time for several years until he married Inis. Together they have shared so many happy memories and experiences." Then, addressing Sister Hunter, he said, "We are grateful beyond expression to you, Inis, for your companionship and your loving and devoted care of him. You brought a sparkle to his eye and joy to him in the crowning years of his life and his ministry."[6]

Teachings of Howard W. Hunter

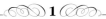

Marriage between a man and a woman is ordained of God and is intended to be eternal.

The Lord has defined marriage for us. He said, "For this cause shall a man leave father and mother, and shall cleave to his wife: and they twain shall be one flesh" (Matthew 19:5).[7]

Life's greatest partnership is in marriage—that relationship which has lasting and eternal significance.[8]

With a knowledge of the plan of salvation as a foundation, a man who holds the priesthood looks upon marriage as a sacred privilege and obligation. It is not good for man nor for woman to be alone. Man is not complete without woman. Neither can fill the measure of their creation without the other (see 1 Cor. 11:11; Moses 3:18).

Marriage between a man and a woman is ordained of God (see D&C 49:15–17). Only through the new and everlasting covenant of marriage can they realize the fulness of eternal blessings (see D&C 131:1–4; 132:15–19).[9]

Marriage is often referred to as a partnership with God. This is not just a figure of speech. If this partnership remains strong and active, the man and woman will love each other as they love God, and there will come into their home a sweetness and affection that will bring eternal success.[10]

The first marriage was performed by the Lord. It was an eternal marriage because there was no such thing as time when that ceremony took place. The ceremony was performed for a couple not then subject to death; thus, under the circumstances the relationship would never be terminated. After the fall, our first parents were driven from the Garden. They were then subject to death, but resurrection was promised to them. At no time was it said that their eternal marriage should come to an end.[11]

In the temple we receive the highest ordinance available to men and women, the sealing of husbands and wives together for eternity. We hope our young people will settle for nothing less than a temple marriage.[12]

Just as baptism is a commandment of the Lord, so is temple marriage. As baptism is essential to admittance to the Church, so temple marriage is essential to our exaltation in the presence of God. It is part of our destiny. We cannot fulfill our ultimate aims without it. Do not be satisfied with anything less.

You wouldn't accept a worldly form of baptism, would you? God has his mode of baptism—by immersion by one who holds the authority. Then would you accept a worldly form of marriage? He has his mode of marriage also: It is temple marriage.[13]

I pray that the Lord will bless us that we may realize the reason for our existence and what we must do to find our way to exaltation and eternal life. Part of the eternal plan is the marriage we hold sacred. If we are willing to comply, the ordinances become permanent forever. What a glorious thing it is to have this understanding and to have revealed to us these truths.[14]

 **2**

When deciding whom to marry, be patient, have faith, and stay worthy of receiving divine assistance.

I think the greatest decision you must make . . . is the decision that's going to shape your life for eternity, and that is your marriage. I'm sure that you would agree with me that this is going to be far more important than anything else you do in life, because your work and your profession or whatever you're going to do is not nearly as important as eternal values. . . . [The decision about marriage is] going to affect you through eternity; it's going to affect you while you live here upon the earth too.[15]

Do not . . . rush into a relationship without proper forethought and inspiration. Prayerfully seek the Lord's guidance on this matter. Stay worthy of receiving that divine assistance.[16]

Many of you . . . worry about courtship, marriage, and starting a family. You probably will not find the name of your future spouse in Nephi's vision or the book of Revelation; you probably will not be told it by an angel or even by your bishop. Some things you must work out for yourself. Have faith and be obedient, and blessings will come. Try to be patient. Try not to let what you don't have blind you to that which you do have. If you worry too much about marriage, it can canker the very possibility of it. Live fully and faithfully as one person before having undue anxiety about living as two.[17]

While waiting for promised blessings, one should not mark time, for to fail to move forward is to some degree a retrogression. Be anxiously engaged in good causes, including your own development.[18]

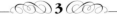 **3**

No blessing will be denied to worthy individuals who are not married.

This is the church of Jesus Christ, not the church of marrieds or singles or any other group or individual. The gospel we preach is the gospel of Jesus Christ, which encompasses all the saving ordinances and covenants necessary to save and exalt every individual who is willing to accept Christ and keep the commandments that he and our Father in Heaven have given.[19]

"While waiting for promised blessings, . . . be anxiously engaged in good causes, including your own development."

No blessing, including that of eternal marriage and an eternal family, will be denied to any worthy individual. While it may take somewhat longer—perhaps even beyond this mortal life—for some to achieve this blessing, it will not be denied. . . .

Now, may I offer a few words of counsel and love.

To you who are *unmarried men:* Don't put off marriage because you are not in a perfect career and financial position. . . . Remember that as a priesthood bearer you have the obligation to take the lead in seeking eternal companionship.

To you *unmarried women:* The promises of the prophets of God have always been that the Lord is mindful of you; if you are faithful, *all* blessings will be yours. To be without marriage and a family in this life is but a temporary condition, and eternity is a long time. President Benson has reminded us that "time is numbered only to man. God has your eternal perspective in mind." (*Ensign,* Nov. 1988, p. 97.) Fill your lives with worthwhile, meaningful activities.

To you who have experienced *divorce:* Don't let disappointment or a sense of failure color your perception of marriage or of life.

Do not lose faith in marriage or allow bitterness to canker your soul and destroy you or those you love or have loved.[20]

Successful marriage requires our best efforts to live the principles of the gospel.

[Marriage] . . . is a learned behavior. Our conscious effort, not instinct, determines the success. The motivating force stems from kindness, true affection, and consideration for each other's happiness and welfare.

Prior to marriage we looked at life from our own point of view, but after stepping over that threshold, we began to consider it from another's viewpoint also. There is a necessity to make sacrifices and adjustments as manifestations of reassurance and love.

It is often said that being happily and successfully married is generally not so much a matter of marrying the right person as it is *being the right person*. Statistics showing the high rate of divorce might indicate unwise choices of partners. If they had married other persons, the particular problem might have been eliminated, but surely another problem would have been in its place. A wise choice of a partner is a large contribution to a successful marriage, yet the conscious effort to do one's part fully is the greatest element contributing to success.[21]

While it is true that worthy couples will obtain exaltation in the celestial kingdom, each man and woman sealed in an eternal relationship must be individually worthy of that blessing.

An eternal marriage will be composed of a worthy man and a worthy woman, both of whom have been individually baptized with water and with the Spirit; who have individually gone to the temple to receive their own endowments; who have individually pledged their fidelity to God and to their partner in the marriage covenant; and who have individually kept their covenants, doing all that God expected of them.[22]

Living the principles of the gospel makes a happy marriage. . . . When two people can live the principles of the gospel, marriage can be sweet and it can be happy.[23]

———————— 〰️ **5** 〰️ ————————

Husbands and wives should work together to strengthen the bonds of marriage.

Charity and patience with imperfections

Most partners have imperfections. . . . Richard L. Evans once said, "Perhaps any of us could get along with perfect people, but our task is to get along with imperfect people" [*Richard Evans' Quote Book* (1971), 165]. We understand in marriage that we are not dealing with perfect people; we are seeking perfection and we are traveling the course in which we hope to find perfection, but we must have understanding, give our best, and make life beautiful. . . .

. . . The Bible tells us: "Charity suffereth long, and is kind" (see 1 Corinthians 13:4). That kind of love, the kind that is not taken lightly, not terminated at pleasure and thrown away like disposable plastic, but which faces all of life's little difficulties hand in hand entwining the souls, is the ultimate expression of human happiness.[24]

Oneness of heart

Surely the happiest marriages are those where your hurt is my hurt, my pain is your pain, my victory, your victory, my concerns, your concerns. The oneness of heart, of soul, of flesh seems to be more of a challenge than ever before in the world in which the question seems to be: "What is there in this for me?" Far too many marriage partners have become merely an ornament on the sleeve rather than a part of the heart.[25]

Fidelity in thought, word, and deed

A man who holds the priesthood shows perfect moral fidelity to his wife and gives her no reason to doubt his faithfulness. A husband is to love his wife with all his heart and cleave unto her and none else (see D&C 42:22–26). President Spencer W. Kimball explained:

"The words *none else* eliminate everyone and everything. The spouse then becomes pre-eminent in the life of the husband or wife and neither social life nor occupational life nor political life nor any other interest nor person nor thing shall ever take precedence over the companion spouse" (*The Miracle of Forgiveness,* Salt Lake City: Bookcraft, 1969, p. 250).

When husband and wife "love each other as they love God, . . . there will come into their home a sweetness and affection that will bring eternal success."

The Lord forbids and his church condemns any and every intimate relationship outside of marriage. Infidelity on the part of a man breaks the heart of his wife and loses her confidence and the confidence of his children (see Jacob 2:35).

Be faithful in your marriage covenants in thought, word, and deed. Pornography, flirtations, and unwholesome fantasies erode one's character and strike at the foundation of a happy marriage. Unity and trust within a marriage are thereby destroyed. One who does not control his thoughts and thus commits adultery in his heart, if he does not repent, shall not have the Spirit, but shall deny the faith and shall fear (see D&C 42:23; 63:16).[26]

Tenderness and respect in intimacy

Keep yourselves above any domineering or unworthy behavior in the tender, intimate relationship between husband and wife. Because marriage is ordained of God, the intimate relationship between husbands and wives is good and honorable in the eyes of God. He has commanded that they be one flesh and that they multiply and replenish the earth (see Moses 2:28; 3:24). You are to love your wife as Christ loved the Church and gave himself for it (see Eph. 5:25–31).

Tenderness and respect—never selfishness—must be the guiding principles in the intimate relationship between husband and wife. Each partner must be considerate and sensitive to the other's needs and desires. Any domineering, indecent, or uncontrolled behavior in the intimate relationship between husband and wife is condemned by the Lord.

Any man who abuses or demeans his wife physically or spiritually is guilty of grievous sin and in need of sincere and serious repentance. Differences should be worked out in love and kindness and with a spirit of mutual reconciliation. A man should always speak to his wife lovingly and kindly, treating her with the utmost respect. Marriage is like a tender flower . . . and must be nourished constantly with expressions of love and affection.[27]

Attentive listening

Many problems could be quickly answered, and many difficult situations resolved, if we could understand that there are times when we need to listen. In school we learned the lesson when we listened, but failed when we refused to give attention. In marriage there is a complete lack of understanding unless we are willing to listen. . . . Of course, we need to talk, but we must listen to the other view in order to increase our understanding sufficiently to make an intelligent decision. A listening ear can oftentimes make the difference.[28]

Selflessness

Friendships cannot endure if they are based on the sands of selfishness. Marriages do not endure when they have no ground except in physical attraction, and do not have the foundation of a deeper love and loyalty.[29]

We hope you who are married will remember the feelings of love which led you to the altar in the house of the Lord. Our hearts are saddened as we learn of many whose love has grown cold or who through reasons of selfishness or transgression forget or treat lightly the marriage covenants they made in the temple. We plead with husbands and wives to have love and respect for each other. Indeed, it would be our fondest hope that each family would be blessed with a mother and father who express love for each other, who are deferential to each other, and who work together to strengthen the bonds of marriage.[30]

Suggestions for Study and Teaching

Questions

- In section 1, President Hunter emphasizes that marriage is or-dained of God and is intended to be eternal. How can knowing this affect your relationship with your spouse? What does it mean to you that marriage is "a partnership with God"? How can we help children and youth prepare to be married in the temple?

- What are your thoughts and impressions as you study President Hunter's counsel about deciding whom to marry? (See section 2.)

- How can President Hunter's promises and counsel in section 3 help persons who are not married? How can we apply President Hunter's message that "this is the church of Jesus Christ, not the church of marrieds or singles"?

- What do you think President Hunter means by saying that mar-riage "is a learned behavior"? (See section 4.) When have you seen that living the principles of the gospel has brought happiness to a marriage? If you are married, consider what you might do to more fully manifest your love to your spouse.

- Ponder President Hunter's counsel in section 5. How can spouses develop greater patience with each other's imperfections? How can spouses develop greater "oneness of heart"? How can spouses show fidelity in marriage through thought, word, and deed?

Related Scriptures

Genesis 2:18, 21–24; Jacob 2:27, 31–33; 4 Nephi 1:11; D&C 42:22; Moses 3:19–24; see also "The Family: A Proclamation to the World," *Ensign,* Nov. 2010, 129

Study Help

"Your gospel study is most effective when you are taught by the Holy Ghost. Always begin your gospel study by praying for the Holy Ghost to help you learn" (*Preach My Gospel* [2004], 18).

Notes

1. In Eleanor Knowles, *Howard W. Hunter* (1994), 72.

2. In Knowles, *Howard W. Hunter*, 79–80.

3. In Don L. Searle, "President Howard W. Hunter, Acting President of the Quorum of the Twelve Apostles," *Ensign*, Apr. 1986, 24–25.

4. Gordon B. Hinckley, "A Prophet Polished and Refined," *Ensign*, Apr. 1995, 34.

5. In Knowles, *Howard W. Hunter*, 270; see also 264, 267, 269.

6. James E. Faust, "Howard W. Hunter: Man of God," *Ensign*, Apr. 1995, 28.

7. *The Teachings of Howard W. Hunter*, ed. Clyde J. Williams (1997), 137.

8. *The Teachings of Howard W. Hunter*, 130.

9. "Being a Righteous Husband and Father," *Ensign*, Nov. 1994, 49.

10. *The Teachings of Howard W. Hunter*, 130.

11. *The Teachings of Howard W. Hunter*, 132.

12. *The Teachings of Howard W. Hunter*, 130.

13. *The Teachings of Howard W. Hunter*, 131–32.

14. "Divine Creation of Women" (address given at the Australia Area Conference, Adelaide, Australia, Nov. 30, 1979), 7, Church History Library, Salt Lake City.

15. *The Teachings of Howard W. Hunter*, 141–42.

16. "The Church Is for All People," *Ensign*, June 1989, 77.

17. "Fear Not, Little Flock" (address given at Brigham Young University, Mar. 14, 1989), 4; speeches.byu.edu.

18. "The Church Is for All People," 77.

19. "The Church Is for All People," 76.

20. "The Church Is for All People," 76–77.

21. *The Teachings of Howard W. Hunter*, 129–30.

22. "The Church Is for All People," 76.

23. *The Teachings of Howard W. Hunter*, 137.

24. *The Teachings of Howard W. Hunter*, 135–36.

25. *The Teachings of Howard W. Hunter*, 137.

26. "Being a Righteous Husband and Father," 50.

27. "Being a Righteous Husband and Father," 51.

28. *The Teachings of Howard W. Hunter*, 129.

29. In Conference Report, Oct. 1967, 12.

30. *The Teachings of Howard W. Hunter*, 130–31.

Preserve and Protect the Family

*"Home may seem commonplace at times
with its routine duties, yet its success should
be the greatest of all our pursuits."*

From the Life of Howard W. Hunter

Howard W. Hunter grew up in a loving, hard-working family, where he learned from his parents that building a happy home often required sacrifice. Shortly before he was married, he made a sacrifice that he felt was necessary for the well-being of his future family.

Howard had developed a love for music at a young age. He first learned to play the piano and violin and then taught himself to play many other instruments. As a teenager, he formed his own band, Hunter's Croonaders, which played at dances and other events around Boise, Idaho. When he was 19, he and his band were hired to provide music for a two-month cruise to Asia.[1]

The year after Howard returned from the cruise, he moved to Southern California, where he continued to play with various bands. In California he also met Claire Jeffs, to whom he proposed marriage in the spring of 1931. Four days before they were married, Howard performed with his band and then packed up his instruments and never played again professionally. Providing music for dances and parties "was glamorous in some respects," he said, "and I made good money," but he felt that parts of the lifestyle were incompatible with the kind of life he envisioned for his family. "This left a void of something I had enjoyed, [but] the decision has never been regretted," he said years later.[2]

Howard and Claire were blessed with three sons, Howard William (Billy), John, and Richard. To their sorrow, Billy died as an infant. As John and Richard grew, the Hunters built a close-knit family.

The family "transcends every other interest in life."

Howard had a full schedule with his law practice and Church callings, but he and Claire made their family a priority. Long before the Church designated Monday night for family home evening, the Hunters set aside that night as a time for teaching the gospel, telling stories, playing games, and going places together. Often the boys were given assignments for the lessons.

Howard and his sons developed common interests, such as model trains. They built the trains from kits and constructed an elaborate railroad with tracks attached to sheets of plywood. He recalled, "One of our favorite pastimes was to go to the railroad yards . . . near the Alhambra station of the Southern Pacific Railroad to get ideas for our switchyards and equipment."[3]

Eventually President and Sister Hunter's family grew to include 18 grandchildren. In addition to extended visits with his children and grandchildren, many of President Hunter's visits were "on the run," during layovers when Church assignments took him through California. Because John often took his children to the airport to see their grandfather during these layovers, they sometimes referred to him as "the grandpa who lives at the airport."[4]

Teachings of Howard W. Hunter

1

The family is the most important unit in society, in the Church, and in eternity.

The family is the most important unit in time and in eternity and, as such, transcends every other interest in life.[5]

The Church has the responsibility—and the authority—to preserve and protect the family as the foundation of society. The pattern for family life, instituted from before the foundation of the world, provides for children to be born to and nurtured by a father and mother who are husband and wife, lawfully married. Parenthood is a sacred obligation and privilege, with children welcomed as a "heritage of the Lord" (Ps. 127:3).

A worried society now begins to see that the disintegration of the family brings upon the world the calamities foretold by the prophets. The world's councils and deliberations will succeed only when

221

President Hunter with his sons, grandchildren, and their families on October 2, 1994, the day after he was sustained as President of the Church

they define the family as the Lord has revealed it to be. "Except the Lord build the house, they labour in vain that build it" (Ps. 127:1).[6]

In seeking after the welfare of individuals and families, it is important to remember that the basic unit of the Church is the family. However, in focusing on the family we should remember that in the world in which we live, families are not restricted to the traditional grouping of father, mother, and children. Families in the Church today also consist of [husbands and wives] without children, single parents with children, and single individuals living alone. . . . Each of these families must receive priesthood watch care. Often those which may need the most careful watch care are those families of the non-traditional structure. Caring and committed home teachers are needed in each home. None should be neglected.[7]

2

Parents are partners in the leadership of the home and are under strict obligation to protect and love their children.

The responsibilities of parenthood are of the greatest importance. The results of our efforts will have eternal consequences for us and the boys and girls we raise. Anyone who becomes a parent is under strict obligation to protect and love [their] children and assist them to return to their Heavenly Father. All parents should understand that the Lord will not hold guiltless those who neglect these responsibilities.[8]

Fathers and mothers have a great responsibility with respect to the children which are entrusted to their care. . . . In the Book of Proverbs we find this admonition to parents:

"Train up a child in the way he should go: and when he is old, he will not depart from it." (Proverbs 22:6.)

The greatest training that can be given to a child is that which comes from the example of parents. Parents need to set the example for young people to follow. Great strength comes from the home where righteous principles are taught, where there is love and respect for each other, where prayer has been an influence in the family life, and where there is respect for those things that pertain to God.[9]

Effective family leadership . . . requires both quantity and quality time. The teaching and governance of the family must not be left . . . to society, to school, or even the Church.[10]

A man who holds the priesthood regards the family as ordained of God. Your leadership of the family is your most important and sacred responsibility. . . .

A man who holds the priesthood leads his family in Church participation so they will know the gospel and be under the protection of the covenants and ordinances. If you are to enjoy the blessings of the Lord, you must set your own homes in order. Together with your wife, you determine the spiritual climate of your home. Your first obligation is to get your own spiritual life in order through regular scriptural study and daily prayer. Secure and honor your priesthood and temple covenants; encourage your family to do the same.[11]

A man who holds the priesthood has reverence for motherhood. Mothers are given a sacred privilege to "bear the souls of men; for herein is the work of [the] Father continued, that he may be glorified" (D&C 132:63).

. . . The priesthood cannot work out its destiny, nor can God's purposes be fulfilled, without our helpmates. Mothers perform a labor the priesthood cannot do. For this gift of life, the priesthood should have love unbounded for the mothers of their children.

[Brethren,] honor your wife's unique and divinely appointed role as a mother in Israel and her special capacity to bear and nurture children. We are under divine commandment to multiply and replenish the earth and to bring up our children and grandchildren in light and truth (see Moses 2:28; D&C 93:40). You share, as a loving partner, the care of the children. Help her to manage and keep up your home. Help teach, train, and discipline your children.

You should express regularly to your wife and children your reverence and respect for her. Indeed, one of the greatest things a father can do for his children is to love their mother.[12]

A man who holds the priesthood accepts his wife as a partner in the leadership of the home and family with full knowledge of and full participation in all decisions relating thereto. Of necessity there must be in the Church and in the home a presiding officer (see D&C 107:21). By divine appointment, the responsibility to preside in the home rests upon the priesthood holder (see Moses 4:22). The Lord intended that the wife be a helpmeet for man (*meet* means equal)—that is, a companion equal and necessary in full partnership. Presiding in righteousness necessitates a shared responsibility between husband and wife; together you act with knowledge and participation in all family matters. For a man to operate independent of or without regard to the feelings and counsel of his wife in governing the family is to exercise unrighteous dominion.[13]

We encourage you, brethren, to remember that priesthood is a righteous authority only. Earn the respect and confidence of your children through your loving relationship with them. A righteous father protects his children with his time and presence in their social, educational, and spiritual activities and responsibilities. Tender expressions of love and affection toward children are as much the responsibility of the father as the mother. Tell your children you love them.[14]

--- ⟨ **3** ⟩ ---

Our homes should be places of love, prayer, and gospel teaching.

We simply must have love and integrity and strong principles in our homes. We must have an abiding commitment to marriage and children and morality. We must succeed where success counts most for the next generation.

Surely that home is strongest and most beautiful in which we find each person sensitive to the feelings of others, striving to serve others, striving to live at home the principles we demonstrate in more public settings. We need to try harder to live the gospel in our family circles. Our homes deserve our most faithful commitments. A child has the right to feel that in his home he is safe, that there he has a place of protection from the dangers and evils of the outside world. Family unity and integrity are necessary to supply this need. A child needs parents who are happy in their relationship to each other, who are working happily toward the fulfillment of ideal family living, who love their children with a sincere and unselfish love, and who are committed to the family's success.[15]

When family home evenings were first introduced as an official program of the Church, the First Presidency said, "If the Saints obey this counsel [to hold family home evenings], we promise that great blessings will result. Love at home and obedience to parents will increase. Faith will be developed in the hearts of the youth of Israel, and they will gain power to combat the evil influence and temptations which beset them." We reaffirm the promised blessings to those who faithfully hold family home evenings.

Monday evenings should be reserved for family home evening. Local leaders should ensure that Church buildings and facilities are closed, that no ward or stake activities are planned for Monday evenings, and that other interruptions to family home evenings be avoided.

The primary emphasis of family home evening should be for families to be together to study the gospel. We remind all that the Lord has admonished parents to teach their children the gospel, to pray, and to observe the Sabbath Day. The scriptures are the most important resource for teaching the gospel.[16]

Pray as families both night and morning. What great blessings come into the lives of children who hear their parents petition the Lord for their welfare. Surely children who come under the influence of such righteous parents will be better protected against the influences of the adversary.[17]

In order that parents and children may better understand each other, a plan has been adopted by the church known as the "Family Council." This council is called and conducted by the parents and attended by all members of the family. It strengthens family ties, assures children they "belong," and convinces them that the parents are interested in their problems. This family meeting teaches mutual respect for each other, eliminates selfishness, and emphasizes the Golden Rule [see Matthew 7:12] in the home and living a clean life. Family worship and prayer are taught, together with the lessons of kindness and honesty. The problem of the family usually confronts one at such close range that its real dimensions and significance are not easily appreciated, but when families are strong and united in the endeavor to serve God and keep His commandments, many of our modern-day problems disappear.[18]

[Brethren,] take seriously your responsibility to teach the gospel to your family through regular family home evening, family prayer, devotional and scripture-reading time, and other teaching moments. Give special emphasis to preparation for missionary service and temple marriage. As patriarch in the home, exercise your priesthood through performing the appropriate ordinances for your family and by giving blessings to your wife and children. Next to your own salvation, brethren, there is nothing so important to you as the salvation of your wife and children.[19]

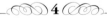

A successful parent is one who has loved, sacrificed, cared for, taught, and ministered to the needs of a child.

General Authorities have the privilege of meeting and getting acquainted with members of the Church all over the world who have consistently lived good lives and raised their families in the

"We must be prayerful and . . . let our children know of our love and concern."

influence of the gospel. These Saints have enjoyed the great blessings and comfort that can come from looking back, as parents, grandparents, and great-grandparents, over long and successful parenting efforts. Surely this is something each of us would like.

However, there are many in the Church and in the world who are living with feelings of guilt and unworthiness because some of their sons and daughters have wandered or strayed from the fold. . . .

. . . We understand that conscientious parents try their best, yet nearly all have made mistakes. One does not launch into such a project as parenthood without soon realizing that there will be many errors along the way. Surely our Heavenly Father knows, when he entrusts his spirit children into the care of young and inexperienced parents, that there will be mistakes and errors in judgment. . . .

. . . Each of us is unique. Each child is unique. Just as each of us starts at a different point in the race of life, and just as each of us has different strengths and weaknesses and talents, so each child is blessed with his own special set of characteristics. We must not

227

assume that the Lord will judge the success of one in precisely the same way as another. As parents we often assume that, if our child doesn't become an overachiever in every way, we have failed. We should be careful in our judgments. . . .

A successful parent is one who has loved, one who has sacrificed, and one who has cared for, taught, and ministered to the needs of a child. If you have done all of these and your child is still wayward or troublesome or worldly, it could well be that you are, nevertheless, a successful parent. Perhaps there are children who have come into the world that would challenge any set of parents under any set of circumstances. Likewise, perhaps there are others who would bless the lives of, and be a joy to, almost any father or mother.

My concern today is that there are parents who may be pronouncing harsh judgments upon themselves and may be allowing these feelings to destroy their lives, when in fact they have done their best and should continue in faith.[20]

A father or mother [whose child has strayed] is not alone. Our first parents knew the pain and suffering of seeing some of their children reject the teachings of eternal life. (See Moses 5:27.) Centuries later Jacob came to know of the jealousy and ill feelings of his older sons toward his beloved Joseph. (See Gen. 37:1–8.) The great prophet Alma, who had a son named Alma, prayed at length to the Lord regarding the rebellious attitude of his son and no doubt was overwhelmed with concern and worry about the dissension and the wickedness his son was causing among those who were within the Church. (See Mosiah 27:14.) Our Father in Heaven has also lost many of his spirit children to the world; he knows the feelings of your heart. . . .

. . . Don't give up hope for a boy or a girl who has strayed. Many who have appeared to be completely lost have returned. We must be prayerful and, if possible, let our children know of our love and concern. . . .

. . . Know that our Heavenly Father will recognize the love and the sacrifice, the worry and the concern, even though our great effort has been unsuccessful. Parents' hearts are ofttimes broken, yet they must realize that the ultimate responsibility lies with the child after parents have taught correct principles.

. . . Whatever the sorrow, whatever the concern, whatever the pain and anguish, look for a way to turn it to beneficial use—perhaps in helping others to avoid the same problems, or perhaps by developing a greater insight into the feelings of others who are struggling in a similar way. Surely we will have a deeper understanding of the love of our Heavenly Father when, through prayer, we finally come to know that he understands and wants us to look forward. . . .

We should never let Satan fool us into thinking that all is lost. Let us take pride in the good and right things we have done; reject and cast out of our lives those things that are wrong; look to the Lord for forgiveness, strength, and comfort; and then move onward.[21]

 **5**

Our homes should be holy places where the principles of the gospel can be lived and where the Spirit of the Lord can dwell.

We hope that you will not be overcome with discouragement in your attempts to raise your families in righteousness. Remember that the Lord has commanded this: "But my disciples shall stand in holy places, and shall not be moved" (D&C 45:32).

While some interpret this to mean the temple, which surely it does, it also represents the homes in which we live. If you will diligently work to lead your families in righteousness, encouraging and participating in daily family prayer, scripture reading, family home evening, and love and support for each other in living the teachings of the gospel, you will receive the promised blessings of the Lord in raising a righteous posterity.

In an increasingly wicked world, how essential it is that each of us "stand in holy places" and commit to be true and faithful to the teachings of the gospel of Jesus Christ.[22]

To reach success in the family, parents must have love and respect for each other. Husbands, the bearers of the priesthood, should hold their wives in the highest esteem before their children, and wives should love and support their husbands. In return, the children will have love for their parents and for each other. The home will then become a hallowed place where the principles of the gospel can be best lived and where the Spirit of the Lord can dwell. To be a successful father or a successful mother is far greater than to rise to leadership or high places in business, government, or worldly affairs. Home may seem commonplace at times with its routine duties, yet its success should be the greatest of all our pursuits in life.[23]

Suggestions for Study and Teaching

Questions

- As you review President Hunter's teachings in section 1, consider the importance of the family. What is the responsibility of the Church for the family? How can we protect and strengthen our families?

- Ponder President Hunter's teachings about parents being partners in the leadership of the home (see section 2). How can these teachings help both fathers and mothers? How can parents become united in raising their children? Consider how you might improve the "spiritual climate" of your home.

- In section 3, President Hunter gives advice for establishing a strong family. How can we build greater "family unity and integrity"? How has family home evening blessed your family? How have family scripture study and family prayer blessed your family?

- How might President Hunter's teachings in section 4 help parents of a child who has strayed? How can parents who are experiencing sorrow and pain turn that to beneficial use? What can parents, grandparents, youth leaders, and others do to help children who go astray?

- After reading section 5, reflect on President Hunter's teachings about making our homes "holy places." What are some challenges we face in doing this? How can we strive to make our homes holy places?

Related Scriptures

Exodus 20:12; Deuteronomy 6:4–7; Psalm 127:3–5; Ephesians 6:1–4; Enos 1:1–3; Mosiah 4:14–15; Alma 56:45–48; 3 Nephi 18:21; D&C 68:25–28; 93:40; 121:41–46

Teaching Help

Ask class members to work in pairs and plan how they would teach a section of the chapter in a family home evening. How could we make the teachings relevant to children and youth? Invite some of the pairs to share their plans with the class.

Notes

1. See Eleanor Knowles, *Howard W. Hunter* (1994), 46–48.

2. In Knowles, *Howard W. Hunter,* 81.

3. In Knowles, *Howard W. Hunter,* 109.

4. In Knowles, *Howard W. Hunter,* 252; see also 251.

5. "Being a Righteous Husband and Father," *Ensign,* Nov. 1994, 50.

6. "Exceeding Great and Precious Promises," *Ensign,* Nov. 1994, 9.

7. *The Teachings of Howard W. Hunter,* ed. Clyde J. Williams (1997), 144.

8. "Parents' Concern for Children," *Ensign,* Nov. 1983, 65.

9. In Conference Report, Apr. 1960, 125.

10. "Being a Righteous Husband and Father," 50.

11. "Being a Righteous Husband and Father," 50, 51.

12. "Being a Righteous Husband and Father," 50.

13. "Being a Righteous Husband and Father," 50–51.

14. "Being a Righteous Husband and Father," 51.

15. "Standing As Witnesses of God," *Ensign,* May 1990, 61–62.

16. First Presidency letter, Aug. 30, 1994 (Howard W. Hunter, Gordon B. Hinckley, and Thomas S. Monson).

17. In Mike Cannon, "'Be More Fully Converted,' Prophet Says," *Church News,* Sept. 24, 1994, 4; see also *The Teachings of Howard W. Hunter,* 37.

18. In Conference Report, Apr. 1960, 125–26.

19. "Being a Righteous Husband and Father," 51.

20. "Parents' Concern for Children," 63, 64–65.

21. "Parents' Concern for Children," 64, 65.

22. *The Teachings of Howard W. Hunter,* 155.

23. *The Teachings of Howard W. Hunter,* 156.

The Ten Commandments include the following admonition: "Thou shalt not bear false witness against thy neighbour" (Exodus 20:16).

We Believe in Being Honest

"If we would have the companionship of the Master and the Spirit of the Holy Ghost, we must be honest with ourselves, honest with God, and with our fellowmen."

From the Life of Howard W. Hunter

While waiting to take a tour of Hearst Castle in California, President and Sister Hunter and another couple drove to a small store. As they were looking around the store, "Elder Hunter went to the counter, counted out some licorice, [and] paid the clerk 10 pennies." The two couples then returned to the car and began driving back to the castle for the tour. On the way, "Elder Hunter passed the licorice around once, and then again, and then suddenly it was apparent to him that he must have miscounted, for we ended up with 11 pieces instead of the 10 he had paid for.

"He could have easily overlooked the error. After all, it was just a penny, and we were in a bit of a hurry now to make the tour. Who would know the difference or care? But he didn't even think twice about it. He wheeled the car around and headed back up the road to the store. . . . He explained the problem to a different attendant, apologized for the error, and paid the extra penny to the surprised clerk."[1]

For Howard W. Hunter, it was important to be honest in small matters as well as large ones.

He taught his sons about integrity by his example. "What I know about honesty and integrity has come in large measure by what people have told me about my father," Richard Hunter said. One time Richard went with his father to a business meeting where a complex project was being discussed. While outside for a break, Richard and one of the men were talking about the meeting. Richard said there would probably be a long wait to begin the project because it would require an immense amount of legal paperwork. The man corrected Richard, telling him the project could proceed before the paperwork was finalized because the people knew that Howard W. Hunter would do whatever he said he would do.[2]

In 1962, President Hunter addressed the youth of the Church and expressed his conviction about the importance of being honest:

"A happy life will come to each of us if we will but be honest—honest with our fathers and mothers, whether it pertains to our dating, our school work, the kids we run with, or attendance at church; honest with our bishops—taking their advice, telling them the truth about ourselves, paying our honest tithing, living a clean, pure life; honest with our schools—never cheating in any part of our activities, whether in class or on the campus; honest in paying our way, whether into games or movies, or in carrying our part of the responsibilities at a party; honest with our boyfriends and girlfriends—never taking advantage of them, never deceiving them, never leading them into temptation; honest with the Lord himself."[3]

Teachings of Howard W. Hunter

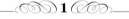

1

The Lord admonishes us to be honest.

Scripture is replete with admonitions to be honest, and commandments are myriad to the effect that we should be honest. We think of them in bold type: THOU SHALT NOT—thou shalt not steal; thou shalt not bear false witness; thou shalt not covet [see Exodus 20:15–17]. . . .

Some of the more common examples of dishonesty are these:

1. *Stealing.* I seldom read a newspaper without finding a number of reports of burglary, robbery, purse-snatching, shoplifting, car theft, and a thousand other things. Even in our chapels there are reports of petty theft.

2. *Cheating.* Newspapers carry similar accounts of fraudulent transactions in security dealings, in business transactions, cheating in investments, and other things that are called to public attention.

There are some who would cheat their way through school and some who would cheat in examinations.

3. *Violations of Word of Wisdom standards.* These are Church standards. They are not violations of the standards of the world. But you have been given the word of the Lord on this subject.

4. *Violation of traffic ordinances.* One cannot be basically honest and violate laws formulated by society and government for the welfare of other persons.[4]

"Thou shalt not bear false witness against thy neighbour" [Exodus 20:16]. Primarily this commandment has reference to false testimony in judicial proceedings, but it is extended to cover all statements which are false in fact. Any untruth which tends to injure another in his goods, person, or character is against the spirit and letter of this law. Suppression of the truth which results in the same injury is also a violation of this commandment.

"Thou shalt not covet thy neighbour's house, thou shalt not covet thy neighbour's wife, nor his manservant, nor his maidservant, nor his ox, nor his ass, nor any thing that is thy neighbour's" [Exodus 20:17]. To covet means to desire, to long for, to crave that which belongs to another person. The desire to acquire good things is not a violation, but the desire to take them away from another unlawfully is a wrong. In this respect it is well for us to understand that good or evil commences not when the act occurs, but when one sets his heart upon a thing.[5]

The Lord hates a proud look, a lying tongue, a heart that deviseth wicked imaginations, feet that be swift in running to mischief, a false witness that speaketh lies, [and] he that soweth discord [see Proverbs 6:16–19]. As Latter-day Saints, can we afford to do anything the Lord hates? How often has he spoken against dishonesty![6]

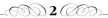

We cultivate honesty in the little, ordinary things of life.

If we are sensitive to our relationship to the Savior, we must be honest in little things as well as the big.[7]

As we strive for achievement and success, so much of our time is consumed in thought and study of the complex that we seldom take time for the simple—the simple things, the little things that are in reality the basis upon which we build and without which a strong foundation cannot exist. A structure may tower to the sky, and we may look at it with awe because of its stature and great height; yet it cannot stand unless its foundation is anchored in rock or in steel and concrete.

Character must have such a foundation. I draw your attention to the principle of honesty. Why is it so many believe in the high and lofty principles of honesty, yet so few are willing to be strictly honest?

[Many] years ago there were posters in the foyers and entries of our chapels that were entitled "Be Honest with Yourself." Most of them pertained to the little, ordinary things of life. This is where the principle of honesty is cultivated.

There are some who will admit it is morally wrong to be dishonest in big things yet believe it is excusable if those things are of lesser importance. . . .

I recall a young man who was in our stake when I served as a stake president. He traveled around with a crowd that thought it was smart to do things that were not right. On a few occasions he was caught in some minor violations. One day I got a call from the police station and was told he was being held because of a traffic violation. He had been caught speeding, as he had on a few other occasions prior to this time. Knowing the things he was doing might prevent him from going on a mission, he straightened up, and when he was 19 years of age, he received his call.

I shall never forget the talk we had when he returned. He told me that while he was in the mission field he had often thought of the trouble he had caused by the mistaken belief that the violation of little things was not important. But a great change had come into his life. He had come to the realization that there is no happiness or pleasure in violation of the law, whether it be God's law or the laws that society imposes upon us.[8]

———— ⟨⟨⟨⟩⟩⟩ 3 ⟨⟨⟨⟩⟩⟩ ————

We can serve God by being honest and fair
in our personal and business dealings.

Religion can be part of our daily work, our business, our buying and selling, building, transportation, manufacturing, our trade or profession, or of anything we do. We can serve God by honesty and fair dealing in our business transactions in the same way we do in Sunday worship. The true principles of Christianity cannot be separate and apart from business and our everyday affairs.[9]

If religion means anything to us, it should be something that motivates our lives. I don't believe religion can be relegated to a minister's sermon for an hour on Sunday and mean anything in our lives. If it doesn't enter into our individual life—our family life—our business life—and everything that we do, then religion means little to us and it becomes merely an idol to be set in a high place and worshipped only occasionally.[10]

What a great change would come over the world if we could all rely upon others as far as honesty is concerned. Men would have perfect confidence in each other in personal and business dealings. There would not be . . . distrust between labor and management. There would be integrity in public office and in government affairs, and nations would exist in peace rather than the turmoil we presently know in the world. . . .

In business dealings there are some who will take a dishonest advantage if it is placed before them. They rationalize and justify their position by saying that in business one is expected to take every offered advantage. Such transactions can amount to large sums of money, but in principle are no different than the failure to return a penny that has been overpaid by the cashier to one who notices the error. It is a form of cheating.[11]

May I suggest a definition of "honorable employment." Honorable employment is honest employment. Fair value is given and there is no defrauding, cheating, or deceit. Its product or service is of high quality, and the employer, customer, client, or patient receives more than he or she expected. Honorable employment is moral. It involves nothing that would undermine public good

Job declared, "I will not remove mine integrity from me" (Job 27:5).

or morality. For example, it does not involve traffic in liquor, illicit narcotics, or gambling. Honorable employment is useful. It provides goods or services which make the world a better place in which to live.[12]

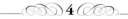

Integrity protects us from evil, helps us be successful, and will save our souls.

The temptations of evil surround us on every side. Without the protection of integrity, we are at the mercy of all kinds of sin and wrongdoings.

Job had no difficulty with these problems. He was protected by his own integrity. This is how he felt:

"All the while my breath is in me, and the spirit of God is in my nostrils;

"My lips shall not speak wickedness, nor my tongue utter deceit. . . .

"My righteousness I hold fast, and will not let it go: my heart shall not reproach me so long as I live" (Job 27:3–4, 6).

How inspiring. Because of his strength, he had no concerns for the trivial temptations before which most people fall. Job had built into his own life a strength and satisfaction that Satan himself could not crash. It is also interesting to see how God was delighted with him: "There is none like him in the earth, a perfect and an upright man, one that feareth God, and escheweth evil[,] and still he holdeth fast his integrity" (Job 2:3).

This great quality of integrity is fully available to us. If effectively used, it will solve all of our problems in government, religion, industry, and our individual lives. It would wipe out the awful scourge of crime, divorce, poverty, and misery. It would make us successful here and save our souls hereafter.

One of the greatest accomplishments of our lives is to promote an honest, earnest integrity within ourselves. This means that we become spiritually sound, intellectually sincere, morally honest, and always personally responsible to God. Integrity is that golden key which will unlock the door to almost any success.[13]

5

True joy results from being honest with ourselves, with others, and with God.

We often speak of that scriptural reference, "Men are, that they might have joy" [2 Nephi 2:25]. There is a joy that comes to one from being honest. Let me tell you how. By this means you can have the companionship of the Master and you can have the Spirit of the Holy Ghost. Violations of the code of honesty will deprive you of these two great blessings. Could you believe that one who would lie or cheat . . . could have the companionship of the Master or have the Spirit of the Holy Ghost?

. . . We should always remember that we are never alone. There is no act that is not observed; there is no word spoken that is not heard; there is no thought conceived in the mind of man that is not known to God. There is no darkness that can conceal the things we do. We must think before we act.

Do you think you can be alone when you commit a dishonest act? Do you think you can be unobserved when you cheat in an examination, even though you are the only person in the room? We must be honest with ourselves. If we would have the companionship of the Master and the Spirit of the Holy Ghost, we must be honest with ourselves, honest with God, and with our fellowmen. This results in true joy.[14]

The Lord knows our innermost thoughts [see D&C 6:16]. He knows each deed we do. We will meet him someday, and we will look him in the face. Will we be proud of our life's record?

We make that record every day. Each act, each thought is a part of it. Will we be proud of it? We will if we have done our best—if we have been honest with ourselves, with our loved ones, with our friends, with all mankind. . . .

Blessed are they who are honest. . . .

Blessed are they who are obedient to the Lord.

They are they who are free—who are happy—who can walk with their heads high. They have their self-respect. They have the respect of those who know them best.

And above all, they have the respect and blessing of our Father in Heaven. Jesus invites us to follow him. His paths are straight and clean and upright and honest. Let us follow him into the abundant life of happiness. It is the only way.[15]

Suggestions for Study and Teaching

Questions
- Review the examples of dishonesty that President Hunter identifies in section 1. What are some consequences of those dishonest practices? What can those consequences teach us about why the Lord places so much emphasis on being honest?

- Ponder President Hunter's teachings about being honest in little things and being honest with ourselves (see section 2). Why do we need to be honest in "little things"? What does it mean to be honest with ourselves? How can we overcome temptations to excuse even seemingly small acts of dishonesty?

- President Hunter emphasizes the need to make religion part of everything we do in our daily lives (see section 3). How can we better live the teachings in this section? How can we effectively teach honesty in our homes?

- In section 4, President Hunter mentions several blessings that come from living with integrity. How does a person develop integrity? How have you been blessed when you have lived true to the Lord's standards?

- How does being honest bring us joy? (See section 5.) Why is being honest necessary for us to have the companionship of the Holy Ghost? How does being honest make us free?

Related Scriptures

Job 27:5; 31:5–6; Psalm 15; Proverbs 20:7; Alma 53:20–21; D&C 10:25–28; 42:20–21, 27; 51:9; 124:15; 136:20, 25–26; Articles of Faith 1:13

Study Help

As you read, "underline and mark words or phrases so that you distinguish between ideas in a single [passage]. . . . In the margins write scripture references that clarify the passages you are studying" (*Preach My Gospel* [2004], 23).

Notes

1. Doug Brinley, "President Hunter Taught Value of a Penny's Worth of Integrity," *Church News,* Dec. 3, 1994, 11; see also "Loved by All Who Knew Him: Stories from Members," *Ensign,* Apr. 1995, 19–20.

2. See Don L. Searle, "President Howard W. Hunter, Acting President of the Quorum of the Twelve Apostles," *Ensign,* Apr. 1986, 24.

3. "We Believe in Being Honest" (transcription of an address given in the Youth Fireside Series, Apr. 10, 1962), 8–9, Church History Library, Salt Lake City; punctuation adapted.

4. "Basic Concepts of Honesty," *New Era,* Feb. 1978, 4–5.

5. In Conference Report, Apr. 1965, 57–58; see also "And God Spake All These Words," *Improvement Era,* June 1965, 511–12.

6. "We Believe in Being Honest," 8.

7. "Basic Concepts of Honesty," 5.

8. "Basic Concepts of Honesty," 4–5.

9. In Conference Report, Oct. 1961, 108.

10. *The Teachings of Howard W. Hunter,* ed. Clyde J. Williams (1997), 261–62.

11. *The Teachings of Howard W. Hunter,* 90–91.

12. "Prepare for Honorable Employment," *Ensign,* Nov. 1975, 122–23.

13. *The Teachings of Howard W. Hunter,* 92.

14. "Basic Concepts of Honesty," 5.

15. *The Teachings of Howard W. Hunter,* 88.

*One way we can show our "total commitment" and
"complete devotion" is to serve those in need.*

Our Commitment to God

*"A successful life . . . requires commitment—
whole-souled, deeply held, eternally cherished
commitment to the principles we know to be
true in the commandments God has given."*

From the Life of Howard W. Hunter

When Howard W. Hunter was called to be a member of the Quorum of the Twelve, he declared, "I accept, without reservation, the call . . . made of me, and I am willing to devote my life and all that I have to this service."[1]

Elder Hunter lived true to his commitment. After he was ordained an Apostle, he returned to California to complete Church and business obligations and to begin preparing to relocate to Salt Lake City. It was difficult for Elder and Sister Hunter to leave their family and friends in California—and for Elder Hunter to leave his law practice. As he concluded his career as an attorney, he wrote:

"Today I finished most of my work at the office. Nearly all of the pending matters are completed. I was alone in the office today with the realization that my practice of law was now at an end. I made notes on a number of files and left them on the desk. . . . I had a sick feeling as I left the office. I have enjoyed the practice of law and it has been my life for the last number of years, but in spite of this I am pleased and happy to respond to the great call which has come to me in the Church."[2]

Elder Hunter knew from personal experience that "submitting to our Father's will is not always easy."[3] Nevertheless, he knew the importance of being fully committed to God. Concerning that commitment, he wrote: "Most people do not understand why persons of our religious faith respond to calls made to serve or the commitment we make to give our all. I have thoroughly enjoyed the practice of law, but this call that has come to me will far overshadow the pursuit of the profession or monetary gain."[4]

Teachings of Howard W. Hunter

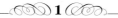 **1**

Our Father in Heaven requires our total commitment, not just a contribution.

As I think of the blessings God has given us and the many beauties of the gospel of Jesus Christ, I am aware that along the way we are asked to make certain contributions in return, contributions of time or of money or of other resources. These are all valued and all necessary, but they do not constitute our full offering to God. Ultimately, what our Father in Heaven will require of us is more than a contribution; it is a total commitment, a complete devotion, all that we are and all that we can be.

Please understand that I do not speak only of a commitment to the Church and its activities, although that always needs to be strengthened. No, I speak more specifically of a commitment that is shown in our individual behavior, in our personal integrity, in our loyalty to home and family and community, as well as to the Church. . . .

Let me recall briefly just one of those magnificent examples from scripture where three relatively young people stood by their principles and held to their integrity even though it seemed apparent that to do so would cost them their lives.

Approximately 586 years before Christ, Nebuchadnezzar, king of Babylon, marched against the city of Jerusalem and conquered it. So impressed was he with the qualities and learning of the children of Israel that he had several of them brought to the king's court [in Babylon].

Trouble came to the Israelites the day Nebuchadnezzar made a golden idol and commanded all in the province of Babylon to worship it, a command that the three young Israelites—Shadrach, Meshach, and Abed-nego—quietly refused. The king was full of "rage and fury" and demanded that they be brought before him.

(Dan. 3:13.) He informed them that if they did not fall down before the golden image at the appointed moment, "ye shall be cast the same hour into the midst of a burning fiery furnace." Then with some self-satisfaction he asked, "And who is that God that shall deliver you out of my hands?" [Dan. 3:15.]

The three young men responded courteously but without hesitation:

"If it be so," they said, "[that you threaten us with death,] our God whom we serve is able to deliver us from the burning fiery furnace, and he will deliver us out of thine hand, O king.

"But if not [if for whatever reason he chooses not to save us from the fire], be it known unto thee, O king, that we will not serve thy gods, nor worship the golden image which thou hast set up." [Dan. 3:17–18.]

Of course Nebuchadnezzar was more furious than ever and ordered that one of the furnaces be heated to seven times its normal temperature. Then he commanded that these three valiant young men be thrown fully clothed into the midst of the fire. Indeed, the king was so insistent and the flame so hot that the soldiers who carried Shadrach, Meshach, and Abed-nego fell dead from the heat of the furnace as they cast their captives forward.

Then transpired one of those great miracles to which the faithful are entitled according to the will of God. These three young men stood and walked about calmly in the midst of the furnace and were not burned. Indeed, when they were later called out of the furnace by the astonished king himself, their clothing was untarnished, their skin was free from any burn, not a hair of their head was singed. Not even the smell of smoke had come upon these courageous, committed young men.

"Blessed be the God of Shadrach, Meshach, and Abed-nego," said the king, "who hath . . . delivered his servants that trusted in him, . . . [who] yielded their bodies, that they might not serve nor worship any god, except their own God.

". . . Then the king promoted Shadrach, Meshach, and Abed-nego, in the province of Babylon." (Dan. 3:28, 30.)

The ability to stand by one's principles, to live with integrity and faith according to one's belief—that is what matters, that is <u>the difference between a contribution and a commitment</u>. That devotion to true principle—in our individual lives, in our homes and families, and in all places that we meet and influence other people—that devotion is what God is ultimately requesting of us. . . .

A successful life, the good life, the righteous Christian life requires something more than a contribution, though every contribution is valuable. Ultimately it requires commitment—whole-souled, deeply held, eternally cherished commitment to the principles we know to be true in the commandments God has given. . . .

If we will be true and faithful to our principles, committed to a life of honesty and integrity, then no king or contest or fiery furnace will be able to compromise us. For the success of the kingdom of God on earth, may we stand as witnesses for him "at all times and in all things, and in all places that [we] may be in, even until death." (Mosiah 18:9.)[5]

 **2**

Be committed to obeying the Lord regardless of what others decide to do.

When Joshua was directed to destroy the city of Jericho that lay before [the tribes of Israel], the great walls of the city stood as an imposing and physically impossible barrier to Israel's success—or at least so it seemed. Not knowing the means, but assured as to the end, Joshua carried out the instructions he had been given by a messenger of the Lord. His commitment was to complete obedience. His concern was to do precisely as he was instructed, that the promise of the Lord would be fulfilled. The instructions no doubt seemed strange, but his faith in the outcome urged him on. The result, of course, was another in a long series of miracles experienced by the Israelites as they were led over many years by Moses, by Joshua, and by many other prophets who were committed to follow the commandments and the directives of the Lord.

As Joshua and his people approached Jericho, the instructions of the Lord were followed precisely, and according to the scriptural account, "the wall fell down flat, so that the people went up into the city, every man straight before him, and they took the city." (Josh. 6:20.)

The record states that after Israel had rested from the wars with their enemies, Joshua, who was now very old, called all Israel together. In his farewell address he reminded them they had been victorious because God had fought for them, but if they now ceased to serve the Lord and keep his law they would be destroyed. . . .

This great military and spiritual leader then urged a commitment, and made one himself and for his family: "Choose you this day whom ye will serve; . . . but as for me and my house, we will serve the Lord." (Josh. 24:15.)

Here was a great statement of full commitment of a man to God; of a prophet to the desires of the Lord; of Joshua the man to his God, who had many times previously blessed his obedience. He was telling the Israelites that regardless of how they decided, he would do what he knew was right. He was saying that his decision to serve the Lord was independent of whatever they decided; that their actions would not affect his; that his commitment to do the Lord's will would not be altered by anything they or anyone else would do. Joshua was firmly in control of his actions and had his eyes fixed on the commandments of the Lord. He was committed to obedience.[6]

 **3**

Decide now to choose the path of strict obedience.

After having come to an understanding of the law of the gospel and the will of the Lord by reading and studying the scriptures and the words of the prophets, then comes the further understanding of the reason why obedience is often referred to as the first law of heaven and why obedience is necessary to be saved. This brings us to the supreme test. Are we willing to become totally obedient to God's law? There comes a time in our lives when a definite decision must be made.[7]

Surely the Lord loves, more than anything else, an unwavering determination to obey his counsel. Surely the experiences of the great prophets of the Old Testament have been recorded to help

*"How pleased the Lord must have been when Abraham . . . did as
he was instructed, without question and without wavering."*

us understand the importance of choosing the path of strict obedience. How pleased the Lord must have been when Abraham, after
receiving direction to sacrifice his only son, Isaac, did as he was instructed, without question and without wavering. The record states
that God said unto Abraham:

"Take now thy son, thine only son Isaac, whom thou lovest, and
get thee into the land of Moriah; and offer him there for a burnt
offering upon one of the mountains which I will tell thee of." (Gen.
22:2.)

The next verse simply states:

"And Abraham rose up early in the morning . . . and took . . .
Isaac his son . . . and went unto the place of which God had told
him." (Gen. 22:3.)

Years later, when Rebekah was asked if she would go with the
servant of Abraham to become Isaac's wife, and no doubt knowing

that the servant's mission had the blessing of the Lord, she simply said, "I will go." (Gen. 24:58.)

A generation after that, when Jacob was instructed to return to the land of Canaan, which meant leaving all for which he had worked many years, he called Rachel and Leah into the field where his flock was and explained what the Lord had said. The reply of Rachel [and Leah] was simple and straightforward and indicative of [their] commitment: "Whatsoever God hath said unto thee, do." (Gen. 31:16.)

We have, then, examples from the scriptures of how we should consider and evaluate the commandments of the Lord. If we choose to react like Joshua, and Abraham, and Rebekah, and Rachel [and Leah], our response will be, simply, to go and do the thing that the Lord has commanded.

There is good reason to make our decision *now* to serve the Lord. On this Sunday morning [of general conference], when the complications and temptations of life are somewhat removed, and when we have the time and more of an inclination to take an eternal perspective, we can more clearly evaluate what will bring us the greatest happiness in life. We should decide now, in the light of the morning, how we will act when the darkness of night and when the storms of temptation arrive.

I pray that we will have the strength to decide now to do what we ought to do. I pray that we will decide now to serve the Lord.[8]

Belief alone is not sufficient; we also need to do Heavenly Father's will.

When speaking to the multitudes, the Master said: "Not every one that saith unto me, Lord, Lord, shall enter into the kingdom of heaven; but he that doeth the will of my Father which is in heaven." (Matt. 7:21.)

As I listen to these words, it seems to me that the Lord is saying, "Just because a person may acknowledge my authority or have a belief in my divine nature, or merely express faith in my teachings or the atoning sacrifice I made, does not mean he shall enter into the kingdom of heaven or attain a higher degree of exaltation." By implication he is saying, "Belief alone is not sufficient." Then he expressly adds, ". . . but he that doeth the will of my Father," that is, he that works and prunes the vineyard that it may bring forth good fruit. . . .

All nature, which is God's domain, seems to portray this same principle. The bee that will not "doeth" will soon be driven from the hive. As I watch the busy ants on the trail and around the ant pile, I am impressed by the fact that they are doers and not just believers. Clucking doesn't produce any seeds for the hen; she must scratch. A stagnant pool, green with algae and the scum of inactivity, is the breeding place of the diseases of the swamp, but the clear mountain stream dashing over the rocks as it winds its way down the canyon is an invitation to drink.

The words of the Master regarding the house without a foundation say to me that a man cannot have a shallow and reckless notion that he is sufficient to himself and can build his own life on any basis that happens to be easy and agreeable [see Matthew 7:26–27]. As long as the weather is fair, his foolishness may not be evident; but one day there will come the floods, the muddy waters of some sudden passion, the rushing current of unforeseen temptation. If his character has no sure foundation in more than just lip service, his whole moral structure may collapse.[9]

James said, "Pure religion and undefiled before God and the Father is this, To visit the fatherless and widows in their affliction, and to keep himself unspotted from the world" (James 1:27).

In other words, religion is more than a knowledge of God or a confession of faith, and it is more than theology. Religion is the doing of the word of God. It is being our brother's keeper, among other things. . . .

We can be religious in worship on the Sabbath day, and we can be religious in our duties on the other six days of the week. . . . [How] important it must be that all of our thoughts, the words we speak, our acts, conduct, dealings with neighbors, business trans-actions, and all of our everyday affairs be in harmony with our religious beliefs. In the words of Paul, "Whatsoever ye do, do all to the glory of God" (1 Corinthians 10:31). Can we therefore eliminate religion from our weekday affairs and relegate it to the Sabbath day only? Surely not, if we follow Paul's admonition.[10]

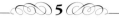

"Living members" strive to have a total commitment.

The Lord revealed in the preface to the Doctrine and Covenants that this is the "only true and living church upon the face of the whole earth." Then he added, "with which I, the Lord, am well pleased, speaking unto the church collectively and not individually" (D&C 1:30). This should raise a question in our minds of eternal significance: We know that this is the true and living church institutionally, but am I a true and living member individually?

. . . When I ask, "Am I a true and living member?" my question is, am I deeply and fully dedicated to keeping the covenants I have made with the Lord? Am I totally committed to live the gospel and be a doer of the word and not a hearer only? Do I live my religion? Will I remain true? Do I stand firm against Satan's temptations? . . .

To answer affirmatively the question, "Am I a living member?" confirms our commitment. It means that we now and always will love God and our neighbors as ourselves. It means our actions will reflect who we are and what we believe. It means that we are every day Christians, walking as Christ would have us walk.

Living members are those who strive to have a total commitment. . . .

Living members recognize their duty to press forward. They are baptized as a first step of their living journey. It is a sign to God, to angels, and to heaven that they will follow God's will. . . .

Living members give heed to the Spirit, which quickens the inner life. They constantly seek its direction. They pray for strength and overcome difficulties. Their hearts are not set upon the things of this world but upon the infinite. Spiritual renewal is not sacrificed for physical gratification.

Living members put Christ first in their lives, knowing from what source their lives and progress come. There is a tendency for man to put himself in the center of the universe and expect others to conform to his wants and needs and desires. Yet nature does not honor that erroneous assumption. The central role in life belongs to God. Instead of asking him to do our bidding, we should seek to bring ourselves into harmony with his will, and thus continue our progress as a living member. . . .

Living members, once they are converted, fulfill the commandment to strengthen their brothers and sisters [see Luke 22:32]. They are anxious to share their joy with others, and they never lose this desire. . . .

Living members recognize the need to put into action their beliefs. These Saints are anxiously engaged in bringing to pass many good and noble works of their own free will and accord [see D&C 58:27]. . . .

Living members love one another. They visit the fatherless and the widows in their afflictions. They keep themselves unspotted from the world [see James 1:27]. . . .

We have a firm belief in the statement that this is the true and living church of the true and living God. The question we have yet to answer is: Am I dedicated and committed, a true and living member?

May we stand firm and be true and living members of the Church and receive the promised reward to be among those spoken of in the Doctrine and Covenants "who are come unto Mount Zion, and unto the city of the living God, the heavenly place, the holiest of all" (D&C 76:66).[11]

Suggestions for Study and Teaching

Questions
- Review President Hunter's teachings about the difference between a "contribution" and "total commitment" (section 1). What difference does it make in our lives when we are totally committed to God? What applications might the story of Shadrach, Meshach, and Abednego have for us?

- Review President Hunter's account of Joshua in section 2. What can you learn from this account about being fully committed to

God? How can we develop a commitment to obey God regardless of what others do? How can we help children and youth develop this commitment?

- What are your impressions as you review the scripture stories in section 3? What other scriptural examples of obedience have influenced you? Why do you think "the Lord loves . . . an unwavering determination to obey his counsel"?

- Ponder President Hunter's teachings in section 4. Why is belief alone "not sufficient"? How does doing Heavenly Father's will help us prepare for times of trouble? How can we apply President Hunter's teachings about living our religion?

- Review each of President Hunter's descriptions of a "living member" in section 5. How do we develop these qualities of "living members"? Consider how you could be a better "true and living member" of the Church.

Related Scriptures

1 Samuel 15:22–23; Psalm 1:1–3; James 2:14–26; 2 Nephi 32:9; Omni 1:26; Mosiah 2:41; Alma 37:35–37; 3 Nephi 18:15, 18–20; D&C 58:26–29; 97:8; Abraham 3:24–26

Teaching Help

Read together several quotations from the chapter. After reading each quotation, ask class members to share examples from the scriptures and from their own experiences that relate to the teachings in the quotation.

Notes

1. In Conference Report, Oct. 1959, 121.
2. In Eleanor Knowles, *Howard W. Hunter* (1994), 153.
3. "The Opening and Closing of Doors," *Ensign,* Nov. 1987, 54.
4. In Knowles, *Howard W. Hunter,* 151.
5. "Standing As Witnesses of God," *Ensign,* May 1990, 60–62.
6. "Commitment to God," *Ensign,* Nov. 1982, 57–58.
7. "Obedience" (address given at the Hawaii Area Conference, June 18, 1978), 5, Church History Library, Salt Lake City.
8. "Commitment to God," 58.
9. In Conference Report, Oct. 1967, 11, 12–13.
10. *The Teachings of Howard W. Hunter,* ed. Clyde J. Williams (1997), 111–12.
11. "Am I a 'Living' Member?" *Ensign,* May 1987, 16–18.

Jesus Christ "taught lessons of love and repeatedly demonstrated unselfish service to others. All were recipients of his love."

Walking the Savior's Path of Charity

"The touchstone of compassion is a measure of our discipleship; it is a measure of our love for God and for one another."

From the Life of Howard W. Hunter

President Howard W. Hunter taught that the Savior "gave us His love, His service, and His life. . . . We should strive to give as He gave."[1] Most particularly, President Hunter encouraged Church members to follow the Savior's example of charity in their everyday lives.

Acts of charity were a defining aspect of Howard W. Hunter's career in the legal profession. A fellow attorney explained:

"He spent a lot of his time giving [free] legal service . . . because he just did not have the heart to send a bill. . . . He was perceived as a friend, guide, counselor, and a professional who was much more concerned about seeing that people got the help they needed than that he got compensated for it."[2]

Charity was also a hallmark of President Hunter's Church service. A woman who said he was her most influential teacher explained some of the reasons:

"I have always observed that this man loved others by putting them in high priority, by listening to understand, and by sharing his experiences with others, which was one of his great enjoyments. He has taught me to understand the importance of these virtues and to feel the joy in practicing them."[3]

Another woman from President Hunter's stake in California paid this tribute:

"President Howard W. Hunter was our stake president years ago when our family lived in the Pasadena Stake. My father had died, leaving my mother to rear my older sister and me. Although we were not a prominent family in the stake, which covered a huge geographical area, President Hunter still knew us personally.

"My most significant memory of him is one that contributed to my sense of self-worth. After each stake conference, we would wait in line to shake hands with him. He always took my mother's hand and said, 'How are you, Sister Sessions, and how are Betty and Carolyn?' It gave me a thrill to hear him call us by name. I knew he knew us and cared about our well-being. The memory still warms my heart."[4]

President Hunter once said, "I feel ours is the mission to serve and to save, to build and to exalt."[5] Comments from his Brethren in the Twelve show how well he fulfilled that mission. "He has a way of making people feel at ease," reported one; "he doesn't dominate them. He is a good listener." Another said, "When you travel with him, he's always watching to be sure that everybody is taken care of and that nobody is being inconvenienced or put out." Still another reported, "He is concerned with and sensitive to others. He has charity and a forgiving heart. He is a student of the gospel, of mankind, of human nature."[6]

Teachings of Howard W. Hunter

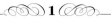 1

The two great commandments are the Lord's touchstone for our discipleship.

In ancient times, one test of the purity of gold was performed with a smooth, black, siliceous stone called a touchstone. When rubbed across the touchstone, the gold produced a streak or mark on its surface. The goldsmith matched this mark to a color on his chart of graded colors. The mark was redder as the amount of copper or alloy increased or yellower as the percentage of gold increased. This process showed quite accurately the purity of the gold.

The touchstone method of testing the purity of gold was quick and was satisfactory for most practical purposes. But the goldsmith who still questioned the purity completed a more accurate test by using a process that involved fire.

I suggest to you that the Lord has prepared a touchstone for you and me, an outward measurement of inward discipleship that marks our faithfulness and will survive the fires yet to come.

On one occasion while Jesus was teaching the people, a certain lawyer approached him and posed this question: "Master, what shall I do to inherit eternal life?"

Jesus, the master teacher, replied to the man, who obviously was well-versed in the law, with a counter-question, "What is written in the law? how readest thou?"

The man replied with resolute summary the two great commandments: "Thou shalt love the Lord thy God with all thy heart, and with all thy soul, and with all thy strength, and with all thy mind; and thy neighbour as thyself."

With approval Christ responded, "This do, and thou shalt live" (Luke 10:25–28).

Eternal life, God's life, the life we are seeking, is rooted in two commandments. The scriptures say that "on these two commandments hang all the law and the prophets" (Matthew 22:40). Love God and love your neighbor. The two work together; they are inseparable. In the highest sense they may be considered as synonymous. And they are commandments that each of us can live.

The answer of Jesus to the lawyer might be considered as the Lord's touchstone. He said on another occasion, "Inasmuch as ye have done it unto one of the least of these my brethren, ye have done it unto me" (Matthew 25:40). He will measure our devotion to him by how we love and serve our fellowmen. What kind of mark are we leaving on the Lord's touchstone? Are we truly good neighbors? Does the test show us to be 24-karat gold, or can the trace of fool's gold be detected?[7]

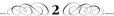

The Savior taught us to love everyone, including those who may be difficult to love.

As if excusing himself for asking such a simple question of the Master, the lawyer sought to justify himself by further inquiring, "And who is my neighbour?" (Luke 10:29).

We all ought to be eternally grateful for that question, for in the Savior's reply came one of his richest and most appreciated parables, one that each of us has read and heard over and over again:

"A certain man went down from Jerusalem to Jericho, and fell among thieves, which stripped him of his raiment, and wounded him, and departed, leaving him half dead.

"And by chance there came down a certain priest that way: and when he saw him, he passed by on the other side.

"And likewise a Levite, when he was at the place, came and looked on him, and passed by on the other side.

"But a certain Samaritan, as he journeyed, came where he was: and when he saw him, he had compassion on him,

"And went to him, and bound up his wounds, pouring in oil and wine, and set him on his own beast, and brought him to an inn, and took care of him.

"And on the morrow when he departed, he took out two pence, and gave them to the host, and said unto him, Take care of him; and whatsoever thou spendest more, when I come again, I will repay thee" (Luke 10:30–35).

Then Jesus asked the lawyer, "Which now of these three, thinkest thou, was neighbour unto him that fell among the thieves?" (Luke 10:36). There the Master holds out the touchstone of Christianity. He asks that our mark be measured on it.

Both the priest and the Levite in Christ's parable should have remembered the requirements of the law: "Thou shalt not see thy brother's ass or his ox fall down by the way, and hide thyself from them: thou shalt surely help him to lift them up again" (Deuteronomy 22:4). And if an ox, how much more should one be willing to help a brother in need. But as Elder James E. Talmage wrote,

"Excuses [not to do so] are easy to find; they spring up as readily and plentifully as weeds by the wayside" (*Jesus the Christ,* 3d ed., Salt Lake City: The Church of Jesus Christ of Latter-day Saints, 1916, p. 431).

The Samaritan gave us an example of pure Christian love. He had compassion; he went to the man who had been injured by the thieves and bound up his wounds. He took him to an inn, cared for him, paid his expenses, and offered more if needed for his care. This is a story of the love of a neighbor for his neighbor.

An old axiom states that a man "all wrapped up in himself makes a small bundle." Love has a certain way of making a small bundle large. The key is to love our neighbor, including the neighbor that is difficult to love. We need to remember that though we make our friends, God has made our neighbors—everywhere. Love should have no boundary; we should have no narrow loyalties. Christ said, "For if ye love them which love you, what reward have ye? do not even the publicans the same?" (Matthew 5:46).[8]

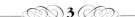

We should love and serve others in their affliction.

Joseph Smith wrote a letter to the Saints, published in the *Messenger and Advocate,* on the subject of loving one another to be justified before God. He wrote:

"Dear Brethren:—It is a duty which every Saint ought to render to his brethren freely—to always love them, and ever succor them. To be justified before God we must love one another: we must overcome evil; we must visit the fatherless and the widow in their affliction, and we must keep ourselves unspotted from the world: for such virtues flow from the great fountain of pure religion. Strengthening our faith by adding every good quality that adorns the children of the blessed Jesus, we can pray in the season of prayer; we can love our neighbor as ourselves, and be faithful in tribulation, knowing that the reward of such is greater in the kingdom of heaven. What a consolation! What a joy! Let me live the life of the righteous, and let my reward be like this!" (*History of the Church,* 2:229).

*The Lord "will measure our devotion to him by
how we love and serve our fellowmen."*

These two virtues, love and service, are required of us if we are to be good neighbors and find peace in our lives. Surely they were in the heart of Elder Willard Richards. While in Carthage Jail on the afternoon of the martyrdom of Joseph and Hyrum, the jailer suggested that they would be safer in the cells. Joseph turned to Elder Richards and asked, "If we go into the cell will you go with us?"

Elder Richards' reply was one of love: "Brother Joseph, you did not ask me to cross the river with you—you did not ask me to come to Carthage—you did not ask me to come to jail with you—and do you think I would forsake you now? But I will tell you what I will do; if you are condemned to be hung for 'treason,' I will be hung in your stead, and you shall go free."

It must have been with considerable emotion and feeling that Joseph replied, "But you cannot."

To which Elder Richards firmly answered, "I will" (see B. H. Roberts, *A Comprehensive History of the Church,* 2:283).

Elder Richards' test was perhaps greater than most of us will face: the test of fire rather than of the touchstone. But if we were asked to do so, could we lay down our lives for our families? our friends? our neighbors?

The touchstone of compassion is a measure of our discipleship; it is a measure of our love for God and for one another. Will we leave a mark of pure gold or, like the priest and the Levite, pass by on the other side?[9]

We need to walk more resolutely the path of charity that Jesus has shown.

In an important message to the Latter-day Saints in Nauvoo just one year before his tragic and untimely martyrdom, the Prophet Joseph Smith said:

"If we would secure and cultivate the love of others, we must love others, even our enemies as well as friends. . . . Christians should cease wrangling and contending with each other, and cultivate the principles of union and friendship in their midst." (*History of the Church*, 5:498–99.)

That is magnificent counsel today, even as it was [then]. The world in which we live, whether close to home or far away, needs the gospel of Jesus Christ. It provides the only way the world will ever know peace. We need to be kinder with one another, more gentle and forgiving. We need to be slower to anger and more prompt to help. We need to extend the hand of friendship and resist the hand of retribution. In short, we need to love one another with the pure love of Christ, with genuine charity and compassion and, if necessary, shared suffering, for that is the way God loves us.

In our worship services, we often sing a lovely hymn with text written by Susan Evans McCloud. May I recall a few lines of that hymn for you?

Savior, may I learn to love thee,
Walk the path that thou hast shown,
Pause to help and lift another,
Finding strength beyond my own. . . .

Who am I to judge another
When I walk imperfectly?

In the quiet heart is hidden
Sorrow that the eye can't see. . . .

I would be my brother's keeper;
I would learn the healer's art.
To the wounded and the weary
I would show a gentle heart.
I would be my brother's keeper—
Lord, I would follow thee.
(*Hymns,* 1985, no. 220.)

We need to walk more resolutely and more charitably the path that Jesus has shown. We need to "pause to help and lift another" and surely we will find "strength beyond [our] own." If we would do more to learn "the healer's art," there would be untold chances to use it, to touch the "wounded and the weary" and show to all "a gentle[r] heart." Yes, Lord, we should follow thee.[10]

Charity is the pure love of Christ and will not fail.

"A new commandment I give unto you," [Jesus] said, "That ye love one another; . . . By this shall all men know that ye are my disciples, if ye have love one to another." (John 13:34–35.) This love that we should have for our brothers and sisters in the human family, and that Christ has for every one of us, is called charity or "the pure love of Christ." (Moro. 7:47.) It is the love that prompted the suffering and sacrifice of Christ's atonement. It is the highest pinnacle the human soul can reach and the deepest expression of the human heart.

. . . Charity encompasses all other godly virtues. It distinguishes both the beginning and the end of the plan of salvation. When all else fails, charity—Christ's love—will *not* fail. It is the greatest of all divine attributes.

Out of the abundance of his heart, Jesus spoke to the poor, the downtrodden, the widows, the little children; to farmers and fishermen, and those who tended goats and sheep; to strangers and foreigners, the rich, the politically powerful, as well as the unfriendly Pharisees and scribes. He ministered to the poor, the hungry, the deprived, the sick. He blessed the lame, the blind, the deaf, and other people with physical disabilities. He drove out the demons and evil spirits that had caused mental or emotional illness. He purified those who were burdened with sin. He taught lessons of love and repeatedly demonstrated unselfish service to others. All were recipients of his love. All were "privileged the one like unto the other, and none [were] forbidden." (2 Ne. 26:28.) These are all expressions and examples of his unbounded charity.

The world in which we live would benefit greatly if men and women everywhere would exercise the pure love of Christ, which is kind, meek, and lowly. It is without envy or pride. It is selfless because it seeks nothing in return. It does not countenance evil or ill will, nor rejoice in iniquity; it has no place for bigotry, hatred, or violence. It refuses to condone ridicule, vulgarity, abuse, or ostracism. It encourages diverse people to live together in Christian love regardless of religious belief, race, nationality, financial standing, education, or culture.

The Savior has commanded us to love one another as he has loved us; to clothe ourselves "with the bond of charity" (D&C 88:125), as he so clothed himself. We are called upon to purify our inner feelings, to change our hearts, to make our outward actions and appearance conform to what we say we believe and feel inside. We are to be true disciples of Christ.[11]

 **6**

Loving others is "a more excellent way."

As a young man, Brother Vern Crowley said he learned something of the crucial lesson the Prophet Joseph had taught the early Saints in Nauvoo when he told them to "love others, even our enemies as well as friends." This is a good lesson for each of us.

After his father became ill, Vern Crowley took responsibility for running the family wrecking yard although he was only fifteen years of age. Some customers occasionally took unfair advantage of the young man, and parts were disappearing from the lot overnight. Vern was angry and vowed to catch someone and make an example of him. Vengeance would be his.

Just after his father had started to recover from his illness, Vern was making his rounds of the yard one night at closing time. It was nearly dark. In a distant corner of the property, he caught sight of someone carrying a large piece of machinery toward the back fence. He ran like a champion athlete and caught the young thief. His first thought was to take out his frustrations with his fists and then drag the boy to the front office and call the police. His heart was full of anger and vengeance. He had caught his thief, and he intended to get his just dues.

Out of nowhere, Vern's father came along, put his weak and infirm hand on his son's shoulder, and said, "I see you're a bit upset, Vern. Can I handle this?" He then walked over to the young would-be thief and put his arm around his shoulder, looked him in the eye for a moment, and said, "Son, tell me, why are you doing this? Why were you trying to steal that transmission?" Then Mr. Crowley started walking toward the office with his arm around the boy, asking questions about the young man's car problems as they walked. By the time they had arrived at the office, the father said, "Well, I think your clutch is gone and that's causing your problem."

In the meantime, Vern was fuming. "Who cares about his clutch?" he thought. "Let's call the police and get this over with." But his father just kept talking. "Vern, get him a clutch. Get him a throwout bearing, too. And get him a pressure plate. That should take care of it." The father handed all of the parts to the young man who had attempted robbery and said, "Take these. And here's the transmission, too. You don't have to steal, young man. Just ask for it. There's a way out of every problem. People are willing to help."

Brother Vern Crowley said he learned an everlasting lesson in love that day. The young man came back to the lot often. Voluntarily, month by month, he paid for all of the parts Vic Crowley had given him, including the transmission. During those visits, he asked Vern why his dad was the way he was and why he did what he did. Vern told him something of their Latter-day Saint beliefs and how much his father loved the Lord and loved people. Eventually the would-be thief was baptized. Vern later said, "It's hard now to describe the feelings I had and what I went through in that experience. I, too, was young. I had caught my crook. I was going to extract the utmost penalty. But my father taught me a different way."

A different way? A better way? A higher way? A more excellent way? Oh, how the world could benefit from such a magnificent lesson. As Moroni declares:

"Wherefore, whoso believeth in God might with surety hope for a better world. . . .

"In the gift of his Son hath God prepared a more excellent way." (Ether 12:4, 11.)[12]

Suggestions for Study and Teaching

Questions

- What does President Hunter mean by referring to the two great commandments as "the Lord's touchstone"? (See section 1.) Reflect on how you would answer the questions President Hunter asks at the end of section 1.

- Review President Hunter's account of the parable of the good Samaritan (see section 2). What can we learn from these teachings about loving our neighbors? How can we increase our love for those who may be "difficult to love"?

- In section 3, President Hunter teaches that we should love and serve others in their times of affliction. How have you been blessed by someone who has loved and served you in a time of need?

- Ponder President Hunter's teachings about following the Savior's example of charity (see section 4). How can we develop greater love for others? What are some ways we can more actively show our love?

- In section 5, President Hunter reviews some of the ways that Christ has shown His love. When have you felt the Savior's love in your life? What blessings have come as you have "exercise[d] the pure love of Christ"?

- What can we learn from President Hunter's telling of the story of Vern Crowley? (See section 6.) How can we replace feelings of "anger and vengeance" with feelings of charity? What experiences have helped you learn that charity is "a more excellent way"?

Related Scriptures

Matthew 25:31–46; 1 Corinthians 13; Ephesians 4:29–32; 1 John 4:20; Mosiah 4:13–27; Alma 34:28–29; Ether 12:33–34; Moroni 7:45–48; D&C 121:45–46

Study Help

"Acting on what you have learned will bring added and enduring understanding (see John 7:17)" (*Preach My Gospel* [2004], 19). Consider asking yourself how you can apply the teachings at home, at work, and in your Church responsibilities.

Notes

1. "The Gifts of Christmas," *Ensign,* Dec. 2002, 18.
2. John S. Welch, in Eleanor Knowles, *Howard W. Hunter* (1994), 119.
3. Betty C. McEwan, "My Most Influential Teacher," *Church News,* June 21, 1980, 2.
4. Carolyn Sessions Allen, in "Loved by All Who Knew Him: Stories from Members," *Ensign,* Apr. 1995, 20.
5. In Thomas S. Monson, "President Howard W. Hunter: A Man for All Seasons," 33.
6. In Knowles, *Howard W. Hunter,* 185.
7. "The Lord's Touchstone," *Ensign,* Nov. 1986, 34.
8. "The Lord's Touchstone," 34–35.
9. "The Lord's Touchstone," 35.
10. "A More Excellent Way," *Ensign,* May 1992, 61.
11. "A More Excellent Way," 61–62.
12. "A More Excellent Way," 62.

Faith and Testimony

"The supreme achievement of life is to find
God and to know that He lives."

From the Life of Howard W. Hunter

Howard W. Hunter began to develop his testimony during his early childhood in Boise, Idaho. Although his father was not then a member of the Church, his mother raised him in the gospel. "It was at her knee that we learned to pray," he recalled. "I received a testimony as a boy at my mother's knee."[1]

Howard's testimony grew over the years. When he was in his 20s and living in Los Angeles, California, he began to recognize the importance of serious gospel study. He wrote: "Although I had attended Church classes most of my life, my first real awakening to the gospel came in a Sunday School class in [the] Adams Ward taught by Brother Peter A. Clayton. He had a wealth of knowledge and the ability to inspire young people. I studied the lessons, read the outside assignments he gave us, and participated in speaking on assigned subjects. . . . I think of this period of my life as the time the truths of the gospel commenced to unfold. I always had a testimony of the gospel, but suddenly I commenced to understand."[2]

Many years later, President Hunter explained: "There comes a time when we understand the principles of our creation and who we are. Suddenly these things are illuminated to us and the cords of our hearts do vibrate. This is the time when testimony enters into our very souls and we know beyond a question of a doubt that God is our father—that he lives, that he is a reality, that we are literally his children."[3]

Concerning President Hunter's faith and testimony, President Gordon B. Hinckley said:

"The greatest quest is a search for God—to determine his reality, his personal attributes, and to secure a knowledge of the gospel of his Son Jesus Christ."

"For President Hunter . . . there was the mighty power of faith. There was the certitude of knowledge of things divine and of things eternal. . . . [He] had a sure and certain testimony of the living reality of God, our Eternal Father. He voiced with great conviction his witness of the divinity of the Lord Jesus Christ, the Redeemer of mankind."[4]

Teachings of Howard W. Hunter

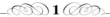 1

Through faith, we can find God and know that He lives.

The supreme achievement of life is to find God and to know that He lives. Like any other worthy accomplishment, this can only be obtained by those who will believe and have faith in that which at first may not be apparent.[5]

As man's thoughts turn to God and the things that pertain to God, man undergoes a spiritual transformation. It lifts him from the commonplace and gives to him a noble and Godlike character. If we have faith in God, we are using one of the great laws of life. The most powerful force in human nature is the spiritual power of faith.[6]

The greatest quest is a search for God—to determine his reality, his personal attributes, and to secure a knowledge of the gospel of his Son Jesus Christ. It is not easy to find a perfect understanding of God. The search requires persistent effort, and there are some who never move themselves to pursue this knowledge. . . .

Whether seeking for knowledge of scientific truths or to discover God, one must have faith. This becomes the starting point. Faith has been defined in many ways, but the most classic definition was given by the author of the letter to the Hebrews in these meaningful words: "Now faith is the substance of things hoped for, the evidence of things not seen." (Heb. 11:1.) In other words, faith makes us confident of what we hope for and convinced of what we do not see. . . . Those who earnestly seek for God do not see him, but they know of his reality by faith. It is more than hope. Faith makes it a conviction—an evidence of things not seen.

The author of the letter to the Hebrews [the Apostle Paul] continues: "Through faith we understand that the worlds were framed by the word of God, so that things which are seen were not made of things which do appear." (Heb. 11:3.) Faith is here described as believing or having the conviction that the world was created by the word of God. Witnesses cannot be produced to prove this fact, but faith gives the knowledge that what we see in the wonders of the earth and in all nature was created by God. . . .

I have a positive conviction that God is a reality—that he lives. He is our Heavenly Father, and we are his spiritual children. He created the heaven and the earth and all things upon the earth and is the author of the eternal laws by which the universe is governed. These laws are discovered bit by bit as man continues his search, but they have existed always and will remain unchanged forever.[7]

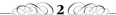

2

To obtain knowledge of the reality of God, we must make a faithful effort, do His will, and pray for understanding.

In order to find God as a reality, we must follow the course which he pointed out for the quest. The path is one that leads upward; it takes faith and effort, and is not the easy course. For this reason many men will not devote themselves to the arduous task of proving to themselves the reality of God. On the contrary, some take the easy path and deny his existence or merely follow the doubter's course of uncertainty. . . .

. . . Sometimes faith means believing a thing to be true where the evidence is not sufficient to establish knowledge. We must continue the probe and follow the admonition: "Ask, and it shall be given you; seek, and ye shall find; knock, and it shall be opened unto you: For every one that asketh receiveth; and he that seeketh findeth; and to him that knocketh it shall be opened." (Matt. 7:7–8.) . . .

It is the general rule that we do not get things of value unless we are willing to pay a price. The scholar does not become learned unless he puts forth the work and effort to succeed. If he is not willing to do so, can he say there is no such thing as scholarship? . . . It is just as foolish for man to say there is no God simply because he has not had the inclination to seek him.

. . . In order for an individual to obtain unwavering knowledge of the reality of God, he must live the commandments and the doctrines announced by the Savior during his personal ministry. . . . Those who are willing to make the search, apply themselves, and do God's will, will have the knowledge come to them of the reality of God.

When a man has found God and understands his ways, he learns that nothing in the universe came by chance, but all things resulted from a divinely prearranged plan. What a rich meaning comes into his life! Understanding which surpasses worldly learning is his. The beauties of the world become more beautiful, the order of the universe becomes more meaningful, and all of God's creations are more understandable as he witnesses God's days come and go and the seasons follow each in their order.[8]

Christ, during his ministry, explained the manner in which one could know the truth about God. He said, "If any man will do his will, he shall know of the doctrine, whether it be of God, or whether I speak of myself." (John 7:17.) The Master also explained the will of the Father and the great commandment in this manner: "Thou shalt love the Lord thy God with all thy heart, and with all thy soul, and with all thy mind." (Matt. 22:37.) Those who will strive to do God's will and keep his commandments will receive personal revelation as to the divinity of the Lord's work in bearing testimony of the Father.

To those who desire understanding, the words of James explain how it may be obtained: "If any of you lack wisdom, let him ask of God, that giveth to all men liberally, and upbraideth not; and it shall be given him." (James 1:5.) It doesn't appear that James was referring to factual knowledge in the sense of science, but rather to the revelation that comes from on high which answers men's questions as the result of following this admonition to pray. . . .

Thus we have the formula for the search for God and the tools to accomplish the quest—faith, love, and prayer. Science has done marvelous things for man, but it cannot accomplish the things he must do for himself, the greatest of which is to find the reality of God. The task is not easy; the labor is not light; but as stated by the Master, "Great shall be their reward and eternal shall be their glory." (D&C 76:6.)[9]

 **3**

We must believe in order to see.

Thomas wanted to see before he would believe.

On the evening of the day of the resurrection, Jesus appeared and stood in the midst of his disciples in the closed room. He showed them his hands through which had been driven the nails and his side which had been pierced by the spear. Thomas, one of the twelve, was not present when this happened, but the others told him they had seen the Lord and that he had spoken to them. . . . Thomas was skeptical, and he said to the disciples:

". . . Except I shall see in his hands the print of the nails, and put my finger into the print of the nails, and thrust my hand into his side, I will not believe." (John 20:25.)

. . . In a sense, Thomas represents the spirit of our age. He would not be satisfied with anything he could not see, even though he had been with the Master and knew his teachings concerning faith and doubt. . . . Faith does not take precedence over doubt when one must feel or see in order to believe.

Thomas was not willing to stand on faith. He wanted positive evidence of the facts. He wanted knowledge, not faith. Knowledge is related to the past because our experiences of the past are those things which give us knowledge, but faith is related to the future— to the unknown where we have not yet walked.

We think of Thomas as one who had traveled and talked with the Master, and who had been chosen by him. Inwardly we wish that Thomas could have turned toward the future with confidence in the things which were not then visible, instead of saying in effect, "To see is to believe." . . .

Faith gives us confidence in things that are not visible.

A week later, the disciples were again together in the same house in Jerusalem. This time Thomas was with them. The door was closed, but Jesus came and stood in the midst of them and said, "Peace be unto you.

"Then saith he to Thomas, Reach hither thy finger, and behold my hands; and reach hither thy hand, and thrust it into my side: and be not faithless, but believing." (John 20:26–27.) . . .

"Jesus saith unto him, Thomas, because thou hast seen me, thou hast believed: blessed are they that have not seen, and yet have believed." ([John] 20:29.)

This occurrence stands as one of the great lessons of all times. Thomas had said, "To see is to believe," but Christ answered: "To believe is to see." . . .

The classic example of faith is ascribed to the Apostle Paul in his Epistle to the Hebrews: "Now faith is the substance of things hoped for, the evidence of things not seen." (Heb. 11:1.)

This statement does not presuppose a perfect knowledge, but describes faith as that which gives to one an assurance or a confidence in things which are yet in the future. These things may be in existence, but it is through faith they are realized. Faith gives a feeling of confidence in that which is not visible or susceptible of positive proof.

It would appear that Thomas had lost his confidence in the future. He looked to the past. He wanted proof of that which was not then visible. Those who lose or lack faith, live in the past—there is loss of hope for the future. What a great change comes into the life of one who finds an abiding faith to give assurance and confidence.

The man born blind did not doubt; he believed in the Savior.

If we turn back to the ninth chapter of John, we read of another incident that took place in Jerusalem in which a man who had been born blind received his sight. It was the Sabbath day, and Jesus was apparently in the vicinity of the temple when he saw the blind man, and his disciples asked him:

". . . Master, who did sin, this man, or his parents, that he was born blind?

"Jesus answered, Neither hath this man sinned, nor his parents: but that the works of God should be made manifest in him.

"I must work the works of him that sent me, while it is day: the night cometh, when no man can work.

"As long as I am in the world, I am the light of the world." (John 9:2–5.)

Jesus then spat on the ground and made clay of the spittle mixed with the dust of the earth. He anointed the eyes of the blind man with the clay and told him to go wash in the pool of Siloam. If this had been Thomas, would he have gone as he had been commanded or would he have asked the question: "What good can come from washing in the stagnant waters of that dirty pool?" or "What medicinal properties are there in saliva mixed with the dust of the earth?" These would seem to be reasonable questions, but if the blind man had doubted and questioned, he would still be blind. Having faith, he believed and did as he was directed. He went and washed in the pool and came back seeing. To believe is to see. . . .

"Blessed are they that have not seen, and yet have believed."

The blind man believed and was permitted to see. Thomas refused to believe until after he could see. The world is full of Thomases, but there are many like the blind man of Jerusalem. Missionaries of the Church meet both of these every day as they carry their message to the world, the message of the restored gospel of Jesus Christ. . . . Some believe, have faith, and are baptized. Some will not accept because they cannot see or feel.

There is no positive, concrete, tangible evidence that God lives, yet millions have a knowledge that he does through that faith which constitutes the evidence of things unseen. Many say to the missionaries, "I would accept baptism if I could believe that Joseph Smith was visited by the Father and the Son." For this fact there is no positive, concrete, tangible evidence, but to those who are touched

"The blind man believed and was permitted to see."

by the Spirit, faith will stand in the place of such evidence of things unseen. Remember the words of the crucified Master as he stood before Thomas:

"Blessed are they that have not seen, and yet have believed." ([John] 20:29.)

Those who believe through faith will see.

I add my witness to the testimonies of the thousands of missionaries that God does live, that Jesus is the Savior of the world, that those who will believe through faith will be caused to see.[10]

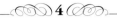

Acting on our faith leads to personal testimony.

As children we accepted as fact the things which were told to us by our parents or our teachers because of the confidence that we had in them. A little boy will jump from a high place without fear if his father tells him that he will catch him. The little fellow has faith that his father will not let him fall. As children grow older, they commence to think for themselves, to question and have doubts about those things which are not subject to tangible proof. I have sympathy for young men and young women when honest doubts enter their minds and they engage in the great conflict of resolving doubts. These doubts can be resolved, if they have an honest desire to know the truth, by exercising moral, spiritual, and mental effort. They will emerge from the conflict into a firmer, stronger, larger faith because of the struggle. They have gone from a simple, trusting faith, through doubt and conflict, into a solid substantial faith which ripens into testimony.[11]

Students spend hours in scientific laboratories experimenting to find the truth. If they will do the same thing with faith, prayer, forgiveness, humility and love, they will find a testimony of Jesus Christ, the giver of these principles.[12]

The gospel of Jesus Christ is not just a gospel of belief; it is a plan of action. . . . He did not say "observe" my gospel; he said "live" it! He did not say, "Note its beautiful structure and imagery"; he said, "Go, do, see, feel, give, believe!" . . .

Action is one of the chief foundations of personal testimony. The surest witness is that which comes firsthand out of personal experience. When the Jews challenged the doctrine Jesus taught in the temple, he answered, ". . . my doctrine is not mine, but his that sent me." Then he added the key to personal testimony, "If any man will do his will, he shall know of the doctrine, whether it be of God, or whether I speak of myself." (John 7:16–17.)

Do we hear the imperative in this declaration of the Savior? "If any man will *do* . . . he shall *know!*" John caught the significance of this imperative and emphasized its meaning in his [epistle]. He said, "He that saith he abideth in him ought himself also so to walk, even as he walked." (1 John 2:6.)

Merely saying, accepting, believing are not enough. They are incomplete until that which they imply is translated into the dynamic action of daily living. This, then, is the finest source of personal testimony. One knows because he has experienced. He does not have to say, "Brother Jones says it is true, and I believe him." He can say, "I have lived this principle in my own life, and I know through personal experience that it works. I have felt its influence, tested its practical usefulness, and know that it is good. I can testify of my own knowledge that it is a true principle."

Many people carry such a testimony in their own lives and do not recognize its worth. Recently a young lady said, "I do not have a testimony of the gospel. I wish I did. I accept its teachings. I know they work in my life. I see them working in the lives of others. If only the Lord would answer my prayers and give me a testimony, I would be one of the happiest persons alive!" What this young lady wanted was a miraculous intervention; yet she had already seen the miracle of the gospel enlarging and uplifting her own life. The Lord *had* answered her prayers. She *did* have a testimony, but she did not recognize it for what it was.[13]

As an ordained Apostle and special witness of Christ, I give to you my solemn witness that Jesus Christ is in fact the Son of God. . . . It is by the power of the Holy Ghost that I bear my witness. I know of Christ's reality as if I had seen with my eyes and heard with my ears. I know also that the Holy Spirit will confirm the truthfulness of my witness in the hearts of all those who listen with an ear of faith.[14]

Suggestions for Study and Teaching

Questions
• President Hunter teaches that "the supreme achievement of life is to find God and to know that He lives" (section 1). What is the role of faith in accomplishing that quest? What experiences have helped you come to find God and know that He lives?

277

- President Hunter says "the task is not easy" and "the labor is not light" in gaining a knowledge of the reality of God. Why do you think devoted effort is necessary for us to gain that knowledge? Why is keeping the commandments important in coming to know God?

- In section 3, President Hunter uses the contrast between Thomas and the man born blind to teach that if we believe, we will be able to see. How might President Hunter's insights into these stories have application in your life? How has exercising faith made it possible for you to see?

- Review President Hunter's teachings that acting on our faith is the key to gaining a testimony (see section 4). What are some ways you can act on your faith? How can faith overcome doubt? How has acting on your faith helped your testimony become stronger?

Related Scriptures

John 17:3; Hebrews 11:1–6; Alma 5:45–48; 30:40–41; 32:26–43; Ether 12:4, 6–22; Moroni 10:4–5; D&C 42:61

Teaching Help

"Ask questions that require learners to find answers in the scriptures and the teachings of latter-day prophets" (*Teaching, No Greater Call* [1999], 62).

Notes

1. In J M. Heslop, "He Found Pleasure in Work," *Church News,* Nov. 16, 1974, 4, 12.

2. In Eleanor Knowles, *Howard W. Hunter* (1994), 70–71.

3. *The Teachings of Howard W. Hunter,* ed. Clyde J. Williams (1997), 48.

4. Gordon B. Hinckley, "A Prophet Polished and Refined," *Ensign,* Apr. 1995, 35.

5. "Faith as the Foundation of Accomplishment," *Instructor,* Feb. 1960, 43.

6. In Conference Report, Apr. 1960, 124–25.

7. "To Know God," *Ensign,* Nov. 1974, 96–97.

8. In Conference Report, Apr. 1970, 7–10.

9. "To Know God," 97.

10. In Conference Report, Oct. 1962, 22–24.

11. "Secretly a Disciple?" *Improvement Era,* Dec. 1960, 948.

12. *The Teachings of Howard W. Hunter,* 48.

13. In Conference Report, Apr. 1967, 115–16.

14. "An Apostle's Witness of Christ," *Ensign,* Jan. 1984, 70.

Teaching the Gospel

"The purpose of teaching . . . [is] that we might
be an instrument in the hands of the Lord in
changing the heart of an individual."

From the Life of Howard W. Hunter

In the April 1972 general conference, Elder Howard W. Hunter, then a member of the Quorum of the Twelve Apostles, was one of the last speakers in one of the sessions. He had prepared a talk, but there was not enough time left in the session for him to give it. "Observing the clock," Elder Hunter said, "I fold the notes that I have prepared and place them in my inside pocket. But let me take just a moment to mention a little incident that made an impression upon me when I was a boy. This came to my mind when it was mentioned that there are with us this afternoon a large group of dedicated people who teach our youth.

"It was on a summer day early in the morning. I was standing near the window. The curtains obstructed me from two little creatures out on the lawn. One was a large bird and the other a little bird, obviously just out of the nest. I saw the larger bird hop out on the lawn, then thump his feet and cock his head. He drew a big fat worm out of the lawn and came hopping back. The little bird opened its bill wide, but the big bird swallowed the worm.

"Then I saw the big bird fly up into a tree. He pecked at the bark for a little while and came back with a big bug in his mouth. The little bird opened his beak wide, but the big bird swallowed the bug. There was squawking in protest.

"The big bird flew away, and I didn't see it again, but I watched the little bird. After a while, the little bird hopped out on the lawn, thumped its feet, cocked its head, and pulled a big worm out of the lawn.

Teaching children at church supports parents' teachings in the home.

"God bless the good people who teach our children and our youth."

Elder Hunter's brief message was later published under the title "A Teacher."[1]

Howard W. Hunter frequently emphasized the importance of good teaching in the Church. He presented principles—such as the importance of teaching by example, illustrated by the story of the birds—that could help teachers become more effective in blessing the lives of those they taught. Often he spoke to teachers of children and youth, helping them understand their sacred responsibility for those of the rising generation. In one such setting, he said:

"Before me now I see some of the choice spirits of the earth. . . . I try to visualize each [of you teachers] at work in your own specific assignment. I wonder what kind of fruit your labor will bring forth. Will some of that fruit be blighted because you have failed to till or cultivate the soil entrusted to your care; or will all the soil be cultivated so it will yield a maximum of good fruit?

"Out in your respective wards and stakes . . . reside many of our Father's children. Like you, they are choice in his sight; but, unlike you, many are inexperienced and many are new in the Gospel. Your responsibility toward them is great indeed. Their lives are pliable, easily bent, easily molded, easily led, if you can gain their confidence and win their hearts. You are their 'shepherd.' You must guide them to 'green pastures.' . . .

"What a challenge, what a joyous task, what a sacred responsibility is yours now! . . . How thoughtful, how considerate, how kind, how tender, how pure in heart, how possessed of that unselfish love as our Lord possessed, how humble, how prayerful you must be as you assume anew your work to feed the lambs as the Lord is telling you to do!"[2]

Teachings of Howard W. Hunter

Help others develop confidence in the scriptures.

I strongly encourage you to use the scriptures in your teaching and to do all within your power to help the students use them and become comfortable with them. I would like our young people to have confidence in the scriptures, and I would like you to interpret that phrase two ways.

First, we want the students to have confidence in the strength and truths of the scriptures, confidence that their Heavenly Father is really speaking to them through the scriptures, and confidence that they can turn to the scriptures and find answers to their problems and their prayers. That is one kind of confidence I would hope you give your students, and you can give it to them if you show them daily, hourly, that you trust in the scriptures just that way. Show them that you yourself are confident that the scriptures hold the answers to many—indeed most—of life's problems. So when you teach, teach from the scriptures.

[A second] meaning implied in the phrase "confidence in the scriptures" is to teach students the standard works so thoroughly that they can move through them with confidence, learning the essential scriptures and sermons and texts contained in them. We would hope none of your students would leave your classroom fearful or embarrassed or ashamed that they cannot find the help they need because they do not know the scriptures well enough to locate the proper passages. Give these young people sufficient experience in the Bible, the Book of Mormon, the Doctrine and Covenants, and the Pearl of Great Price that they have both of the kinds of confidence I have just mentioned.

I have often thought that our young people in the Church would be very much like other young people outside of the Church if they do not establish some mastery and command of the standard works. All of you remember the verses the Prophet Joseph wrote from his confinement in Liberty Jail. Among them he wrote, "For there are many yet on the earth among all sects, parties, and denominations, who are blinded by the subtle craftiness of men, whereby they lie in wait to deceive, and *who are only kept from the truth because they know not where to find it*" (D&C 123:12; emphasis added).

We have a great responsibility as [teachers] in the Church to make sure our own members, our own young people, do not fall into that unfortunate category of being blinded, of being good, fine, worthy young men and women who are kept from the truths of the scriptures because they do not know where to find those truths and because they do not possess confidence [in using] their standard works.[3]

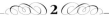

2

Teach with the Spirit.

Prepare and live in such a way that you have the Spirit of the Lord in your teaching. There is so much in our world that destroys the feeling of the Spirit and so much that would keep us from having the Spirit with us. We need to do all we can for these young people who are assaulted and barraged by worldliness all around them. We need to do everything possible to let them feel the sweet, reassuring presence of the Spirit of the Lord. . . .

In one of the most basic revelations of this dispensation, the Lord said, "And the Spirit shall be given unto you by the prayer of faith; and if ye receive not the Spirit ye shall not teach" (D&C 42:14).

I take this verse to mean not only that we *should not* teach without the Spirit, but also that we really *cannot* teach without it. Learning of spiritual things simply cannot take place without the instructional and confirming presence of the Spirit of the Lord. Joseph Smith would seem to agree: "All are to preach the Gospel, by the power and influence of the Holy Ghost; and no man can preach the Gospel without the Holy Ghost" [*Teachings of Presidents of the Church: Joseph Smith* (2007), 332].

. . . I get concerned when it appears that strong emotion or free-flowing tears are equated with the presence of the Spirit. Certainly the Spirit of the Lord can bring strong emotional feelings, including tears, but that outward manifestation ought not to be confused with the presence of the Spirit itself.

I have watched a great many of my brethren over the years and we have shared some rare and unspeakable spiritual experiences together. Those experiences have all been different, each special in its own way, and such sacred moments may or may not be accompanied by tears. Very often they are, but sometimes they are accompanied by total silence. Other times they are accompanied by joy. Always they are accompanied by a great manifestation of the truth, of revelation to the heart.

Give your students gospel truth powerfully taught; that is the way to give them a spiritual experience. Let it come naturally and as it will, perhaps with the shedding of tears, but perhaps not. If what you say is the truth, and you say it purely and with honest conviction, those students will feel the spirit of the truth being taught them and will recognize that inspiration and revelation has come into their hearts. That is how we build faith. That is how we strengthen testimonies—with the power of the word of God taught in purity and with conviction.

Listen for the truth, hearken to the doctrine, and let the manifestation of the Spirit come as it may in all of its many and varied forms. Stay with solid principles; teach from a pure heart. Then the Spirit will penetrate your mind and heart and every mind and heart of your students.[4]

Invite students to seek God the Father and Jesus Christ directly.

I am sure you recognize the potential danger of . . . your students build[ing] an allegiance to you rather than to the gospel. . . . That is why you have to invite your students into the scriptures themselves, not just give them your interpretation and presentation of them. That is why you must invite your students to feel the Spirit of the Lord, not just give them your personal reflection of that. That is why, ultimately, you must invite your students directly to Christ, not just to one who teaches his doctrines, however ably. You will not always be available to these students. . . .

Our great task is to ground these students in what *can* go with them through life, to point them toward him who loves them and

"Try the best you can to think of [students] individually, to let them feel something personal and special in the concern of you, their teacher."

can guide them where none of us will go. Please make sure the loyalty of these students is to the scriptures and the Lord and the doctrines of the restored Church. Point them toward God the Father and his Only Begotten Son, Jesus Christ, and toward the leadership of the true Church. . . . Give them the gifts that will carry them through when they have to stand alone. When you do this, the entire Church is blessed for generations to come.[5]

 4

Strive to reach the individual.

I have always been impressed that the Lord deals with us personally, individually. We do many things in groups in the Church, and we need organizations of some size to allow us to administer the Church well, but so many of the important things—the most important things—are done individually. We bless babies one at a time, even if they are twins or triplets. We baptize and confirm children one at a time. We take the sacrament, are ordained to the priesthood, or move through the ordinances of the temple as individuals—as one person developing a relationship with our Father in Heaven. There may be others nearby us in these experiences, just as there are others in your classroom, but heaven's emphasis is on each individual, on every single person.

When Christ appeared to the Nephites, he said:

"Arise and come forth unto me, that ye may thrust your hands into my side, and also that ye may feel the prints of the nails in my hands and in my feet. . . .

"And it came to pass that the multitude went forth, and thrust their hands into his side, and did feel the prints of the nails in his hands and in his feet; and this they did do, *going forth one by one* until they had all gone forth, *and did see with their eyes and did feel with their hands,* and did know of a surety and did bear record" (3 Nephi 11:14–15; emphasis added).

That experience took time, but it was important that each individual have the experience, that each set of eyes and each pair of hands have that reaffirming, *personal* witness. Later Christ treated the Nephite children exactly the same way. "He took their little children, *one by one,* and blessed them, and prayed unto the Father for them" (3 Nephi 17:21; emphasis added).

It will be hard for you to give all of the personal attention some of your students both want and need, but try the best you can to think of them individually, to let them feel something personal and special in the concern of you, their teacher. Pray to know which student needs what kind of help, and remain sensitive to those promptings when they then come. . . . Remember that the very best teaching is one on one and often takes place out of the classroom. . . .

In your search for individually teaching each student, you will most certainly discover that some are not doing as well as others and that some are not making it to class at all. Take personal interest in such students; give extra-mile effort to invite and help the lost sheep back into the fold. "Remember the worth of souls is great in the sight of God" (D&C 18:10). An incalculable price has been paid by our Savior for every one of us, and it is incumbent on us to do all we can to assist him in his work. It is incumbent on us to make sure that the gift of the Atonement is extended to every young man or woman we have responsibility for. In your situation, that means keeping them in full activity in your classes.

Give special attention to those who may be struggling, and go out as necessary to find the lost sheep. A written postcard, a telephone call, or, if possible, a personal visit to a home in many cases will have a wonderful result. Personal attention to a young person just beginning to stray may save hours and hours—indeed, years and years—of effort later in our attempt to reclaim that person to activity. Do all you can to fortify the strong one and reanchor the wayward ones at this age.[6]

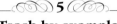 **5**

Teach by example.

It is so needful for us [as teachers] to set the proper example, to be diligent and vigilant in our own lives, to keep the Sabbath Day holy, to honor the leadership of the ward, the stake, and the Church. Nothing unseemly should come from our lips that would give any child the right or the privilege to do wrong. Surely <u>if we say or do something wrong, the children have license to follow.</u>

Example carries with it an influence much more forceful than precept. He who would persuade others to do right should do right himself. It is true that he who practices good precepts because they are good and does not suffer himself to be influenced by the unrighteous conduct of others will be more abundantly rewarded than one who says and does not. . . . Children are prone to imitate those in whom they place confidence. The greater their confidence, the more readily they are influenced for good or for evil. Every good Saint respects genuine goodness wherever it is seen and will try to imitate all good examples.[7]

The formula for a great teacher is not only to live the commandments of the Lord and to advocate the commandments of the Lord, but to obtain the spirit of teaching by prayer. When we obtain that spirit and observe the commandments of the Lord, walking in obedience before Him, then the lives of those whom we touch will be changed and they will be motivated to live lives of righteousness.[8]

Effective gospel teaching leads to "the transformation of the human soul."

Every teacher must have a personal testimony that God lives, of the divine mission of Jesus Christ, and that the appearance to Joseph Smith of the Father and the Son was a reality. Not only must he have that knowledge and testimony, but he should be anxious to express his belief without equivocation to those who come to learn.[9]

◠◠◠ 6 ◠◠◠

Be an instrument in the Lord's hands in helping students experience a miraculous change of heart.

When a teacher performs as the Lord intended, a great miracle does take place. The miracle of the Church today is not the healings which are so profuse, not that the lame shall walk, the blind see, the deaf hear, or the sick be raised up. The great miracle of the Church and kingdom of God in our day and in our time is the transformation of the human soul. As we journey throughout the stakes and missions of the Church, this is what we see—the transformation of the human soul because someone has taught the principles of truth.

It is as Alma proclaimed, in his day in teaching the people, when he said: "And now behold, I ask of you, my brethren [and sisters] of the church, have ye spiritually been born of God? Have ye received his image in your countenances? Have ye experienced this mighty change in your hearts?" (Alma 5:14.) This is the purpose of teaching. This is the reason we labor so hard, seek the Spirit, and prepare our minds with good things as the Lord has commanded, that we might be an instrument in the hands of the Lord in changing the heart of an individual. Our aim is to plant in the hearts of children the desire to be good, the desire to be righteous, the desire to keep the commandments of the Lord, the desire to walk in humility before Him. If we can be an instrument in the hands of the Lord in bringing to pass this mighty change in the hearts of the children, then we have accomplished the great miracle of a teacher. And truly, it is a miracle. We do not understand how the Lord changes the hearts of men, but He does. . . .

I bear you my witness of the regenerating power of the Spirit in the lives of members of the Church. I plead with you . . . to labor unceasingly in righteousness and holiness before the Lord in accomplishing the task that has been assigned to you."[10]

Suggestions for Study and Teaching

Questions

Note: You might want to discuss some of the following questions from the point of view of parents teaching their children.

- President Hunter encourages teachers to help students gain "confidence in the scriptures" (section 1). When have the scriptures helped you in your own life? When have you found answers to your questions in the scriptures? How can we help others, including those in our homes, learn to love the scriptures and benefit from their power?

- What can we learn from section 2 about teaching by the Spirit? What experiences have you had with teaching and learning by the Spirit? What are some things you can do to help you teach by the Spirit?

- How can a teacher help students build loyalty to the scriptures and the gospel, not to himself or herself? (See section 3.) How can a teacher help point students toward Heavenly Father and Jesus Christ? How can a teacher help students become grounded in the gospel so they remain strong "when they have to stand alone"?

- Ponder President Hunter's teachings about the importance of each individual (see section 4). How can you help those you teach develop a testimony that God knows and loves them individually? Consider what you, as a teacher, can do to reach those you teach individually.

- President Hunter emphasizes the importance of teaching by example (see section 5). Why is our example more powerful than our words? How have you been blessed by a teacher who was a good example? How does the example of parents teach their children?

- When have you experienced the "great miracle" that President Hunter describes in section 6, either as a teacher or a learner? Reflect on some teachers who have been a good influence in your life. What made them an effective influence? How can we teach the gospel with greater power—whether at home, in a classroom, or in another setting?

Related Scriptures

John 21:15–17; 1 Corinthians 12:28; 2 Timothy 3:14–17; 2 Nephi 33:1; Alma 17:2–3; 31:5; D&C 11:21–22; 50:17–22; 88:77–80

Teaching Help

On different pieces of paper, write questions from the end of the chapter or other questions that relate to the chapter. Invite class members to select a question and search the chapter for teachings that help answer it. Ask them to share what they learned.

Notes

1. "A Teacher," *Ensign*, July 1972, 85.
2. *The Teachings of Howard W. Hunter,* ed. Clyde J. Williams (1997), 210–11.
3. "Eternal Investments" (address to CES religious educators, Feb. 10, 1989), 2; si.lds.org.
4. "Eternal Investments," 3–4.
5. "Eternal Investments," 2–3.
6. "Eternal Investments," 4–5.
7. "Formula for a Great Teacher" (address given at Primary conference, Apr. 1965), 3–4, Church History Library, Salt Lake City.
8. "Formula for a Great Teacher," 1.
9. *The Teachings of Howard W. Hunter,* 188.
10. "Formula for a Great Teacher," 4–6.

"No Less Serviceable"

*"Most of us will be quiet, relatively unknown folks
who . . . do our work without fanfare. To those of
you who may find that . . . unspectacular, I say,
you are 'no less serviceable' than the most
spectacular of your associates."*

From the Life of Howard W. Hunter

President Howard W. Hunter was known not only as a dedicated
leader and beloved prophet, but also for the quiet way in which he
served. He knew that the service itself was important, not whether
he received any recognition. Elder Neal A. Maxwell of the Quorum
of the Twelve once said of him, "President Howard W. Hunter is a
meek man. . . . This is the same lowly man, when I awakened after
a weary and dusty day together with him on assignment in Egypt,
who was quietly shining my shoes, a task he had hoped to complete
unseen."[1]

President Thomas S. Monson first noticed President Hunter's humble way of serving when the Los Angeles California Temple was
dedicated in 1956, several years before either of them was called as
an Apostle. He recalled:

"My . . . introduction to President Hunter was when he served as
president of the Pasadena California Stake and had responsibility to
coordinate local arrangements for the dedication of the Los Angeles
(California) Temple. It was my privilege to print the tickets. His assignment was mammoth. I saw only that portion which pertained
to the tickets, which were color coded, intricately labeled, and numbered in the most orderly fashion I had ever seen. He generously
gave credit to others and insured that his name was not excessively
featured, even though he had been a driving force behind these
monumental undertakings."[2]

Life-changing service is rendered by many "who are not seen in the limelight, who do not receive the attention of the world."

Elder James E. Faust of the Quorum of the Twelve further observed: "He had no ego needs. With all his wisdom, he could sit among his brethren and say very little. He was at complete peace with himself."[3]

President Hunter understood that every act of service is important in God's eyes, no matter how unheralded or inconspicuous. Several weeks before President Hunter passed away, a friend asked, "Dear President, what is the most exalted position or calling—that of a dear and trusted friend, or that of a prophet of God?" After hearing the question, "the President pondered silently for what seemed like minutes; then slowly grasping the hand of his friend and turning his head squarely toward him, with a tear trickling down his frail cheek, he responded, 'they are *both* sacred callings of trust.'"[4]

Teachings of Howard W. Hunter

 **1**

Those who serve quietly and inconspicuously are "no less serviceable" than those who receive the world's acclaim.

It was said of the young and valiant Captain Moroni: "If all men had been, and were, and ever would be, like unto Moroni, behold, the very powers of hell would have been shaken forever; yea, the devil would never have power over the hearts of the children of men." (Alma 48:17.)

What a compliment to a famous and powerful man! I can't imagine a finer tribute from one man to another. Two verses later is a statement about Helaman and his brethren, who played a less conspicuous role than Moroni: "Now behold, Helaman and his brethren were no less serviceable unto the people than was Moroni." (Alma 48:19.)

In other words, even though Helaman was not as noticeable or conspicuous as Moroni, he was as serviceable; that is, he was as helpful or useful as Moroni.

Obviously, we could profit greatly by studying the life of Captain Moroni. He is an example of faith, service, dedication, commitment, and many other godly attributes. Rather than focusing on this magnificent man, however, I have chosen to look instead at those who are not seen in the limelight, who do not receive the attention of the world, yet who are "no less serviceable," as the scripture phrased it.

Not all of us are going to be like Moroni, catching the acclaim of our colleagues all day every day. Most of us will be quiet, relatively unknown folks who come and go and do our work without fanfare. To those of you who may find that [thought] lonely or frightening or just unspectacular, I say, you are "no less serviceable" than the most spectacular of your associates. You, too, are part of God's army.

Consider, for example, the profound service a mother or father gives in the quiet anonymity of a worthy Latter-day Saint home. Think of the Gospel Doctrine teachers and Primary choristers and Scoutmasters and Relief Society visiting teachers who serve and bless millions but whose names will never be publicly applauded or featured in the nation's media.

Tens of thousands of unseen people make possible our opportunities and happiness every day. As the scriptures state, they are "no less serviceable" than those whose lives are on the front pages of newspapers.

The limelight of history and contemporary attention so often focuses on the *one* rather than on the *many*. Individuals are frequently singled out from their peers and elevated as heroes. I acknowledge that this kind of attention is one way to identify that which the people admire or hold to be of some value. But sometimes that recognition is not deserved, or it may even celebrate the wrong values.

We must choose wisely our heroes and examples, while also giving thanks for those legions of friends and citizens who are not so famous but who are "no less serviceable" than the Moronis of our lives.[5]

―――――――――――――――― ⨭⨭⨭ **2** ⨭⨭⨭ ――――――――――――――――

In the scriptures, many people who served in the shadow of others made important contributions.

Perhaps you could consider with me some interesting people from the scriptures who did not receive the limelight of attention but who, through the long lens of history, have proven themselves to be truly heroic.

Many who read the story of the great prophet Nephi almost completely miss another valiant son of Lehi whose name was Sam. Nephi is one of the most famous figures in the entire Book of Mormon. But Sam? Sam's name is mentioned there only ten times. When Lehi counseled and blessed his posterity, he said to Sam:

"Blessed art thou, and thy seed; for thou shalt inherit the land like unto thy brother Nephi. And thy seed shall be numbered with his seed; and thou shalt be even like unto thy brother, and thy seed like unto his seed; and thou shalt be blessed in all thy days." (2 Ne. 4:11.)

Sam's role was basically one of supporting and assisting his more acclaimed younger brother, and he ultimately received the same blessings promised to Nephi and his posterity. Nothing promised to Nephi was withheld from the faithful Sam, yet we know very little of the details of Sam's service and contribution. He was an almost unknown person in life, but he is obviously a triumphant leader and victor in the annals of eternity.

Many make their contributions in unsung ways. Ishmael traveled with the family of Nephi at great personal sacrifice, suffering "much affliction, hunger, thirst, and fatigue." (1 Ne. 16:35.) Then in the midst of all of these afflictions, he perished in the wilderness. Few of us can even begin to understand the sacrifice of such a man in those primitive times and conditions. Perhaps if we were more perceptive and understanding, we too would mourn, as his daughters did in the wilderness, for what a man like this gave—and gave up!—so that we could have the Book of Mormon today.

The names and memories of such men and women who were "no less serviceable" are legion in the Book of Mormon. Whether it

*After Abish (left) touched the hand of the Lamanite queen,
the queen arose from the ground (see Alma 19:15–29).*

be Mother Sariah or the maid Abish, servant to the Lamanite queen, each made contributions that were unacknowledged by the eyes of men but not unseen by the eyes of God.

We have only twelve verses of scripture dealing with the life of Mosiah, king over the land of Zarahemla and father of the famous King Benjamin. Yet his service to the people was indispensable. He led the people "by many preachings and prophesyings" and "admonished [them] continually by the word of God." (Omni 1:13.) Limhi, Amulek, and Pahoran—the latter of whom had the nobility of soul not to condemn when he was very unjustly accused—are other examples of people who served selflessly in the shadow of others' limelight.

The soldier Teancum, who sacrificed his own life, or Lachoneus, the chief judge who taught people to repent during the challenge of the Gadiantons, or the virtually unmentioned missionaries Omner and Himni, were all "no less serviceable" than their companions, yet they received very little scriptural attention.

We don't know much about Shiblon, the faithful son of Alma whose story is sandwiched between those of Helaman, the future leader, and Corianton, the transgressor; but it is significant that he is described as a "just man [who] did walk uprightly before God." (Alma 63:2.) The great prophet Nephi, mentioned in the book of Helaman, had a brother named Lehi, who is seemingly mentioned only in passing but is noted as being "not a whit behind [Nephi] as to things pertaining to righteousness." [Helaman 11:19; see also verse 18.][6]

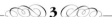 **3**

Even though we may not be well known, we can render great service in the kingdom.

Of course, there are examples of these serviceable individuals in our dispensation as well. Oliver Granger is the kind of quiet, supportive individual in the latter days that the Lord remembered in section 117 of the Doctrine and Covenants. Oliver's name may be unfamiliar to many, so I will take the liberty to acquaint you with this early stalwart.

Oliver Granger was eleven years older than Joseph Smith and, like the Prophet, was from upstate New York. Because of severe cold and exposure when he was thirty-three years old, Oliver lost much of his eyesight. Notwithstanding his limited vision, he served three full-time missions. He also worked on the Kirtland Temple and served on the Kirtland high council.

When most of the Saints were driven from Kirtland, Ohio, the Church left some debts unsatisfied. Oliver was appointed to represent Joseph Smith and the First Presidency by returning to Kirtland to settle the Church's business. Of this task, the Doctrine and Covenants records: "Therefore, let him contend earnestly for the redemption of the First Presidency of my Church, saith the Lord." (D&C 117:13.)

He performed this assignment with such satisfaction to the creditors involved that one of them wrote: "Oliver Granger's management in the arrangement of the unfinished business of people that have moved to the Far West, in redeeming their pledges and thereby sustaining their integrity, has been truly praiseworthy, and has entitled him to my highest esteem, and every grateful recollection." (Horace Kingsbury, as cited in Joseph Smith, *History of the Church,* 3:174.)

During Oliver's time in Kirtland, some people, including disaffected members of the Church, were endeavoring to discredit the First Presidency and bring their integrity into question by spreading false accusations. Oliver Granger, in very deed, "redeemed the First Presidency" through his faithful service. . . . The Lord said of Oliver Granger: "His name shall be had in sacred remembrance from generation to generation, forever and ever." (D&C 117:12.) "I will lift up my servant Oliver, and beget for him a great name on the earth, and among my people, because of the integrity of his soul." (*History of the Church,* 3:350.)

When he died in 1841, even though there were but few Saints remaining in the Kirtland area and even fewer friends of the Saints, Oliver Granger's funeral was attended by a vast concourse of people from neighboring towns.

Though Oliver Granger is not as well known today as other early leaders of the Church, he was nevertheless a great and important man in the service he rendered to the kingdom. And even if no one but the Lord had his name in remembrance, that would be a sufficient blessing for him—or for any of us.[7]

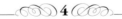 4

Nephi is an example of remembering God as the source of his strength and blessings.

I think we should be aware that there can be a spiritual danger to those who misunderstand the singularity of always being in the spotlight. They may come to covet the notoriety and thus forget the significance of the service being rendered.

We must not allow ourselves to focus on the fleeting light of popularity or substitute that attractive glow for the substance of true but often anonymous labor that brings the attention of God, even if it does not get coverage on the six o'clock news. In fact, applause and attention can become the spiritual Achilles' heels of even the most gifted among us.

If the limelight of popularity should fall on you sometime in your life, it might be well for you to follow the example of those in the scriptures who received fame. Nephi is one of the great examples. After all he accomplished traveling in the wilderness with his family, his attitude was still fixed on the things that matter most. He said:

"And when I desire to rejoice, my heart groaneth because of my sins; nevertheless, I know in whom I have trusted.

"My God hath been my support; he hath led me through mine afflictions in the wilderness; and he hath preserved me upon the waters of the great deep.

"He hath filled me with his love, even unto the consuming of my flesh.

"He hath confounded mine enemies, unto the causing of them to quake before me." (2 Ne. 4:19–22.)

The limelight never blinded Nephi as to the source of his strength and his blessings.[8]

 **5**

When we understand why we serve, we won't be concerned about where we serve.

At times of attention and visibility, it might also be profitable for us to answer the question, Why do we serve? When we understand why, we won't be concerned about where we serve.

President J. Reuben Clark, Jr., taught this vital principle in his own life. At general conference in April 1951, President David O. McKay was sustained as President of the Church after the passing of President George Albert Smith. Up to that time, President Clark had served as the First Counselor to President Heber J. Grant and then to President George Albert Smith. President McKay had been the Second Counselor to both men.

During the final session of conference when the business of the Church was transacted, Brother Stephen L Richards was called to the First Presidency and sustained as First Counselor. President J. Reuben Clark, Jr., was then sustained as the Second Counselor. After the sustaining of the officers of the Church, President McKay explained why he had chosen his counselors in that order. He said:

"I felt that one guiding principle in this choice would be to follow the seniority in the Council [of the Twelve]. These two men were sitting in their places in that presiding body in the Church, and I felt impressed that it would be advisable to continue that same seniority in the new quorum of the First Presidency." (In Conference Report, 9 April 1951, p. 151.)

President Clark was then asked to speak following President McKay. His remarks on this occasion were brief but teach a powerful lesson: "In the service of the Lord, it is not where you serve but how. In The Church of Jesus Christ of Latter-day Saints, one takes the place to which one is duly called, which place one neither seeks nor declines. I pledge to President McKay and to President Richards the full loyal devoted service to the tasks that may come to me to the full measure of my strength and my abilities, and so far as they will enable me to perform them, however inadequate I may be." (Ibid., p. 154.)

The lesson that President Clark taught is expressed in another way in this poem by Meade McGuire, which has been repeated many times:

"Father, where shall I work today?"
And my love flowed warm and free.
Then He pointed out a tiny spot
And said, "Tend that for me."
I answered quickly, "Oh no; not that!
Why, no one would ever see,
No matter how well my work was done;
Not that little place for me."
And the word He spoke, it was not stern;
He answered me tenderly:
"Ah, little one, search that heart of thine.
Art thou working for them or for me?
Nazareth was a little place,
And so was Galilee."

We are "most happy and successful in life" when our "interests are coupled with giving assistance to others and helping them find the way."

[See *Best-Loved Poems of the LDS People,* comp. Jack M. Lyon and others (1996), 152.]

King Benjamin declared: "Behold, I say unto you that because I said unto you that I had spent my days in your service, I do not desire to boast, for I have only been in the service of God. And behold, I tell you these things that ye may learn wisdom; that ye may learn that when ye are in the service of your fellow beings ye are only in the service of your God." (Mosiah 2:16–17.)[9]

6

We should serve faithfully and quietly, being on guard regarding the praise of others.

He is the most happy and successful in life whose interests are coupled with giving assistance to others and helping them find the way.

The sign at the railroad crossing that warns us to stop, look, and listen could be a guide for us. Stop as we rush through life. Look for all the friendly, thoughtful, courteous things we can do, and all the little human needs we can fill. Listen to others and learn of their hopes and problems so that we will be able to contribute in little ways to their success and happiness.[10]

President Ezra Taft Benson said . . . : "Christlike service exalts. . . . The Lord has promised that those who lose their lives serving others will find themselves. The Prophet Joseph Smith told us that we should 'wear out our lives' in bringing to pass His purposes. (D&C 123:13.)" (*Ensign,* Nov. 1989, pp. 5–6.)

If you feel that much of what you do does not make you very famous, take heart. Most of the best people who ever lived weren't very famous, either. Serve and grow, faithfully and quietly. Be on guard regarding the praise of men. Jesus said in the Sermon on the Mount:

"Take heed that ye do not your alms before men, to be seen of them: otherwise ye have no reward of your Father which is in heaven.

"Therefore when thou doest thine alms, do not sound a trumpet before thee, as the hypocrites do in the synagogues and in the streets, that they may have glory of men. Verily I say unto you, They have their reward.

"But when thou doest alms, let not thy left hand know what thy right hand doeth:

"That thine alms may be in secret: and thy Father which seeth in secret himself shall reward thee openly." (Matt. 6:1–4.)

May our Father in Heaven so reward you always.[11]

Suggestions for Study and Teaching

Questions

- What is President Hunter trying to help us understand by emphasizing that Helaman and his brethren were "no less serviceable" than Captain Moroni? (See section 1.) How can this understanding help you?

- What can the scriptural examples in section 2 teach us? How can these examples influence our own feelings as we serve? How have you been blessed by others who have served in quiet, unsung ways?

- What can we learn from the story President Hunter tells about Oliver Granger? (See section 3.) Why should we not be concerned about receiving recognition when we serve?

- How can "the limelight of popularity" or fame be dangerous? (See section 4.) What can Nephi's example teach you about how to stay "fixed on the things that matter most"?

- Review the account of President J. Reuben Clark Jr. in section 5. What impresses you about President Clark's attitude and words? Consider your answer to the question "Why do I serve?" How can we develop an attitude of giving our best regardless of where we serve?

- In section 6, President Hunter refers to the Lord's promise that "those who lose their lives serving others will find themselves" (see Matthew 10:39; 16:25). What does this mean? How have you found this to be true? How has service brought you happiness?

Related Scriptures

Matthew 6:2–7, 24; 20:25–28; James 1:27; D&C 76:5–7; 121:34–37

Study Help

"Share what you learn. As you do this, your thoughts will become clearer and your power of retention will increase" (*Teaching, No Greater Call* [1999], 17).

Notes

1. Neal A. Maxwell, "Meek and Lowly" (Brigham Young University devotional, Oct. 21, 1986), 8; speeches.byu.edu.

2. Thomas S. Monson, "President Howard W. Hunter: A Man for All Seasons," *Ensign,* Apr. 1995, 31.

3. James E. Faust, "Howard W. Hunter: Man of God," *Ensign,* Apr. 1995, 27.

4. Jon M. Huntsman Sr., "A Remarkable and Selfless Life," *Ensign,* Apr. 1995, 24.

5. "No Less Serviceable," *Ensign,* Apr. 1992, 64–65.

6. "No Less Serviceable," 65.

7. "No Less Serviceable," 65–66.

8. "No Less Serviceable," 66.

9. "No Less Serviceable," 66–67.

10. *The Teachings of Howard W. Hunter,* ed. Clyde J. Williams (1997), 267.

11. "No Less Serviceable," 67.

"If we are to follow the example of Christ and walk in his footsteps, we must seek to do the same things after the pattern he set."

Following the Example of Jesus Christ

"We should at every opportunity ask ourselves, 'What would Jesus do?' and then be more courageous to act upon the answer."

From the Life of Howard W. Hunter

President Thomas S. Monson, who served as second counselor to President Hunter, said that he "lived as he taught, after the pattern of the Savior whom he served."[1]

A close friend observed that "the traits embodied by our Lord and Savior, Jesus Christ, were beautifully characterized in President Hunter's remarkable and selfless life. All mankind were his friends."[2]

Another associate who worked closely with President Hunter for more than three decades said, "[He] knew instinctively the course he would follow. That course would be to emulate the character of his Savior Jesus Christ."[3]

Throughout his ministry, President Hunter lovingly encouraged Church members to follow the Savior's example. In his first statement as President of the Church, he said:

"I would invite all members of the Church to live with ever more attention to the life and example of the Lord Jesus Christ, especially the love and hope and compassion He displayed.

"I pray that we might treat each other with more kindness, more courtesy, more humility and patience and forgiveness. We do have high expectations of one another, and all can improve. Our world cries out for more disciplined living of the commandments of God. But the way we are to encourage that, as the Lord told the Prophet Joseph in the wintry depths of Liberty Jail, is 'by persuasion, by long-suffering, by gentleness and meekness, and by love unfeigned; . . . without hypocrisy, and without guile' (D&C 121:41–42)."[4]

Teachings of Howard W. Hunter

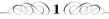 **1**

Jesus Christ set the perfect example for us.

To be a light is to be an exemplar—one who sets an example and is a model for others to follow. . . . [We have covenanted] to follow Christ, the great exemplar. We have the responsibility to learn of him, the things he taught and the things he did during his earthly ministry. Having learned these lessons, we are under commandment to follow his example, and these are some of the examples he set for us:

1. Christ was obedient and valiant in the premortal life, thus gaining the privilege of coming into mortality and receiving a body of flesh and bones.

2. He was baptized in order that the door to the celestial kingdom would be opened.

3. He held the priesthood and received all the saving and exalting ordinances of the gospel.

4. Jesus served for about three years in a ministry of teaching the gospel, bearing witness of the truth, and teaching men what they must do to find joy and happiness in this life and eternal glory in the world to come.

5. He performed ordinances including the blessing of children, baptisms, administering to the sick, and ordinations to the priesthood.

6. He performed miracles. At his command the blind were given sight, the deaf heard, the lame leaped, and the dead returned to life.

7. In conformity with the mind and will of the Father, Jesus lived a perfect life without sin and acquired all of the attributes of Godliness.

8. He overcame the world; that is, he bridled every passion and has risen above the carnal and sensual plane so that he lived and walked as guided by the Spirit.

9. He brought to pass the Atonement, thereby ransoming men from the [spiritual and physical] death caused by the fall of Adam.

10. Now, resurrected and glorified, he has gained all power in heaven and in earth, has received the fullness of and is one with the Father.

If we are to follow the example of Christ and walk in his footsteps, we must seek to do the same things after the pattern he set.[5]

It is important to remember that Jesus was capable of sinning, that he could have succumbed, that the plan of life and salvation could have been foiled, but that he remained true. Had there been no possibility of his yielding to the enticement of Satan, there would have been no real test, no genuine victory in the result. If he had been stripped of the faculty to sin, he would have been stripped of his very agency. It was he who had come to safeguard and ensure the agency of man. He had to retain the capacity and ability to sin had he willed so to do.[6]

To the very end of his mortal life Jesus was demonstrating the grandeur of his spirit and the magnitude of his strength. He was not, even at this late hour, selfishly engrossed with his own sorrows or contemplating the impending pain. He was anxiously attending to the present and future needs of his beloved followers. He knew their own safety, individually and as a church, lay only in their unconditional love one for another. His entire energies seem to have been directed toward their needs, thus teaching by example what he was teaching by precept. He gave them words of comfort and commandment and caution.[7]

During both his mortal ministry among his flock in the Holy Land and in his postmortal ministry among his scattered sheep in the Western Hemisphere, the Lord demonstrated his love and concern for the individual.

In the press of a multitude, he sensed the singular touch of a woman who sought relief for an ailment from which she had suffered for some twelve years. (See Luke 8:43–48.) On another occasion, he saw beyond the narrowly focused prejudice of a condemning crowd and the sin of her who stood accused. Perhaps sensing her willingness to repent, Christ chose to see the worth of the individual

307

and sent her forth to sin no more. (See John 8:1–11.) On another occasion, "he took their little children, *one by one,* and blessed them, and prayed unto the Father for them." (3 Ne. 17:21; italics added.)

As the trials of Gethsemane and Calvary fast approached, with much weighing heavily upon his mind, the Savior took time to notice the widow casting in her mite. (See Mark 12:41–44.) Similarly, his gaze took in the small-statured Zacchaeus who, unable to see because of the size of those congregating around the Savior, had climbed a sycamore tree for a view of the Son of God. (See Luke 19:1–5.) While hanging in agony upon the cross, he overlooked his own suffering and reached out in caring concern to the weeping woman who had given him life. (See John 19:25–27.)

What a marvelous example for us to follow! Even in the midst of great personal sorrow and pain, our Exemplar reached out to bless others. . . . His was not a life focused on the things he did not have. It was a life of reaching out in service to others.[8]

Let us follow the Son of God in all ways and walks of life.

One of the most important questions ever asked to mortal men was asked by the Son of God himself, the Savior of the world. To a group of disciples in the New World, a group anxious to be taught by him and even more anxious because he would soon be leaving them, he asked, "What manner of men ought ye to be?" Then in the same breath he gave this answer: "Even as I am" (3 Ne. 27:27).

The world is full of people who are willing to tell us, "Do as I say." Surely we have no lack of advice givers on about every subject. But we have so few who are prepared to say, "Do as I do." And, of course, only One in human history could rightfully and properly make that declaration. History provides many examples of good men and women, but even the best of mortals are flawed in some way or another. None could serve as a perfect model nor as an infallible pattern to follow, however well-intentioned they might be.

Only Christ can be our ideal, our "bright and morning star" (Rev. 22:16). Only he can say without *any* reservation, "Follow me, learn of me, [and] do the things you have seen me do. Drink of my water and eat of my bread. I am the way, the truth, and the life. I am the law and the light. Look unto me and ye shall live. Love one another as I have loved you" (see Matt. 11:29; 16:24; John 4:13–14; 6:35, 51; 7:37; 13:34; 14:6; 3 Ne. 15:9; 27:21).

My, what a clear and resonant call! What certainty and example in a day of uncertainty and absence of example. . . .

. . . How grateful we should be that God sent his Only Begotten Son to earth . . . to set a perfect example of right living, of kindness and mercy and compassion, in order that all of the rest of mankind might know how to live, know how to improve, and know how to become more godlike.

Let us follow the Son of God in all ways and in all walks of life. Let us make him our exemplar and our guide. We should at every opportunity ask ourselves, "What would Jesus do?" and then be more courageous to act upon the answer. We must follow Christ, in the best sense of that word. We must be about his work as he was about his Father's. We should try to be like him, even as the Primary children sing, "Try, try, try" (*Children's Songbook,* p. 55). To the extent that our mortal powers permit, we should make every effort to become like Christ—the one perfect and sinless example this world has ever seen.[9]

Again and again during our Lord's mortal ministry he issued a call that was at once an invitation and a challenge. To Peter and his brother Andrew, Christ said, "Follow me, and I will make you fishers of men." (Matt. 4:19.) To the rich young man who asked what he must do to have eternal life, Jesus answered, "Go and sell that thou hast, and give to the poor . . . and come and follow me." (Matt. 19:21.) And to each of us Jesus says, "If any man serve me, let him follow me." (John 12:26.)[10]

Let us study the Master's every teaching and devote ourselves more fully to his example. He has given us "all things that pertain unto life and godliness." He has "called us to glory and virtue" and has "given unto us exceeding great and precious promises: that by these [we] might be partakers of the divine nature" (2 Pet. 1:3–4).[11]

Those who follow Christ seek to follow his example. His suffering on behalf of our sins, shortcomings, sorrows, and sicknesses should motivate us to similarly reach out in charity and compassion to those around us. . . .

. . . Seek opportunities for service. Don't be overly concerned with status. Do you recall the counsel of the Savior regarding those who seek the "chief seats" or the "uppermost rooms"? "He that is greatest among you shall be your servant." (Matt. 23:6, 11.) It is important to be appreciated. But our focus should be on righteousness, not recognition; on service, not status. The faithful visiting teacher, who quietly goes about her work month after month, is just as important to the work of the Lord as those who occupy what some see as more prominent positions in the Church. Visibility does not equate to value.[12]

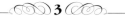

3

Our salvation depends on our commitment to following the Savior.

The Lord's invitation to follow him is individual and personal, and it is compelling. We cannot stand forever between two opinions. Each of us must at some time face the crucial question: "Whom say ye that I am?" (Matt. 16:15.) Our personal salvation depends on our answer to that question and our commitment to that answer. Peter's revealed answer was "Thou art the Christ, the Son of the living God" (Matt. 16:16). Many, many witnesses can give an identical answer by the same power, and I join with them in humble gratitude. But we must each answer the question for ourselves— if not now, then later; for at the last day, every knee shall bow and every tongue shall confess that Jesus is the Christ. Our challenge is to answer correctly and live accordingly before it is everlastingly too late. Since Jesus is indeed the Christ, what must we do?

Christ's supreme sacrifice can find full fruition in our lives only as we accept the invitation to follow him [see D&C 100:2]. This call is not irrelevant, unrealistic, or impossible. To follow an individual means to watch him or listen to him closely; to accept his authority, to take him as a leader, and to obey him; to support and advocate his ideas; and to take him as a model. Each of us can accept this

One way we can pattern our lives after the Savior's example is to follow His command to Peter: "Feed my lambs. . . . Feed my sheep" (John 21:15–17).

challenge. Peter said, "Christ also suffered for us, leaving us an example, that ye should follow his steps" (1 Pet. 2:21). Just as teachings that do not conform to Christ's doctrine are false, so a life that does not conform to Christ's example is misdirected, and may not achieve its high potential destiny. . . .

Righteousness must start in our own individual lives. It must be incorporated into family living. Parents have the responsibility to follow the principles of the gospel of Jesus Christ and teach them to their children [see D&C 68:25–28]. Religion must be part of our living. The gospel of Jesus Christ must become the motivating influence in all that we do. There must be more striving within in order to follow the great example set by the Savior if we are to become more like him. This becomes our great challenge.[13]

If we can pattern our life after the Master, and take his teachings and example as the supreme pattern for our own, we will not find it difficult to be consistent and loyal in every walk of life, for we will be committed to a single, sacred standard of conduct and belief.

Whether at home or in the marketplace, whether at school or long after school is behind us, whether we are acting totally alone or in concert with a host of other people, our course will be clear and our standards will be obvious. We will have determined, as the prophet Alma said, "to stand as witnesses of God at all times and in all things, and in all places that [we] may be in, even until death." (Mosiah 18:9.)[14]

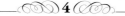

4

We should make room for Christ.

On that night in Bethlehem there was no room for him in the inn, and this was not the only time during the thirty-three years of his sojourn in mortality that there was no room for him. Herod sent soldiers to Bethlehem to slay the children. There was no room for Jesus in the domain of Herod, so his parents took him to Egypt. During his ministry, there were many who made no room for his teachings—no room for the gospel he taught. There was no room for his miracles, for his blessings, no room for the divine truths he spoke, no room for his love or faith. He said to them, "The foxes have holes, and the birds of the air have nests; but the Son of man hath not where to lay his head" (Matthew 8:20).

Even in our day, although two thousand years have passed, there are many who say the same thing that was said on that night in Bethlehem. "There is no room, no room" (see Luke 2:7). We make room for the gifts, but sometimes no room is made for the giver. We have room for the commercialism of Christmas and even pleasure-seeking on the Sabbath day, but there are times when there is not room for worship. Our thoughts are filled with other things—there is no room.[15]

While it will be a beautiful sight to see the lights of Christmas . . . , it is more important to have human lives illuminated by an acceptance of him who is the light of the world [see Alma 38:9; D&C 10:70]. Truly we should hold him up as our guide and exemplar.

On the eve of his birth, angels sang, "And on earth peace, good will toward men" (Luke 2:14). If men would follow his example, it would be a world of peace and love toward all men.[16]

What is our responsibility today as members of The Church of Jesus Christ of Latter-day Saints? It is to see that our individual lives reflect in word and deed the gospel as taught by our Lord and Savior, Jesus Christ. All that we do and say should be patterned after the example of the one sinless person to walk the earth, even the Lord Jesus Christ.[17]

Suggestions for Study and Teaching

Questions
- Review the many ways the Savior has set the example for us, as outlined in section 1. How has the Savior's example influenced you? What can we learn from His example during the last part of His mortal life?

- President Hunter counsels us to "ask ourselves, 'What would Jesus do?' and then be more courageous to act upon the answer" (section 2). Consider how you can be more courageous in following the Savior's example. How can we teach this principle in our families?

- What can the teachings in section 3 help us understand about following Jesus Christ? How might your life be different if you did not have the influence of the Savior's teachings and example? How can we make our religion more a part of our daily living?

- Ponder what President Hunter says about there being "no room" for the Savior (section 4). How can we make more room for the Savior in our lives? How have you been blessed as you have made more room for Him?

Related Scriptures
Matthew 16:24–27; John 10:27–28; 14:12–15; 1 Peter 2:21–25; 2 Nephi 31:12–13; 3 Nephi 12:48; 18:16; 27:20–22; D&C 19:23–24

Teaching Help
Provide hymnbooks for each person. Invite participants to find and share a hymn that relates to specific passages they read in the chapter.

Notes

1. Thomas S. Monson, "President Howard W. Hunter: A Man for All Seasons," *Ensign,* Apr. 1995, 33.

2. Jon M. Huntsman Sr., "A Remarkable and Selfless Life," *Ensign,* Apr. 1995, 24.

3. Francis M. Gibbons, *Howard W. Hunter: Man of Thought and Independence, Prophet of God* (2011), 152.

4. In Jay M. Todd, "President Howard W. Hunter: Fourteenth President of the Church," *Ensign,* July 1994, 4–5.

5. *The Teachings of Howard W. Hunter,* ed. Clyde J. Williams (1997), 40–41.

6. "The Temptations of Christ," *Ensign,* Nov. 1976, 19.

7. "His Final Hours," *Ensign,* May 1974, 19.

8. "The Church Is for All People," *Ensign,* June 1989, 76–77.

9. "What Manner of Men Ought Ye to Be?" *Ensign,* May 1994, 64; see also

"He Invites Us to Follow Him," *Ensign,* Sept. 1994, 2–5; "Follow the Son of God," *Ensign,* Nov. 1994, 87.

10. "An Apostle's Witness of Christ," *Ensign,* Jan. 1984, 69.

11. "Exceeding Great and Precious Promises," *Ensign,* Nov. 1994, 8.

12. "To the Women of the Church," *Ensign,* Nov. 1992, 96–97.

13. "He Invites Us to Follow Him," 2, 4; see also "An Apostle's Witness of Christ," 69–71; Conference Report, Oct. 1961, 109.

14. "Standing As Witnesses of God," *Ensign,* May 1990, 60.

15. *The Teachings of Howard W. Hunter,* 41–42.

16. *The Teachings of Howard W. Hunter,* 44–45.

17. *The Teachings of Howard W. Hunter,* 45.

List of Visuals

Index

A

Adversity
  the Atonement helps us with, 44–47, 51–58, 66–67, 103
  be optimistic during, 66
  can humble and refine us, 29, 62, 64, 80
  experienced by Howard W. Hunter, 29, 33–34, 99
  experienced by Joseph Smith, 64–65
  is a necessary part of mortality, 45, 56
  is for our growth and experience, 64–65
  is part of God's plan for our progress, 62–65
  persevering through, brings true greatness, 162–63
  turn to the Savior during, 29, 44–47, 54–58, 66–67

Atonement. *See* Jesus Christ, Atonement of

B

Baptism
  correct form of, 210
  covenant of, 128, 170, 174
  of Howard W. Hunter, 4–5, 197
  of Howard W. Hunter's father, 6–7, 177
  of Jesus, 306

Baptism for the dead, 184, 190–91

Book of Mormon, 144, 151–52

Brigham Young University Jerusalem Center for Near Eastern Studies, 22–24, 49, 123

C

Charity
  brings us peace, 53
  encompasses all other godly virtues, 262
  of Howard W. Hunter, 255–56
  in marriage, 214
  walk the path of, more resolutely, 261–62
  will not fail, 262–63
  world would benefit greatly from, 263
  See also Love

Chastity, 181

Children
  parents' responsibilities for, 221–30
  teaching, by example, 279, 281, 287
  teaching, the gospel, 281
  teaching, about the temple, 184
  who have strayed, 227–29

Christ. *See* Jesus Christ

Church of Jesus Christ of Latter-day Saints, The
  has a mission to teach the gospel to all nations, 125–27
  is guided by revelation, 114, 115, 117–18
  Jesus Christ is the head of, 111, 113
  was reestablished through the Prophet Joseph Smith, 90–91

Commitment
  of Abraham, 248–49

were chosen before they were born, 114

R

Resurrection, 43, 46, 99, 101, 104–9, 203

S

Sacrament
Howard W. Hunter passes and blesses, 4–5, 197, 199
instituted by the Savior, 102, 201–3
renew covenants by partaking of, 128, 203–5

Scriptures
example of in-depth study, 149–51
help others develop confidence in, 282–83
studying, brings us closer to Christ, 151–52
studying, in families, 144–45, 146, 147, 148
studying, helps us be taught from on high, 76–79
studying, helps us learn and obey God's will, 145–46
studying, is the most profitable of all study, 144–45
teach from, 284–85
understanding of, requires consistent, prayerful study, 147–49

Seminary program, 14

Service
be concerned with why, not where, 299–301, 310
be on guard about the praise of others in, 301–2
brings happiness, 301
brings peace, 54
brings true greatness, 155, 157, 160, 162–63

is a measure of our devotion to God, 257
to others in their affliction, 259–61
quiet and inconspicuous, 291, 293–98, 301–2
seek opportunities for, 310
in small and simple ways, 293–98

Smith, Joseph
adversity experienced by, 64–65
cared for and served others, 160–62
Church reestablished through, 90–91
example of, in prayer, 76–79
example of, in turning to the scriptures, 76–79
First Vision of, 76–79, 89–90
life and works of, 94–97
was a prophet, seer, and revelator, 92–94

T

Teachers
help students develop confidence in the scriptures, 282–83
help students experience a change of heart, 288–89
invite students to seek God the Father and Jesus Christ, 284–85
should not build allegiance to themselves, 284–85
strive to reach the individual, 285–87
teach by example, 279, 281, 287
teach with the Spirit, 283–84

Teaching
by example, 279, 281, 287
importance of good, in the Church, 279–89
with the Spirit, 283–84

Temple
baptisms for the dead in, 190–91